Graduates' W
Organisational change and students' attributes

Lee Harvey, Sue Moon and Vicki Geall

with Ray Bower

Centre
for
Research
into
Quality

Graduates' Work: Organisational change and students' attributes

Lee Harvey, Sue Moon and Vicki Geall
with Ray Bower

© Lee Harvey, Sue Moon and Vicki Geall, 1997

Centre for Research into Quality
The University of Central England in Birmingham
90 Aldridge Road, Perry Barr, Birmingham B42 2TP

All rights reserved. No part of this publication may be reproduced, stored in a retrieval system, or transmitted, in any form or by any means, electronic, mechanical, photocopying, recording or otherwise, without the prior permission of the publisher. The publication may, however, be reproduced in part without permission by academics in HEFCE, HEFCW and SHEFC funded institutions wishing to make multiple copies of sections for the use of members of their own institutions.

British Library Cataloguing-in-Publication Data
A catalogue record for this book is available from the British Library
ISBN 1-85920 111 3

Project Directors: Lee Harvey and Sue Moon

Project Researchers: Vicki Geall, Ray Bower, Lindsey Bowes and Gloria Montague

Project Administrator: Lesley Plimmer

Additional interviews: Melissa Weatherly and Robert Plimmer

Additional interview transcription: Val Bates

Jointly published by Centre for Research into Quality and The Association of Graduate Recriuiters

Contents

Overview		1
Chapter 1	Purposes, aims and approach	5
Chapter 2	The changing organisation	9
Chapter 3	Flexibility, empowerment and transformation	17
Chapter 4	Changes in graduate careers: implications of flexibility	35
Chapter 5	Recruitment policy and practices	50
Chapter 6	Attributes of graduates	65
Chapter 7	Benefits of a degree	80
Chapter 8	Work placements	94
Chapter 9	HE–employer links	103
Chapter 10	Training and lifelong learning	112
References		123
Appendix 1	Outline details of respondents	127
Appendix 2	Defining the size of organisations	132

Acknowledgements

We are indebted to the 258 respondents who gave up their time to participate in the research. We also want to take this opportunity to thank all the people in the organisations who helped us to arrange interviews.

We have had invaluable support from the Project Steering Committee at all stages of this research: Kate Orebi Gann, Roly Cockman, Patrick Coldstream, Keith McMaster, Elizabeth Maddison, Claire Matterson, Matthew Farrow, Derek Pearce, Richard Garrett, George Taylor, Margaret Wallis, Peter Wright and the late Jeremy Gibson. Words cannot express our sorrow at his untimely death.

Many thanks to Lesley Plimmer for all her hard work as research administrator supporting the researchers and transcribing many of the in-depth interviews.

The following organisations* have taken part in the research:
ABPM, AFE Technologies, Andersen Consulting, Aston Manor Brewery, Automotive Products Borg and Beck/Lockheed, Bank of England, Barclays Bank, BBC Pebble Mill, Beard Dove, Beds and Herts Ambulance and Paramedics, BGC, Birmingham City Council Housing Department, Birmingham Youth Service, BNFL, Bournville Village Trust, BP, British Gas Transco, British Steel, BT, Brittannnic Assurance, Burton and Jackson, Cabinet Office, Cadbury, Canon UK, Carfax, Carnegie Health Trust, Central Office of Information, Deloitte and Touche, Delta, Diomed, Don Valley High School, Doncaster Health Authority, Esso, First Class Design, Flag Communications, Futura, Glaxo Wellcome, GMTV, Grantham, Brundell and Farron, Grau, Guinness/United Distillers, Hallam FM, Handsworth Viewpoint, Hoskyns (Compuware), ICL, Irwin Mitchell, Iveco Ford, Keepmoat Holdings, Kesslers, KPMG, Landsdowne Centre, Loadhaul (Rail), Lovell, White Durrant, Low Pay Unit, Lucas, Marks & Spencer, McDonalds, MEL Research, Mercedes Benz, Midland Bank (HSBC), Monocon International, NatWest Bank, Norton Rose, Oxfam, Oxford Mail, Pauffley PRL, Price Waterhouse, Rank Xerox, Rare Design, Sainsbury's, Scotland Yard, Serck, Servern Trent Systems, Shell, Shelter, Sir Alexander Gibb, Smith & Nephew, Swallow Hotels, The Dome, The Drum, Theodore Goddard, Unilever (Unipath), University Hospital, UUNET Pipex, Wakemans, West Midlands Arts, West Midlands Fire Service, Wilsic Hall School, WMCCA, Yorkshire Arts Circus, Yorkshire Bank.

---

* informal designations

Overview

Employer organisations have changed rapidly over the last decade and they are likely to continue to evolve into the 21st Century. Respondents suggested a variety of scenarios and, although there is little agreement on the nature of future changes, there is overwhelming agreement that things will continue to change, both in terms of internal organisational structure and the focus, objectives and future strategies of organisations. These changes will be prompted by the continuing information revolution, by a growing awareness of the need to be responsive to customers, clients and other stakeholders, and by the need to adopt an international perspective.

Graduates should no longer expect stability and a linear career progression and they need to be alert to the growing and varied range of graduate opportunities, often in non-traditional areas. Graduates are being employed in areas that were formerly staffed by non-graduates. However, the jobs are not the same, they are evolving over time and the expectation is that this will continue. There is a symbiosis between the changing nature of jobs as a result of organisational change (delayering, for example, requiring a wider range of job functions and communication with a broader range of people) and the abilities, desire and enthusiasm of graduates to 'grow' jobs.

Employers want people who are going to be effective in this future, changing world. Employers indicate that what they want now, and in the foreseeable future, are intelligent, flexible adaptable employees who are quick to learn and who can deal with change. Graduates are much more likely than non graduates to meet these criteria. In a future world of uncertainty employers do not want people who are unable to work on a range of tasks simultaneously, people who are resistant to new approaches or who are slow to respond to cues.

In the delayered, downsized, information-technology driven, innovative organisation there is likely to be less and less time for new recruits to 'get up to speed'. Employers want people who can rapidly 'fit in' to the workplace culture, work in teams, exhibit good interpersonal skills, communicate well, take on responsibility for an area of work, and perform efficiently and effectively to add value to the organisation – they want *adaptive* recruits.

However, employers want more than that; they also want employees who can use their abilities and skills to evolve the organisation. They want people who exhibit an ability to learn and add to knowledge and skill and the ability to use their knowledge and skills in face of change. They want people who have bright ideas, who are able to communicate them to others, develop them in teams and persuade colleagues to attempt new approaches: *adaptable* people.

Ultimately, employers are looking for people who can do more than respond to change. They want people to anticipate and lead change, to help them transform their organisations. People who can use higher-level skills, such as analysis, critique, synthesis, and multi-layered communication to facilitate innovative teamwork: *transformative* employees.

Employers want adaptive, adaptable and transformative people to help them maintain, develop and ultimately transform their organisations in response to, and preferably in anticipation of, change.

Although employers and recent graduates agree that an undergraduate experience is enormously beneficial in terms both of personal development and workplace effectiveness, they are generally of the view that a degree course does not prepare students for work. Younger, full-time students, other than those who have had a significant placement experience on their course, leave university with little idea of the nature and culture of the workplace and find it initially difficult to adjust. This period of adjustment – the time it takes for a graduate to become effective in the workplace – is, increasingly, a cost that graduate employers are unable or unwilling to bear. Many small and medium-sized organisations want new recruits to be effective from the outset. A significant number of larger organisations are moving away from a general, leisurely, 'fast-track' introductory training to more job-specific recruitment requiring more rapid effectiveness. Some future projections suggest that all firms, large and small, are likely to expect graduates to be immediately effective. The implication of this is that higher education programmes will need to better prepare graduates for workplace culture.

Higher education needs to be aware of the changing nature of the workplace and of the requirements of employing organisations. It needs to be responsive to these changes and demands. Higher education has a responsibility to its principal stakeholders – students – to equip them with more than a profound knowledge of an academic subject area. Higher education has a responsibility to students that includes encouraging and enabling them to develop, through their academic study, a range of explicit attributes, which allow them to subsequently engage effectively in the world of work.

Respondents overwhelmingly endorsed work-based placements as a means of helping students develop attributes that would help them to be successful at work. A work-based placement not only helps develop specific 'work-related' skills but also provides a foretaste of workplace culture and thus helps graduates to be effective more quickly. To be a worthwhile experience for both student and employing organisation, the placement should ideally be for an academic year during the course of the programme. If there was to be a single recommendation to come from the research, it would be to encourage all undergraduate programmes to offer students an option of a year-long work placement and employers to be less reluctant to provide placement opportunities.

Respondents were of the view that graduates are cost-effective and that a degree education is both beneficial for the graduates as well as adding value to the organisation. The expectation is that graduates will continue to be cost-effective in the future and that, for some employers, graduate employment will not only increase but will be fundamental to future development. However, it is increasingly incumbent on higher education to ensure that graduates have a clear idea of the world of work and are equipped with an explicit range of skills and abilities, in addition to knowledge, so that they can rapidly play an effective role in a workplace organisation.

However, higher education should not simply respond to the perceived requirement of employers for a range of adaptive, adaptable and transformative people by producing graduates who slot into different points on the continuum. Higher education should continue to strive to enhance and empower *all* graduates as critical, reflective, transformative people.

The critical, analytic and reflective element of higher education constitutes, arguably, the essence of a graduate programme (HEQC, 1996). To deny this in any part of the higher education system is to short-change stakeholders (students, parents, employers).

Respondents want graduates who can add value rapidly rather than inflexible graduates unable to cope with change. They also want graduates who have the potential to do more than add short-term value. Among graduate-level recruiters, there is relatively little interest in alternatives to the current degree education: there was no widespread enthusiasm for higher level (G)NVQ recruits, and the idea of shorter degree programmes or interim, diploma-style, pre-degree qualifications was thoroughly disliked.

Numerous comments have suggested that, while employers are looking for adaptive people who fit in, they also want them to be intelligent, rounded people who have a depth of understanding, can apply themselves, take responsibility and develop their role in the organisation – to be educated rather than trained.

Most respondents were of the view that, for young people, an extended period away from home helps them become mature, develop a broader perspective, enhance interpersonal skills and self-confidence and generally assists them to become 'a more rounded person'. These self-sufficient dispositions, developed in a university setting, will be increasingly important in flatter organisational structures (where communication will be with a wider range of people) and in the future global economy where it will be necessary to be sensitive to cultural sensibilities and local politics.

Furthermore, some employers had considerable misgivings about 'mix-and-match' semesterised, modular programmes. Although they might provide graduates with a breadth of view and perhaps enhance their ability to 'fit-in' to an organisation, 'mix-and-match' programmes are sometimes viewed as insufficiently academically rigorous, failing to produce critical, analytic reflective thinkers.

However, it is a mistake to assume that particular types of courses, institutions, degree subjects, or even degree classification in any way parallels the difference between adaptive, adaptable and transformative graduates. It is important to relate attributes to their use in practice in the organisational setting. A transformative graduate not only needs a range of transformative attributes but has to be able to use them to work with others to innovate, cope with change and ultimately help transform the organisation. As one strategic manager noted, using a sporting analogy, it is captains on the pitch, not managers in the stand that are required. Degree classification and institutional reputation are not good indicators of such transformative potential.

Employers need to rethink their recruitment strategy and presuppositions. Far too much recruitment procedure is guided by prejudice, preconceptions and bureaucratic pragmatism, directed towards reproduction of the prevailing culture. It is predominantly 'safe' and oriented towards adding value, rather than 'risky' aiming at recruitment of transformative employees. This is a particular problem for large employers but also evident amongst small employers. The response to the increasing numbers of graduates is not to consider the wider range of potential transformative agents, but to narrow down the choice on the basis of spurious criteria such as A-level grades, degree-classification, or reputation of higher education institution. Placements provide a useful and more appropriate recruitment process for organisations who provide work-based experiences for undergraduates.

In essence, employers expect a degree to provide a profound, broad education rather than attempt to train someone for a specific job. In some cases, particular knowledge and understanding of a subject area is a bonus, as are specific technical skills. An understanding of the world of work, some commercial awareness, some appreciation of work culture and the ability to work in teams, communicate well and exhibit confidence (but not arrogance) in interpersonal relations is a considerable enhancement. However, there is no evident desire for an undergraduate education to become more closely linked to specific vocational qualifications. In short, then, employers as much as students and educators expect an undergraduate programme to produce analytic, critical, reflective, transformative graduates.

Although employers want adaptive, adaptable and transformative people, these are not distinct types of employees. All employees, in different contexts, need to be adaptive, adaptable and transformative. It may be that in certain circumstances there is more emphasis on the 'fitting in' and a 'doing the job' while in other situations, employees are expected to spend a lot of time motivating themselves and others to innovate and reconceptualise ways of working. However, the organisation of the future is unlikely to expect graduate-level employees either to merely 'fit in' or, conversely, to be constantly 'transforming'.

Similarly, the adaptive-adaptable-transformative continuum is cumulative: one starts at the value-added end and progresses along. That is, people cannot be effective at the transformative end of the continuum unless they also have the skills and abilities to add-value. To be merely 'transformative' without adding value takes an individual off the continuum. Such an individual would be a 'loose cannon', working alone and failing to harness the transformative potential to organisational culture and structures. In essence, 'transformation ability' without added value is likely to be destructive rather than transformative.

So, although employers may appear to want an array of adaptive, adaptable and transformative graduates, higher education should not be tempted to produce 'quotas' of each type.

On the other hand, higher education should not simply read this as *carte blanche* to continue to pursue rigorous subject specialism, albeit making the higher level intellectual skills more explicit, on the grounds that this will provide an endless stream of potentially transformative graduates. To do so is to opt out of a wider set of stakeholder responsibilities, not least a responsibility to students who will need the skills and abilities to both fit in quickly and add value effectively as well as generate new ideas and help the organisation anticipate and deal with change.

In short, higher education needs to be responsive to wider stakeholder concerns, while at the same time maintaining the essence of the higher educative process.

So higher education needs to work with employers to identify what is necessary in a graduate education to develop added value but also to ensure that the essential transformative element of a degree programme is retained and enhanced. The agenda is to empower students as critical, reflective citizens while also making them aware of the organisational imperatives and modes of working that will allow them to add value.

Most employers want, in principle, to develop closer links with higher education. There are practical constraints that restrict the amount of effort that can be put into developing such links. Most employers see links in terms of recruitment and training. Some see links in terms of providing placement experience. Few consider it their role to directly or indirectly affect curriculum content and delivery, although some think it would be mutually beneficial if employers became more involved in programmes of study, offering guest lecturers, hosting open days, and so on. There is a good case for using employers' experience of skills training and competence assessment in course development – although any inclusion of a more explicit range of abilities needs to be integrated fully into the content of a programme, with appropriate assessment, and not presented as an optional add-on.

Ways forward

The research suggests several ways in which higher education and employers could help students be successful at work. These are not prescriptive recommendations but some ideas of what needs to be done in order to move things forward.

- Programmes should continue to produce critical, reflective and potentially transforming students who can help organisations deal with change. However they should not neglect to prepare students to fit into organisational culture and add value through working effectively with others. Graduates need help to be adaptive as well as transformative.

- Personal and interactive skills should be explicitly developed as an integral part of the programme of study and they should be included as part of the assessment of student achievement. It may be appropriate to use the expertise of employers to develop ways of assessing these skills.

- A positive commitment to academic staff development will be necessary in order to achieve the above.

- Opportunities for work experience should be developed so that students can become acquainted with work-place culture and develop higher-level academic abilities in a work setting. Overall, employers benefit from providing work-place learning opportunities and should continue to be encouraged to become more involved.

- The higher education experience goes beyond the formal programme of study and students should be enabled to recognise the skills developed through informal learning opportunities, experience of part-time work and other extra-curricular activities.

- As the academic world changes employers will need to develop more sophisticated criteria than A-level scores, degree classification and university reputation when undertaking initial filtering of applications. Higher education and employers might want to co-operate in developing a more appropriate set of indicators of graduates' suitability for the workplace.

1 Purposes, aims and approach

Purposes

> Most British people, most educators and most students now believe that it is one of higher education's purposes to prepare students well for working-life. (CIHE, 1996)

Employers and their representatives consistently say that, to succeed at work, most people in future must develop a range of personal and intellectual attributes beyond those traditionally made explicit in programmes of study in higher education institutions. The need for developing a range of personal and intellectual attributes beyond specific expertise in a disciplinary field is becoming increasingly important and is likely to be more pressing in the working world of the 21st Century.

The research reported here has systematically explored the views of a wide range of employers and recent graduates to identify the nature and extent of the knowledge abilities and skills that graduates will need in the 21st Century if they are to be successful at work.

The research explores recent and expected changes in the organisation of the workplace, the recruitment practices of large, medium and small organisations, the graduate attributes required by employers, the extent to which an undergraduate experience helps to develop them, the benefits and cost effectiveness of an undergraduate education, the benefits and desirability of postgraduate study, the links that employers have with HE, and the ways that it and employers might work together to enhance the HE experience, thus further helping students towards success at work.

The report can be read in three ways:

- as providing an analysis and overview of the changing world of graduate career opportunities;
- as identifying the range of knowledge, skills and attitudes that will help graduates to acquire jobs and then to be successful through their working life;
- as exploring the complex inter-relationship between the development of graduate skills, student learning, employee progression, workplace structures and changing organisational ethos.

The implications of changes and projections for the future are identified and recommendations for future action by students, academics and employers are suggested.

Context

There is increasing pressure on HE to contribute directly to economic regeneration and growth (Ball, 1989, 1990). Increasingly, national and international assessments of the role and purposes of education indicate a need for HE to contribute significantly to 'meeting the needs of the economy' (DES, 1987; EC, 1991). A significant element of that contribution is the future competitiveness of economies or groupings of nation states.

A central element of the more explicit involvement of HE in meeting the needs of the economy is the promotion of HE–employer links to enhance the skills and abilities of graduates. For example, the Industrial Research and Development Advisory Committee of the European Commission draws a direct link between the attainment of economic objectives and the development of human resources: 'The output of education and training systems (including, in particular, HE) in terms of both quantity and quality of skills at all levels, is the prime determinant of a country's level of industrial productivity and hence competitiveness' (IRDAC, 1990, 1994).

Similarly, the DTI and the CIHE reported in 1990 that chief executives of many companies point to their need for highly educated and skilled people. This is seen as the crucial factor in determining the success of their business.

The CIHE (1992) has constantly advanced the view that 'those charged with overseeing the "quality" of HE should seek employers' views not only on the skills they immediately need but on the long-term demands of employment, including flexibility and adaptability, which students must be prepared to meet'.

Skills gap

Analytic studies of the labour market suggest that there is a skills gap between the labour requirements of an industrially developed society and the outputs from the education system. That has prompted various attempts at planning educational provision to match projected skills shortages but rapid change has led to forecasts being inexact[1]. Nonetheless, the perception of a skills gap and the 'spectre' of continual change has led to a variety of 'manifestos' and policy statements:

> One feature of current skills shortage is the *widespread lack of important generic skills* and social skills such as quality assurance skills, problem-solving skills, learning efficiency, flexibility and communication skills. These are in addition to *shortages of critical scientific and technological skills*. In the 1990s the skills content of work is expected to increase. There will be a greater proportion of workers needing communications, language, management and organisational skills.
> (EC, 1991, p. 4)

Harvey with Green (1994) argue that the perceived skills gap occurs for four reasons. First, a view that education is a 'once-and-for-all' activity, which ignores the need for life-long learning and skills updating. Second, a lack of communication between HE and commerce and industry. Third, the indifference and inconsistency of industrialists in identifying what they want (Cannon, 1986; Davies, 1993). Fourth, the perceived threat to academic autonomy and freedom posed by closer links to commerce and industry.

Research aims

The research, aimed at helping students towards success at work, is designed to provide a firmer base on which HE might respond to employer perceptions. It has been clear that, although industry and commerce have frequently identified the kinds of skills and abilities needed, there has been inconsistency in the messages. It is not clear from the rapidly growing number of lists of attributes, core skills and competencies exactly what it is that employers most desire. Furthermore, the lists of attributes that employers specify as desirable appear to be growing and presenting a daunting challenge to students and academics.

The confusion has also been accentuated at different levels within organisations; the abilities sought by graduate recruiters may not coincide with the immediate requirements of line-managers, which in turn may differ from the longer-term strategic requirements of senior executives.

There have been many studies that have attempted to prioritise skills required by employers in general, or in specific sectors[2]. What these studies have tended to show is that 'skills' such as communication, teamworking, interpersonal skills, problem solving and analysis are accorded high priority alongside attitudes or dispositions such as flexibility, adaptability, willingness to learn, motivation and various self-skills. However, most of these studies rely on quantitative data collection methods such as questionnaires or content analysis of job advertisements. While

---

1 Studies of a skills gap include O'Leary (1981), Lindley (1981), Teichler (1989), TUC (1989), PSI (1990), IOD (1991, 1996), Khawaja (1991) and attempts at manpower planning can be found in Pearson (1976), DE (1981), IMS (1981), Fulton, Gordon and Williams (1982).

2 Examples of such studies include Greenwood et al. (1986), Green, S. (1990), Phillips-Kerr (1991), Harvey Burrows and Green (1992), NBEET (1992), BT (1993), Binks, Exley and Grant (1993), Harvey with Green (1994).

these are indicative, they tend to suffer from a major problem: terminological confusion and imprecise clarification of concepts. What one organisation means by 'communication skill' may be entirely different from another, which in turn may differ substantially from what a teacher in HE implies by the term.

The research attempts to address these issues in three ways:

- by exploring in depth, what it is that employers think significant, and recent graduates regard as important in their development, to enable new recruits to become successful at work;
- by identifying why particular attributes are important in the current, and likely future, workplace organisation;
- by adopting a qualitative approach designed to get behind the meaning of the skills, competencies and abilities – rather than generate yet more lists – to explore what they involve, in practice, in the work setting.

In short, the research lets employers and recent graduates speak for themselves to get an idea of the 'real' work context, the roles played by graduates and thus the holistic set of attributes necessary to be successful in different work settings.

The research has been funded by the Association of Graduate Recruiters, the Council for Industry and Higher Education, and the Department for Education and Employment. It provides the empirical support for the 'Declaration of Intent' of the Employment Skills Overview Group whose members are additionally drawn from the following: Confederation of British Industry, TEC National Council, National Council for Vocational Qualifications, Association of Graduate Careers Advisory Services, Higher Education Quality Council, Standing Conference of Principals, Committee of Vice-Chancellors and Principals of the Universities of the United Kingdom and the Funding Councils for England, Scotland and Wales, the Universities of Bradford, Middlesex and Teesside, Rover Group Ltd and Lucas Industries plc.

It is important that the research feeds into HE policy decisions. The intention is to provide practical suggestions for future development. Employers have been consulted on many occasions in the past and there is a feeling, whether warranted or not, that nothing much ever changes:

> I understand that this research will be input for a discussion about what should higher education do and do differently in order to deliver products that are geared to what business wants. So how committed is the educational system to doing that? ... Business has made quite a lot of pleas over the last decade and things have apparently not happened to the extent that business would like. (57A: senior executive, multi-national brewing company)

Conversely, RSA's 1995 study, *Tomorrow's Company*, suggested that employers are not sure what they really need, or will need in the future and have paid little heed to wake-up calls in the past.

Methodology

Semi-structured, in-depth interviews have been carried out with 84 strategic managers, 55 line managers, 84 graduates and 35 non-graduate employees in 91 organisations. A total of 258 face-to-face interviews of between 30 and 85 minutes have been recorded and transcribed.

The transcribed conversations have been entered onto a qualitative database and systematically analysed. A number of main themes have been identified, which correspond to the chapters of this report. The data has been analysed in detail to explore nuances of meaning and context and reported using indicative quotes to allow the respondents to speak for themselves. Where appropriate, broad statistical indicators have been included to give an indication of the prevalence of particular views.

A brief description of each organisation and the job-title of respondents is provided in Appendix 1. The names of respondents and of organisations have been omitted from this report. Quotes in the text have been referenced using a numbering system to enable cross-referencing with Appendix 1.

The sample

The organisations in the sample vary in size and type. The interviews were carried out in a variety of locations in England and Scotland, although the majority were in London, Yorkshire and the West Midlands (Table 1.1).

Table 1.1   Interview location by respondent type

Region	A	B	C	D	Total
South and East England	32	24	27	8	91
Midlands	31	19	33	14	97
North England and Scotland	21	12	24	13	70
Total	**84**	**55**	**84**	**35**	**258**

A = strategic manager,   B = line manager,   C = recent graduate,   D = non-graduate

Organisations included vary from large multi-nationals through to small organisations, from the manufacturing and service sectors, both private and public (Table 1.2). Classifying the size of organisations is not easy (see Appendix 2 for details). The main activity of an organisation is not always easy to specify, which causes problems when allocating to sector. Many large organisations undertake a variety of manufacturing and service activities and where this occurs, the main activity of the organisation, as described by the respondents, is used for classification purposes. In two cases, large organisations that are both clearly service and manufacturing organisations have been classified in the latter category.

Table 1.2   Size and sector of organisations in the sample

Size	Private Service	Manufacturing	Public Service	Total
Small	14	2	9	25
Medium	9	6	5	20
Large	22	16	8	46
Total	**45**	**24**	**22**	**91**

About half the interviews were in large organisations and a similar proportion were in private service sector organisations (Table 1.3).

Table 1.3   Interviews by size, sector, and type of respondent

Size	Sector	A	B	C	D	Total
Small	Private manufacturing	2	1	2	0	5
	Private service	14	10	13	6	43
	Public service	7	2	7	1	17
	Subtotal small	*23*	*13*	*22*	*7*	*65*
Medium	Private manufacturing	5	3	5	4	17
	Private service	8	4	8	4	24
	Public service	4	4	6	3	17
	Subtotal medium	*17*	*11*	*19*	*11*	*58*
Large	Private manufacturing	16	11	14	8	49
	Private service	21	16	22	7	66
	Public service	7	4	7	2	20
	Subtotal large	*44*	*31*	*43*	*17*	*135*
Total		**84**	**55**	**84**	**35**	**258**

A = strategic manager, B = line manager, C = recent graduate, D = non-graduate

2 The changing organisation

There were very few respondents whose organisation had not undergone significant change over the last ten years or who foresaw no significant changes of structure in the next ten years. Many organisations had already experienced downsizing, delayering, outsourcing, decentralisation or recentralisation, mergers and take-overs. Few respondents were prepared to predict future changes, although many presupposed that all these things would be continuing features of working life.

> I am sure [the organisation] will change a lot. Quite how it does I think will depend very much on how the market and the business develops. I think the general rule is that any business planning is usually out of date three months after it has been written.
>
> (23A: chief executive, small medical lasers manufacturer)

In short, the future is far from certain, and the presupposition is that rigid organisational structures will not be able to respond quickly enough. Much more important than attempting to predict change is to have an organisation in place that can adjust to change. It is, as one respondent put it, about 'learning to live with change. We try to be adaptable we have to respond very quickly to things. Everything changes so fast.' (20A). Not only do organisations need to respond to financial imperatives, but also to the advent of global markets, the need to consolidate in areas of maximum penetration, the ever changing and unpredictable impact of information technology and shifting emphases towards clients, customers and employees.

Terms like 'downsizing', 'delayering' 'outsourcing' and 'homeworking' are often used in relation to graduate career prospects. This chapter attempts to explore what the terms mean in 'real' settings and in Chapter 4, the implications for graduate jobs and careers are explored.

Downsizing

Downsizing is a euphemism for reducing the number of employees in an organisation without necessarily reducing the work or the output. Downsizing has been a feature of the 1980s and 1990s and many organisations, large and small alike, believe that they have become 'leaner' and 'fitter' as a result.

Downsizing attracts headlines when large numbers of employees are made redundant. However, much downsizing has taken place more gradually without headline-grabbing redundancy notices:

> We regard it as a management failure if we suddenly have to announce X thousand redundancies. Just to give you one example, the UK soap and detergent business, in 20 years, that employs about a fifth of the people it did, something in that order, and that has been done without a single compulsory redundancy. That has been done by natural wastage – not replacing staff who retire or leave.
>
> (11A: vice-president, multi-national food manufacturers)

Some respondents thought that downsizing had reached its limit while a significant number thought that further reductions in personnel would take place. For some, cost-reduction is a constant process.

> I think probably as important for total employment level is how you try to keep up in the race for becoming every year more efficient, because on the one hand you are talking about

growth, new product development and maintaining market positions, on the other hand you have to fund it with advertising. In a stable position, one way to fund that is cutting costs out of the business, which means getting heads out of the business. That is not going to be dramatic but it is a constant process where every year you take out X hundred people from a total of 40,000 – that's in *quantity* terms. If you are talking *quality* terms, you have a different discussion. There it is not new product development that is significant, it is the way you run the business that is significant in terms of the people you need. What type of people do you need in the business at different levels within the strategic complex.

(57A: senior executive, large brewing company)

As this suggests, downsizing is not uniform in its impact as it tends to affect different areas of the workforce in different ways:

There are two sides to downsizing. I think we will probably reduce our manufacturing arm by over 50% over the next five years. You look at the staff side and I think we will become much more analytical. I see us becoming much more reliant on good computer systems but then much more reliant on very high calibre people who can analyse what comes out instead of spending a lot of time putting stuff in. So in my department, I have something like 18 people in here, my guess is in five years I will have five or six, but they will all probably be paid 10 or 15 grand more than they are now and they will all be completely different calibre and much more senior people.

(29A: supply manager, medium-sized health product manufacturer)

What I think will happen is the support processes will change significantly as we automate, computerise and control from remote locations more and more. We will need fewer and fewer people. I can foresee where we will have a very limited semi-skilled work force and everybody else will be a staff employee with craft or graduate qualifications. And the manual or semi-skilled role will be taken by contracting companies, we are moving that way and we will move even faster.

(40B: production manager, large steel manufacturer)

The implication of these and many other comments is that there will be a growth in 'symbolic-analytic services' (Reich, 1991). Reich argues that three broad types of work are emerging in post-industrial economies: routine production services, in-person services and symbolic-analytic services.

Routine production services are 'repetitive tasks performed by the old foot soldiers of American capitalism in the high-volume enterprise' (Reich, 1991, p. 175) and include routine supervisory jobs performed by foremen, line-managers and clerical supervisors as well as the assembly work of those on the production-line. Projected changes see not only a reduction in the numbers of production-line workers (as robotics displace people) but a significant change in old supervisory roles and a less controlling and more empowered structure. In essence, routine production services are being, and will continue to be, transformed.

I think we are certainly in for some quite significant changes within this business. I suspect we will become more product-based rather than works-oriented. I think that the functional support will be slimmer. In the past, department heads didn't have to worry about the finance, the supplies, the transport, personnel issues: they were [central] functions. These days we realise that a line manager has to own a lot of those processes himself. He can't say, as a departmental manager, that the responsibility for training is the training department, it isn't. The responsibility lies with that manager, team leader or supervisor... I think the outcome of that will be different types of jobs. The overall objective is to have a slimmer, more efficient, more streamlined, smoother organisation, but we will still need to recruit people who can meet whatever spec. we need for that new structure.

(40A: manager of training and development, large steel manufacturer)

Other detailed case-study research has suggested the increase in empowerment predicted by Reich's model has not occurred in routine-production work in the UK (Smith and Elger, 1996).

In-person services are routine, closely supervised services provided on a person-to-person basis, such as waiters, retail outlet workers, taxi-drivers, nurses and car-mechanics. This is a rapidly growing area of employment in the burgeoning service sector. It is also an area of rapidly growing graduate employment as the large numbers of graduates in the labour market provide the impetus to evolve these jobs.

Symbolic-analytic services include 'problem-solving, problem-identifying, and strategic brokering activities' by people such as research scientists, design engineers, software engineers, public relations executives, investment bankers, lawyers, quantity surveyors, energy consultants, advertising executives, systems analysts, television producers, and so on. It is this expanding symbolic-analytic area that will require graduate calibre employees.

This view reflects recent projections collated by the Department for Education and Employment in *Labour Market and Skills Trends: 1996/1997*. It notes that 'gains and losses in different industries will not be spread evenly across all occupations' (DfEE, 1996a, para. 2.16) and suggests that, while there is a projected decline in employment in manufacturing, the number of managers and professionals is expected to increase.

In the traditional manufacturing areas, economic pressures have led to downsizing preceding the reconceptualisation and restructuring processes. In other, more buoyant areas, the process has gone on simultaneously, leading in this case to a shift from non-graduate to graduate-level employees.

> The company has gone through a massive downsizing programme. We have gone from 225,000 people to 130,000, in five or six years. So it has been vital to bring in new blood. It's like exiting one end and bringing graduates in. People who were losing their jobs had great difficulty understanding how come they were going but yet somebody new was coming.
> (32B: recruitment and development manager, large telecommunications organisation)

Delayering

Downsizing is often closely linked to delayering, which is the process of removing layers of management to change the organisation from one with a rigid hierarchical framework with numerous layers of supervisory grades into a 'flatter' organisation with minimal layers of management. Such organisations tend to emphasise teamworking, with people taking on different roles in different teams.

The vast majority of organisations in the sample have undergone significant delayering during the 1980s and 1990s. Most expected this process to continue, but at a slower rate, as many thought they were approaching the feasible limit of delayering.

> Some layers of management have gone. My understanding and expectation would be for the time being that is probably it as far as we are concerned. I think there is still some 'fat' in our head office, that is, the centralised departments. But [delayering] is now evolutionary rather than revolutionary.
> (36B: area manager, large financial institution)

For most organisations, delayering involved a combination of removing 'unnecessary' layers of middle managers and giving managers a broader portfolio:

> We have a flat structure between the manufacturing director of this operation and the hourly paid people there is one level of management. We have taken out at least two or three layers of middle management. That has some major benefits, it is cost effective and it speeds up the communication process. Writers talk about the lean manufacturing organisation, but there is a view that lean means fragile, because it is now very reliant upon key people within it.
> (76A: senior executive, multi-national motor component manufacturer)

Although many organisations have been through significant periods of downsizing and delayering, to the extent that they are suffering from 'corporate anorexia', some still think the process will continue.

> The management is becoming flatter and that process began in the early '80s for us. I am sure there will be some more delayering in the future.
>
> (70A: strategic manager, multi-national petro-chemical company)

> We had very hierarchical management structures until about two years ago, and we have had to flatten it out basically because we had to put as much money as we could in the front line. And all NHS trusts now, anyway, are charged with making year-on-year savings of managers. So, by my calculations, by the year 2010 there will be no managers at all.
>
> (77A: director of human resources, paramedic ambulance trust)

One strategic manager suggested that delayering and other structural changes were not one-off shifts to better management but an ongoing process. This reflects changing circumstances but also acts as a galvanising process because 'no management system is perfect forever. It meets the requirement of the time and if that requirement disappears or it is satisfied, then it is time to change the structure otherwise you stagnate' (63B).

Reducing the full-time complement

Delayering tends to be associated with the development of more 'flexible' contractual arrangements including:

- part-time and short-term contracted employees;
- bought-in contractees;
- outsourcing;
- home working.

These arrangements are primarily designed to enhance the responsiveness of the organisation rather than to empower the individual, although they may suit certain types of workers and provide them with the flexibility of employment they need.

Part-time and short-term contracts

Britain, along with Holland and the Scandinavian countries, has the highest rate of part-time employment in Europe (Hutchinson and Brewster, 1994). However, our respondents suggested that it would be fixed-term contracts and, in some cases, consultancy contracting that would be the main form of flexible working arrangements that would affect graduates.

In some organisations, fixed-term contracts act as probationary periods. In most, though, part-time and short-term contracts were used to provide employers with a degree of flexibility to deal with unpredictable changes in workloads:

> ...if we hit a peak, we have, in the past, employed a number of people temporarily to get over that peak. This business is so difficult to try and keep a steady work-force load, you can get a 'phone call tomorrow which will bring you in work for 10 or 15 people.
>
> (44A: business development manager, large international highway design engineers)

For others, a degree of flexibility through fixed-term contracts enables speculative ventures and provides an opportunity for fresh ideas:

> The majority of our employment is permanent, and I believe it will remain so, because there has to be a mutual commitment to each other to get the best out of people, particularly on intellectual, patentable property. But we are, for a number of reasons, bringing people in on temporary contracts, at Ph.D. and at graduate level. That is partly to provide a continual pipeline and refreshment of skills without permanency, and secondly, truthfully, it is to get

extra headcount in on particular projects without necessarily committing permanently either to the individual or the project. You know we will do speculative things with temporary resources for two or three years, see if it is working and then commit to it.

(63A: human resources manager, large pharmaceutical manufacturers)

Some respondents, while not discounting a shift towards short-term contracts, regarded it as inadvisable because of the cost of recruitment and training and lack of commitment from staff:

I still believe that we will be employing people longer term. I don't think we want to put all of this time and effort into recruiting people, training people, developing them and then getting rid of them. We can't afford it, we want the expertise and the talent coming through, staying with us, growing with us and contributing more as they progress through. I don't think we are going down the route of part-time, short-time temporary contracts.

(40A: manager of training and development, large steel manufacturer)

In some cases, organisations are reversing a policy of employing people on short-term contracts in order to increase motivation and loyalty:

We now have fewer short-term contracts. There has been a drive in the last year or two to get rid of that culture. We were basically stringing people along all the time, and losing them, because if they are very good they are going to move to somebody else for better security who will at least give them a year.

(43A: specialist journalist manager, large public broadcasting organisation)

In some, usually public, organisations funding arrangements are so unpredictable that fixed-term contracts are the only viable option, for example: 'I've got National lottery money to employ two workers for three years at the end of which that money runs out, so they have to be fixed-term contracts' (05D). However, such arrangements are not regarded as conducive to effective working because uncertainty about continued employment is 'very stressful' (41A).

Outsourcing, contractors and consultants

Outsourcing means contracting-out aspects of the work of the organisation, previously done in-house, to specialist providers. Outsourcing is often targeted on support functions such as IT or low-level clerical or secretarial support, or on specialist activities where there is not the work for a full-time employee: a publishing firm, for example, contracts-out proof reading.

The use of contractors, sometimes more splendidly known as consultants, is reasonably widespread and is an alternative to taking on employees on fixed-term contracts. Contractors differ from employees in that they are self-employed or employed by a consultancy firm and contracted for a defined period of work, for a number of sessions a year, or for a specific task.

We do employ contractors today. Like all companies we try to be cost effective and therefore we don't carry labour to meet our peaks, nor our troughs. When we need to buy more labour, typically we buy contractors and that will almost certainly continue.

(39B: team manager, medium-sized software services contractor)

In some areas where small, high-skill organisations predominate, there is a need for contract work because the range of abilities required is wide but the ongoing work-load is small.

I think more employers will deal with freelance on short-term contracts rather than employing people. With our particular business you need to be able to call on a lot of different skills: you might need a cartoonist one day, the next day you might need an illustrator, and you can't expect someone to sit in the corner and be able to do all those things, the same as you can't afford to have a cartoonist sitting there for 40 hours a week hoping the work might come in.

(14A: owner, small design and print agency)

Contractors tend to be more expensive than employees, but are supposedly fully trained and 'up-to-speed' and provide flexibility in periods of uncertainty:

> When we started the company there were two of us and ten contractors and we ran that system for about a year, until we knew that we were sufficiently confident in what we had been doing that we could consider committing to full-time. It cost us more to have contractors, but it gave us a lot of flexibility and we didn't have fixed overheads and commitments.
>
> (23A: chief executive, small medical lasers manufacturer)

Several disadvantages of using contractors were identified including not being able to train contractees, wasting time fitting them into the organisational culture and a lack of loyalty and personal investment in the organisation.

A few respondents thought that contracting and outsourcing would become more important in the future. Organisations would retain a small core of employees, supported by a range of peripheral contracted services, such as technical support 'bought in as and when we need it' (43A). For example, an executive of a Regional Arts Board thought the organisation would be reduced to a 'small core managing contracts and undertaking development work' (07A), while a graduate recruiter in a multinational organisation expected that, among other things, 'personnel and finance will be outsourced' to specialist organisations (32C).

> We have cut our workforce by about 50% over the last ten years, and I think the likelihood is that we will cut it further. We will also contract out much more of what we do, until we finally end up with a much smaller organisation, which will probably be defined as areas that no-one else can do. So if we can contract it in why shouldn't we?
>
> (66A: recruitment manager, multi-national petro-chemical company)

However, overall, the respondents were rather more muted about the projected development of contractors and outsourcing than in some recent studies. There was little expectation that activities, other than peripheral ones, would be outsourced, and the use of contractors was closely linked to fixed-term working to deal with fluctuations in work load.

Home working and the portfolio worker

Much has recently been made of the emergence of the 'portfolio worker', a self-employed, self-reliant worker who will increasingly play a major role in organisations as the core workforce shrinks and more work is outsourced (AGR, 1995). The portfolio worker is so-called because they have a portfolio of skills and experience that enables them to attract outsourced, consultancy work. Despite speculation and anecdote suggesting a rise in portfolio working, there is relatively little sign from projected statistics; for example self-employment is expected to rise from 13.1% of all employment in 1994 to just 13.9% by 2001 (DfEE, 1996a), and this increase is not necessarily attributable to the increase in portfolio workers. Although our research was based on employees, there was little indication that they intend to move towards portfolio working. This coincides with recent research that suggests that portfolio working is a 'tip in search of an iceberg' (Thompson, 1996).

Although portfolio workers are not necessarily 'home workers' they will, in theory, be disengaged from a particular workplace and normally operating, at least part of the time, from a home base. A minority of respondents considered homeworking, of any type, to be a serious employment alternative in the near future. This coincides with other research on 'teleworking' – various arrangements by which employees spend some or all of their working week at home – which, in the mid-1980s, was forecast to rise dramatically (NEDO, 1986). However, less than one per cent of the European workforce are involved in teleworking and, although there are suggestions that the rate is higher in Britain, there is little indication of the massive increases predicted (Hutchinson and Brewster, 1994).

Where respondents envisaged any shift to 'homeworking' it tended to be in terms of a locational rather than contractual shift. It is important, in discussing 'homeworking' to draw a distinction between working *at* home, working *from* home and self-employed homeworking. Typically, respondents were sceptical that there would be any significant growth in 'homeworking'.

Working at home

A number of respondents referred to working at home in certain circumstances. For example, where a person needs to work alone to complete a task, such as writing up a report, then working at home is a viable option on a job-specific basis.

> For as long as I can remember people have worked from home on particular projects in our service. It's become more fashionable now, so people think there is more of it, but in relative terms I don't think there is. (05A: principal officer for policy, publicly funded youth service)

> Home working is pretty well impossible in the scientific environment. You can't develop drugs in the kitchen sink. We do allow informal homeworking to finish reports, to write up things, but that is about all that can be done. (63A: HR manager, large pharmaceutical manufacturers)

For many people, 'homeworking' is nothing more than a euphemism for unpaid 'overtime' at home.

> We don't have any formal home working, although I have an office at home so that I can work there in the evening. And we do have mailing, we have dial-in links here, for one or two people to be able to work from home, but that is more related to if something needs to be done. People like to get home and see the kids before they go to bed and then carry on, rather than just arrive home late at night, having missed the family.
> (23A: chief executive, small medical lasers manufacturer)

Working from home

Working from home is an established practice in one or two organisations especially in sales departments: 'most of the fax salesmen work from home' (26C).

> I don't think we will have a huge number of people working from home, largely because we have a high street operation that needs to be manned. The only parts of our network who could potentially work from home are our sales people... The sales team for the credit-card operation is home-based right across the country, but it is a small part of our organisation.
> (36A: senior manager, large financial institution)

For most respondents, 'homeworking' conjured up images of working from home via information technology links, but as an employee not as a self-employed contractor.

> I think there will be more homeworking or hot desking and things like that. And I quite like that. We are already doing it. You know, we've got Powerbook Macs and we've got modem links. All of which means you can work from home. And I love that. Work in my pyjamas. (28C: project manager, small design and communications company)

> I can envisage that theoretically we might not, in a few years' time, have any office at all. It is a business that could lend itself to home working or offices in different places, so that is a major people-issue that we have to address. And the communication is already increasingly by electronic means. Our business, as lawyers, is all about information access, it is central to our business, and that lends itself to electronic transfer.
> (12A: personnel director, large law firm)

Homeworking

Despite some vague projections that 'homeworking' might increase, very few respondents projected a scenario where jobs could be transformed into homeworking in the sense of being self-employed and working from home on a contractual basis:

> A lot of my work I could do at home with a machine. I even said "Why not employ me as a consultant and I'll come in as and when training is needed," but at the moment they don't have enough expertise internally to identify training needs, so I'd have to do that as well.
>
> (01A: training and safety officer, medium-sized private leisure and entertainment complex)

> I think companies will get smaller and more people will end up working for themselves. The Internet means everyone can work at home and it's a collective of people working together on the Internet.
>
> (14B: studio manager, small design and print agency)

In the main 'homeworking' is seen as a location issue and one that is driven by information technology. For one company, it is not home but the client's premises that is the base for remote work; home would merely provide a secure locus for electronic communication:

> A lot of our staff actually work on client sites, it is very difficult to communicate with them, because obviously we may want to send them some information but it may be client sensitive... We will encourage our employees, possibly with interest-free loans, to buy PCs, have it installed at home, so that when they get home there will be stuff on the Internet. We have got it working in Holland.
>
> (46A: senior consultant, multi-national computer service company)

Home, therefore, is just one of a number of different off-site locations from which employees might operate, but remote working has a clear downside – the lack of effective teamworking:

> We are taking IT concepts on but we are not considering the implications for home life, the liaison and contacts you have within work and the relationships that develop there. It is easier to get things done face-to-face than talking over the telephone or via computers, but I think that is the way the world is going. Hot desking could be a concept here.
>
> (50C: performance analyst, large freight company)

Summary

- Most organisations have undergone significant change in the last decade and most are developing structures and practices to enhance their flexibility for further change.

- The assumption is that organisations will need to be flexible in the future if they are going to be responsive in a world of rapid and unpredictable change.

- Most respondents expected continual change but, apart from short-term extrapolation, few were inclined to predict the future.

- Downsizing has been a feature of the last decade and many organisations, large and small alike, believe that they have become 'leaner' and 'fitter'.

- Some respondents are of the view that downsizing had reached its limit while others think that further reductions in personnel will take place, although this is likely to affect 'routine production services' more adversely than 'symbolic-analytic services'.

- The vast majority of organisations in the sample have undergone significant delayering in the last decade and most expected this process to continue, but at a slower rate.

- For most organisations, delayering involved a combination of removing 'unnecessary' layers of middle managers and giving managers a broader portfolio.

- Flexible contractual arrangements, including part-time and short-term contracts, outsourcing and home working were expected to increase but not to the extent that some forecasters predicted.

Flexibility, empowerment and transformation

As the previous chapter has shown, organisations have been forced to change. Many businesses are concluding that modification and reconceptualisation of bureaucracies are not enough to meet the demands of the next century. More fundamental changes are needed.

Throughout the interviews with respondents the underlying theme of organisational change was the need to be 'flexible' in order to respond to, or even anticipate, change. Equally, respondents talked about the need for flexible employees and, in a delayered, downsized environment, the need for employees who could take more responsibility.

Organisational flexibility

The interviews suggest that flexibility is a complex notion, by no means restricted to flexible working arrangements. Although cost concerns predominate in the interviews, it is possible to identify a continuum of flexibility concerns ranging from 'cost-flexibility' through 'response flexibility' to 'stakeholder flexibility'. The inflexible organisation, that resists change and considers its operating practices and culture as adequate, is a rarity. Organisations that espoused such sentiments were entirely absent from the sample.

Cost-flexibility

Cost-flexibility refers to the ability of an organisation to respond to financial imperatives. There is considerable pressure for organisations to become 'cost-flexible' in order to establish, retain or maximise their market position: be it measured by market share, turnover, profits, competitive edge or ability to demonstrate accountability and effectiveness in artificial public sector 'markets'.

In essence, a cost-flexible organisation is better able to adjust its expenditure to meet actual or forecast changes in its variable income. It does this by reducing the proportion of its total costs that are fixed costs. Cost-flexibility is rooted in the idea that labour is treated as the major fixed cost. Flexibility is thus achieved through contractual arrangements that enable the organisation to adjust its labour costs to match the flow of income-generating work. In some cases this involves literally adjusting the numbers of paid workers through the use of short-term and part-time contracts to meet peaks and troughs in work activity (see Chapter 2).

In other organisations, flexibility is based on contractual arrangements that permit changes in the *workload* of a relatively stable workforce in response to changing work flows. It is such contractual arrangements that the Chancellor of the Exchequer claimed, in his recent Budget Speech, would be Britain's 'flexible friend' underpinning future growth (Clark, 1996).

Cost-flexibility is heavily driven by financial measures of performance, conformity to established added-value practices and a considerable degree of self-management. Communication is usually in the form of top-down requests for information and bottom-up syntheses and recommendations for action. Opportunities for employees to control their working situation tend to be constrained by well-established parameters.

Response flexibility

Response flexibility begins to shift the emphasis away from financial costs and addresses flexibility in terms of a wider range of responses. The perceived growing need for organisations to be more responsive to customers, clients or stakeholders requires a different type of flexible organisation, one that acknowledges a range of concerns beyond shareholder dividends. Response flexibility values employee, customer and client loyalty. It is an approach that attempts to develop mutual respect for a range of stakeholders. Response flexibility moves towards a culture in which diverse views are considered and which emphasises leadership towards a common purpose rather than controlling management towards a singular objective.

In practice, response flexibility permits a considerable degree of project working, local management control and encourages local leadership. The response-flexible organisation is cost-conscious but also attempts to develop partnerships with client groups to secure a mutually beneficial longer-term future.

> There is a lot of talk at the moment about transferring over to an organisational structure in line with what we call a trading unit. This involves looking at what is profitable and what is not, working out where we fit in that chain and reorganising along the lines of profit. It is also an attempt to be customer-focused, reduce costs and increase revenue. What is actually happening is a lot more project-management-type jobs, where a person would be responsible for a project drawing in resources from across the company. This is something I know is happening in other companies too. So you might not be in a line-management position but you are having to gain co-operation and pull together a group from across lots of different departments. So the emphasis is on dragging down costs and maximising output and being that much more customer focused. (32D: programme manager, large telecommunications organisation)

Stakeholder flexibility

Stakeholder flexibility embraces not just a culture conducive to flexibility but the establishment of a structure that effectively engages stakeholders in the organisation's strategic decision making, direction and ethos. As an approach it perceives flexibility as necessary for more than cost-adjustment purposes. Stakeholder flexibility is characterised by openness and dialogue, a range of success criteria in addition to financial indicators, and a supportive environment for innovatory facilitating leadership. It is compatible with what the RSA (1995) have recently referred to, in *Tomorrow's Company*, as an 'inclusive' approach. Among other things the 'inclusive' approach:

- communicates its clearly defined purposes and values to all those important to the company's success;
- realises that by learning from all those who contribute to the business it is best able to improve returns to shareholders;
- builds reciprocal relationships with customers, suppliers and other key stakeholders, through a partnership approach.

There is a preoccupation in Britain with financial performance but to be able to predict changes and be able to discover what changes will be needed in three-to-four years time requires changing attention from the 'financial health of the organisation to its strategic health' (BOC/LBS, 1994, p. 23). By itself, financial performance does not gauge the overall health of the business. For example, of the top 11 most profitable companies in Britain in the 1980s, four subsequently collapsed and two were acquired. Companies that have profits as their major goal are less profitable, in the long run, than people-centred organisations (Waterman, 1994).

Research also suggests that there is a strong correlation between issues concerning people and sustainable business success. For example, corporate cultures that emphasise a range of stakeholders have better long-term profitability (Kotter and Heskett, 1992). Close and stable relationships with employees, customers and suppliers are essential for a flexible and co-operative response to change (Kay, 1993). Furthermore, employee and customer loyalty are closely correlated: 'For large companies like Marks and Spencer with 15 million customers and 50,000 employee shareholders, BT with 25 million customers, many of whom are shareholders, and Abbey National with 2.5 million shareholders, most of whom are customers, these interdependencies are self-evident' (RSA, 1995, p. 6). They are equally real for many smaller companies (Reichheld, 1993, 1994; Weiser, 1995).

Only through 'deepened relationships with employees, customers, suppliers, investors and the community,' argues the RSA, 'will companies anticipate and adapt fast enough, while maintaining public confidence' (RSA, 1995, p. 6). Some implicit sympathy with this approach emerged from the interviews. However, cost-flexibility remains a dominant concern, especially in commercial organisations. Despite the cost-reduction and accountability pressures on public organisations, stakeholder-flexibility and responsiveness are more explicit:

> Our slogan is that everyone has a story to tell and we find ways of helping them tell it. What that is about is providing access to the arts, and encouraging participation, particularly for those who would not normally find a means of expressing themselves through the arts. And that is very strong in the organisation, it is at all levels. So it could just be part of a very big project, or it could be just someone who wanted to find employment through the arts. With that in mind, what we want to do is to really expand what we can offer, which is part of what our application to the lottery is about – it's to do with extending our resources, keeping up to date, so that we are not part of some backward-looking, one-foot-in-the-past kind of organisation, which is the perception that we have to work against. Fundamental to what we are about, is the fact that community art is quality art and not about some little sub-section of the arts. It's about producing something of quality at every level of involvement.
>
> (58A: development co-ordinator, small publicly funded arts publishers)

Flexibility not only requires a workforce that engages change in a contractual sense (cost-flexibility) but one that operates at a 'higher' level, especially in terms of the development of symbolic-analytic services. Flexibility is not just about employees being flexible to suit the financial imperatives of the organisation. It is also about the organisation being flexible to maximise the potential of the workforce. Indeed, in the 'inclusive' approach, the flexibility orientation is widened to include a range of clients and customers as well as employees.

Empowerment

Expansion, restructuring and reorganisation, alongside more intensive use of information technology and the emphasis of a client-oriented approach, provide the impetus for a shift towards a more empowered workforce. While implicit in many comments, about 10 per cent of the sample explicitly related delayering to the empowerment of the workforce. However, empowerment means different things in different organisational contexts. Empowerment can be seen to fall into three broad categories: 'self-regulatory'; 'delegated'; and, 'stakeholder' approaches.

Self-regulatory empowerment

In many areas, empowerment appears to equate with the encouragement of self-management which ranges from 'taking a lot of responsibility for your own actions' (29C) through to 'allowing people who can do a job to manage it themselves' (50A).

> We are a very flat management structure here anyway, and I think that has worked very well. We have a management policy where everyone is a manager, basically, everyone is responsible and accountable for their own work. I think that has been one of our strengths – encouraging people and empowering people.
>
> (42A: training and personnel manager, medium-sized private broadcasting company)

'Self-regulatory' empowerment involves training staff to take on responsibility and to develop a wider set of organisation-determined competencies. 'Self-regulatory' empowerment improves communication in as much as there are fewer levels to block the flow of information. Furthermore, a single manager may be responsible for a wide range of areas in which there are often cross-cutting teams so there is less departmentalisation to inhibit communication. However, this does not necessarily lead to better communication beyond the next level up and employees in such organisations could be as ill-informed about strategic changes and the evolution and status of the company as employees in a 'traditional' layered organisation. 'Self-regulatory' empowerment leads, in theory, to a greater feeling of ownership of the work situation but in practice, overloading self-regulatory employees or teams with too much work and responsibility means that they are not able to plan, prioritise, or be proactive: their whole time is spent meeting the next deadline and feeling overwhelmed by the number of balls they have to keep juggling at once. Employees are likely to feel only nominally empowered with little sense of real ownership and therefore exhibit little deep-seated loyalty.

In some organisations, where self-regulatory empowerment is a novel departure, some radical reconceptualisation is required:

> I am led to believe the Americans like a flat structure and empowerment pushed down as far as possible. They really like, as far as possible, people who can do a job, to do it. We can't do this. We are not up to it, everyone will do as much as they can, and they will be trained accordingly. (50A: planning and analysis manager, large freight company)

Delayering is thus likely to work effectively if the workforce are educated and sufficiently self-assured to take on the roles formerly entrusted to intermediate managers. Indeed, there is a presumption in some organisations that, with an increase in the number of graduates, there will be a more educated workforce able to take up responsibility and take the initiative.

Delegated empowerment

One manifestation of empowerment linked to delayering is the delegation of responsibility to managers to develop appropriate strategies at the local level.

> We have removed completely one level of hierarchy, the senior supervisor has gone and each of the area managers now look after eight, nine or ten restaurants so what we have tried to do is flatten the hierarchy, give more responsibility to the line manager and ultimately more responsibility to the actual restaurant manager. (61A: operations manager, international fast-food chain)

Delegated empowerment provides a good deal of local control and feeling of ownership.

> Increasingly you are more in charge of your own destiny, so long as you work within the regulations of the bank then you can almost reorganise your own branch or job and move it in the direction you want, so you are given a lot more power at grass roots level to develop the business how you see fit. In years gone by you were given five or six different things that you've got to do, whereas now it's a lot looser and that can blow the mind a little bit when you are not given any standards or procedures that you have to go by to organise your branch. That brings its own pressures in that if you have changed things and you don't perform then there is only you responsible. (36D: branch manager, large financial institution)

However, it is a limited ownership in which local control is constrained by a centrally-imposed framework. Empowerment may amount to nothing much more than delegation to select appropriate options suited to the local context.

> Our parent company really think that we should be having more responsibility. At the moment a lot of our decisions have to be referred back to them. They will be delegating down to us certain sorts of decisions, but in terms of things like support services it is quite likely that those will be concentrating more, things like advertising support, customer information, help-lines, those could be organised at a Pan-European level. On the other hand more decision-making at the sharp end, so that means when we are recruiting graduates they have got to be capable of standing on their own feet and making the decisions and be really responsible for performance. (72A: strategic manager, automobile supply company)

In the main, this delegated empowerment involves providing people with a framework within which to work but leaving them to make decisions, show initiative and develop ideas provided they remain within the parameters.

> Our mission statement is all about making our brand the number one brand. One of the ways in which we are trying to grab market share is in the whole area of competencies and making our managers make the difference. This involves outlining some of the key skills and behaviours that are needed to be the agents of change to meet the challenges of the 1990s: innovation, empowerment, continuous improvement, results-orientation. So those kinds of things will affect the kinds of things we are looking for in our graduate trainees, bearing in mind those graduate trainees are future senior managers, future directors and executives of the company.   (47A: personnel manager, multi-national food manufacturer)

In another sense, delegated empowerment is equated with the ability to report directly to, or engage in dialogue with, senior managers, which, at least potentially, 'greatly enhances information flows' (13D). However, one respondent working in a flat structure was rather more cynical of the empowerment philosophy and suggested that it could be counterproductive:

> Staff actually want easier access to a knowledgeable manager who can give them a decision quickly. If that manager is so stretched trying to cover so many functions that they can't do it either because they are so busy or they just don't know – due to the fact that they have such a wide-ranging span – then it is no good to anyone. And also the notion that someone is really empowered because they report to a very, very senior manager – I don't think is entirely valid.   (35B: research and policy officer, local authority landlord)

Stakeholder empowerment

'Stakeholder empowerment' involves broad-ranging development and training of employees. It sees people as the key resource in the organisation, one that needs nurturing beyond the immediate utilitarian requirements imposed by seeing training as an investment requiring a return.

At one extreme, investment in employee development and training is seen as investing in the development of effective 'critical' reflective citizens. Slightly less altruistically, organisations are seeking to include a range of stakeholders in order to stimulate ideas, encourage loyalty and develop a culture of communal involvement in coping with change. The company ethos is communicated to all stakeholders and innovation is encouraged in a secure environment. Ownership is embodied in leadership rather than management and is disengaged from formal structures being located in team project working.

Stakeholder empowerment is thus compatible with an 'inclusive' approach in which employees, amongst others, are given a larger stake and involvement in the determination of the purpose and direction of the organisation. Some organisations in our sample were moving in that direction:

> In the UK at the moment we have got five million charge-card holders which is a phenomenal number. People are wishing to buy in different ways, shopping in the town centre is still popular, but shopping out of town is also popular, electronic shopping on the Internet, which is at the moment in the early stages, will also affect the structure of this business.
>
> We will have to become more aware as a business of environment and interest groups in total, and in terms of the company structure it will become less paternalistic, it will also, and I know this is an overworked word, become flatter as well. Taking note of the environment and interest groups affects the type of people we will need to employ. We will need to employ people who have an awareness outside. In the past you could have been a good buyer and if you bought fashionable fabrics and fashionable colours that was great news. Now they need to be environmentally friendly fabrics. We should be employing the sort of wide-thinking boss who anticipates the next environmental issue, and we should be onto it before our competitors.
>
> The organisation is becoming more global, the world is becoming smaller and people need to be able to be flexible. It is a skill that you did not have to have some years ago. They have got to have the ability to learn from other cultures. In terms of the skills and

abilities that we need, whatever job they do here they have got to be able to get a buzz out of retail and put themselves in the customer's position. They have also got to be able to relate to the community in that if they are in store or regional management they have got to be able to build a rapport with the Chief Executive of the Council and high-ranking officials – so the presentation skills would be very important. They have got to be able to give and accept criticism both internally and externally.

We have got better at understanding the potential in people and pressing the right buttons and therefore getting people to use some of the skills they have, whereas for too many years it was all about conforming. (54A: assistant to deputy chairman, large international retailers)

At the very least, stakeholder empowerment is about appointing staff who are able to empathise with and contribute to a developmental organisational ethos.

Looking at our five-year plan we will treble the number of graduates we take on through that period. We kicked graduate recruitment off again last year and we are continuing it this year. We need to get better-qualified people and people who can actually take the company on in a manner which it historically has not, to meet new challenges. The business world is not going to get any better. But you will have to continuously improve performance and one thing that can do that for you, is people. So we need better people.

(60A: director commercial operations, large vehicle manufacturer)

In essence, empowerment of the workforce, in whatever form, is about finding ways to actively involve employees in dealing with change.

Adaptive, adaptable and transformative

Employers want employees who can deal with change and they regard graduates as having the capacity to do that (see Chapters 4 and 7). The sample respondents suggested that, at one end of the spectrum, coping with change involves responding to cost-flexible pressures. At the other end, employers want transformative agents who are empowered to deal with change.

In *Employer Satisfaction* (Harvey with Green, 1994) it was argued that employers take on graduates because they add value and, potentially, help transform the organisation. A model of the impact of the transformative graduate was suggested along an enhancement continuum (Figure 3.1). It was suggested that 'the more that graduate employees are able to operate along the continuum the greater the potential evolution of the organisation'. At one end are the attributes that add value, and at the other are transformative attributes. Employers want people who can 'fit-in' and be effective as rapidly as possible within a given context. Employers want people who adapt to the organisation, understand the job requirement and produce work that has a clear return as quickly as possible. In short, they are looking for *adaptive* graduate recruits. The

Figure 3.1 Enhancement continuum

Adaptive: knowledge and skills brought to the organisation. Ability to fit-in to organisational culture.

Adaptable: ability to learn and add to knowledge and skill, ability to use knowledge and skills in face of change. To interact effectively, work in teams and communicate at a variety of levels.

Transformative: the use of 'high level' skills (analysis, critique, sysnthesis, multi-layered communication) to facilitate innovative teamwork.

Adding → **Transforming**

Evolution of the organisation

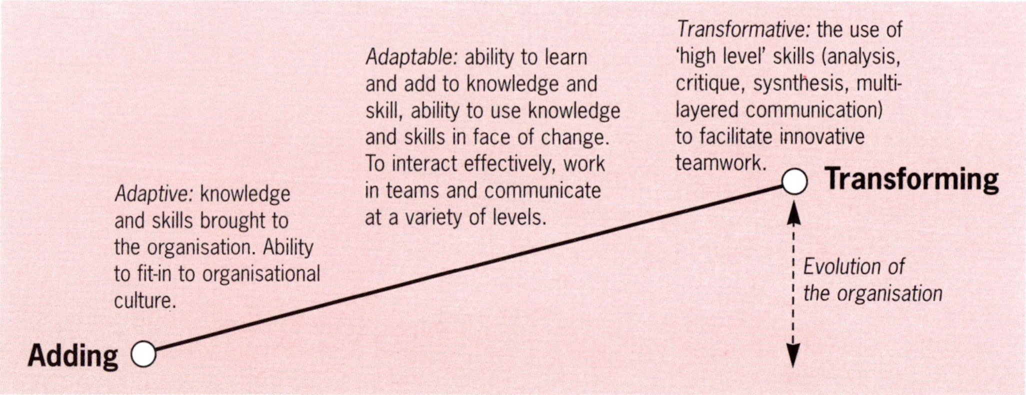

Adapted from Harvey with Green, 1994, p. 16

adaptive employee tends to take few risks, does the required job competently, tends to avoid questioning established procedures, which they are able to imitate and adapt to changing circumstances. They have high expectations that if they please others they will succeed. Adding value, especially in the short-term, relies on knowledge, speed of learning, ability to play a role in teams and generally adjusting to the culture of the organisation.

> But what you do need is people with the basic ingredients who are self-starters, to fit into this industry, to fit into the culture that we have.
>
> (40A: manager of training and development, large steel manufacturer)

> We are looking for what we call, suitability to [our organisation], which is actually specific to our culture... The culture we have here is very much a professional one. I suppose that ethos would be work hard, play hard, in that order. Client requirement would always come first, as it does in any service function, as we are really. But when that deal is done we will relax, we will celebrate, we will pop those champagne corks. The team will have fun, temporarily, in terms of letting their hair down.
>
> (09B: graduate recruiter and training manager, large law firm)

What most employers want are people who can get to the start of the continuum quickly – add value from day one – and have the potential to move up the continuum rapidly, thus helping to transform their flexible organisation.

> It's rare to get people coming straight out of university who are so familiar with working life and what it's like to be in it, and understand what the business is all about, that they can just immediately slot in. We would rather recruit somebody who has experience who can add value to us straight away. We are prepared to add value to them by giving them training and developing their skills but we need to have some immediate benefit from those people.
>
> (04A: owner, small corporate literature specialists)

Employers also want people who can take their organisation forward and who see change as an opportunity not a threat. They want, in short, 'transformative agents', who can help the organisation evolve. Transformative attributes tend to include such things as critique, synthesis, and enabling leadership. Transformative agents by definition, have ideas, 'look outside the box', cause friction and look ahead.

> We did a study about 30 years ago which tried to identify what it was that managers needed in [the company]. We identified four qualities at that time which were called analysis, imagination, sense of reality and, what we called, a 'helicopter' – being able to keep a sense of perspective whilst also looking at detail. About eight years ago we expanded that to an additional six competencies covering such things as achievement, motivation, delegation, organisation and planning – those sort of things. Recently, we have condensed them down again to just three core criteria: capacity, which is intellectual capability; wide-range relationships, which is the ability to work with people, to inspire people; and achievement, which is setting the most demanding targets and actually meeting them.
>
> (66A: recruitment manager, multi-national petro-chemical company)

Transformative agents recognise their own power, can define their own life path and can take responsibility for their actions. A clear sense of direction, and the ability to express it, is likely to impress employers.

> ...they need to work out their deal, I think, with this company. They need to decide what the company is giving them and how they will respond... It all seems trivial but it's about working out your deal with the company. What will you give? The deal with the company is pretty loose, you are employed at X thousand pounds a year, your working hours are X a week, your holidays are X. That is the deal from the company. But I think underneath it you need to work out what your personal deal is, what you will be prepared to do, and I think

you need to share that with your line manager as well. That can be as much or as little as you want, and I think you need to decide what you want to get out of it.

(32B: recruitment and development manager, large telecommunications organisation)

Transformative people can be seen as threatening, as rocking the boat, but maybe as necessary to promote and steer change:

> The objection that some of the professional personnel people had to them was that they were a little too dominant, too abrasive, and I actually quite liked that... I actually need people who can be a bit aggressive, who, if need be, can force through a policy in spite of the opposition.
> (40B: production manager, large steel manufacturer)

However, despite the different emphasis on skills and abilities, ranging from the imitative to the iconoclastic, the difference between adding value and transforming is not primarily a different set of skills but the difference between having abilities and putting them into practice. It is about the way a range of skills and abilities are applied. It is the difference between fitting into a team, working in a team, and getting the team to push the boundaries. It is the difference between adding value by bringing knowledge to a situation and reconceptualising by asking appropriate questions. It is the difference between having the interpersonal skills to get on with clients, customers, colleagues and using interpersonal skills to 'include' a range of stakeholders.

Graduate status itself is no guarantee that the employee will be adaptive or transformative.[1] In a sense, graduate status adds some immediate value through knowledge and higher-level skills such as analysis. However, there may be counter tendencies that reduce the value or at least delay it: *viz.* failure to understand organisational culture, commercial pressures, or lack of prior opportunity to put theory into practice.

The kind of person required by organisations who emphasise transformation are those who can lead, rather than manage, who can work with and get the best out of other people, maximising their potential and their ideas rather than controlling them through setting specific tasks or tight frames of reference.

> I want leaders, I want captains of teams rather than managers of teams. I want that captain to be on the pitch and not the manager up in the stand. And that is a very peculiar animal, and a very difficult animal to find. I'm not sure university can actually give them the attitude of mind that means they are going to be leaders, that they are going to be risk-takers, that they are going to actually create teams around them and drive those teams, both by helping and by delegating. You tend to get a guy, if he is very good he moves forward himself, he does everything himself, he becomes the proverbial manager – too busy to do anything – and subsequently he doesn't make his team do anything at all.
>
> The British automotive industry is extremely traditional, and it can't afford to be, and it has got to break out. The only way it breaks out is by having strategically-placed people at various levels of management, all of whom sing from the same hymn sheet, all of whom believe in the same basic freedom, but actually have got balls – even ladies, yes – who actually

---

[1] The adaptiveness – adaptability – transformation continuum also reflects different styles of learning with the former compatible with behaviourist-style learning, which emphasises assimilation of dominant culture, conforming to standard ways of doing things, disinclination to go back to first principles, imitative practices that allow for a rapid delegation of responsibility to deal with mundane issues, undertake standard work, and deal with unexceptional problems. The value-added end of organisational development requires learners who can rapidly assimilate 'normal' procedures and be effective in 'doing the job'. The transformative end is more likely to be facilitated by the critical-structural learner who engages the structures, tries to get beneath the surface to understand processes. Critical-structural learners tend to push against the boundaries. This is a potentially dangerous activity as there is a fine line between transformation and devastation. Critical-structural learning is about deconstruction of ideas and concepts and reconstruction of alternatives: transformation. Where it slips into demolition without a considered practical reconceptualisation it is a destructive process.

Behaviourist learning encourages reactive development whilst critical-structural learning is more likely to encourage proactive development. Critical structuralists approach encourages deep learning and the ability to think conceptually, to link theory and practice through reflection. There is 'intrinsic worth' in the educative process, valuing the process, and recognising the responsibility of the learner, whether the participants are individuals or organisations. (Atkins, *et al.*, 1993; Brown and Knight, 1994; Harvey and Knight, 1996).

> go and do things and are not worried about taking risks and they create the same environment around their people. So the people know that they are trusted, they will be supported, and they will take risks... And I need people who have got that about them, who want to do something but most of them don't make it because they just don't have the perseverance, they don't have the drive, they don't necessarily have the skills, but they need to develop.
>
> Everybody talks about man-management skills, it's the biggest load of nonsense I have every heard in my life. You have got to treat people like you want to be treated, and you just have to have the ability to work *with* people, not have people work *for* you. Now and then you have got to be the boss – now and then – and certainly you have got to give directions, strategic thought, but then, for Christ's sake, you have got to be able to take your hands off and have confidence that the people that you have got will actually take your basic direction, translate it into what they have got to do and go off and do it.
>
> (60A: director commercial operations, large vehicle manufacturer)

Although some employees may be more inclined to one end of the spectrum than the other, people are unlikely to be just adaptive or transformative, they are likely to slide along the continuum between one end and the other depending on circumstances and context. Most of the time they will be somewhere between the limits – they will be *adaptable* (Figure 3.1) – able and willing to learn and add to their knowledge and skills, demonstrating initiative within the pre-set framework; able and confident enough to use their knowledge and skills in the face of change; and interacting effectively to motivate teams and to communicate at a variety of levels:

> Somebody who can work in a team and on their own, is not afraid to ask questions if they get stuck. Also providing fresh ideas. No one person has a handle on all good ideas. So not being afraid to push their own ideas forward, but also, a big thing we look for is, being able to compromise as well.
>
> (81A: software development manager, small, operator-systems design firm)

Individuals cannot act alone to transform organisations, they can only operate within the context provided by the organisation. The organisation needs to provide the environment for the application of transformative skills and abilities. An 'inclusive approach' provides a framework to encourage transformative initiatives as it provides a context to support the development of a broader flow of ideas from a wide range of stakeholders rather than close control and insecurity that comes from financially-dominated (cost-flexible) organisations, in which intellectual space to develop is limited (Barnett, 1994).

There is a tension between 'fitting the organisation' and being able to innovate, anticipate change and helping develop for the future. In any social setting some level of adaptation is necessary.

Organisations and businesses have to adapt to market needs to keep pace with their competitors. Similarly, individuals have to learn to adjust, to 'fit in' with what is there. However, a distinction can be seen between the adaptable individual who adjusts to a fast-changing situation and an adaptive individual who, in fitting in with the expectations of others, may lose what makes them unique. Taken to its extreme, the adaptive individual loses the core sense of self in order to please significant others, perhaps parents, tutors or employers.

> There's a certain degree of contradiction in the requirement – my job as a manager is to try to keep this explosive pot bubbling – if it goes flat you get people very stale, follow the rules but they just do what they're told. That's no good for us. If everybody is off on their own thing we simply fall apart.
>
> (53A: chief executive, small private research organisation)

There is then a potential clash between the need for adaptive employees and the underlying requirement for people who can deal with and, preferably, lead change. This poses a dilemma for an organisation. To what extent should they employ adaptive people who may rapidly add value to the organisation and to what extent should they risk employing people who may help transform the organisation?

Loyalty

When an organisation's main focus is responding to financial imperatives there is little opportunity to exhibit loyalty to employees. A guarantee of lifetime employment is increasingly unrealistic in many organisations. If this is linked to instrumental training, it can leave the employee feeling undervalued, or valued only in terms of their cost-effectiveness. It also fosters an environment in which the employee's loyalty is primarily dependent on motivating factors such as earnings, promotion or status. Short-term vision by the organisation does not cultivate long-term vision from the employee, and there is no incentive to be committed to the collectivity.

This issue is compounded by the desire, in many organisations, for a loyal, committed workforce that is also flexible and mobile. Mobile, flexible workers are not wedded to a particular job. While this is invaluable within the 'cost-flexible' organisation that has to respond to change, it is also a drawback when the mobile, flexible worker considers that job horizons go beyond the employing organisation. Furthermore, adaptive, mobile, flexible workers tend to be attractive to other organisations.

> I was one of eight graduate recruits in 1992. Since then six of them have moved on as they felt they weren't getting the opportunities that they wanted. They were attracted by more money and more glamorous companies.
>
> (76B: business manager, medium-sized, motor component manufacturer)

Thus, matching the lack of organisational loyalty to the individual, mobile individuals are unlikely to be loyal to the organisation. If the organisation has carefully selected 'cost-flexible' recruits who 'move around a lot' when given the 'opportunity to move' (46B) then these same recruits could just as easily move to another organisation and 'fit in' there.

> I don't think there is much job security any more, and that is the same in [this organisation] as anywhere. So it is up to me to make sure I am all right. I don't think the organisation is going to make sure I'm all right, its not a job for life any more.
>
> (43C: news producer, large public broadcasting organisation)

Graduates, traditionally, had expectations of rapid career advancement through a clearly defined career path within an organisation leading to senior management positions. Even where graduates have a 'realistic' appraisal of the situation in a delayered organisation, they still expect to 'progress':

> I think the expectations that the business has of graduates have risen in recent years. I think equally the frustrations that graduates have had in previous years about not being able to progress as quickly as they would have wished have largely diminished now because we have got to the stage where we have a scheme running in the bank that puts people into management positions within 24 months. That's probably about as quickly as we can do it.
>
> (36A: senior manager, large financial institution)

Where progression is lacking, adaptive, value-adding graduates are likely to follow incentives, such as pay or status, which may mean moving to other organisations or become consultants – contracting in their 'added-value' skills, knowledge and experience.

> Because they got rid of so many layers of management only one in twenty people get promoted to the next grade up. So it is just a case of progressing as high as you can up this massive grade and then when you get to something like 40 thinking "I've had enough, I want to do something different". That's how it works with a lot of people. That's the way I see it being for my generation really. But that's not necessarily a bad thing just because you can't progress in the organisation you are in, doesn't mean you can't progress in your life...
>
> (27D: equity markets analyst, large public financial institution)

An overemphasis on cost-flexibility means that there is no incentive for good mobile flexible employees to stay. And so the cost-flexible firm is in danger of losing its investment in adaptive people. There is thus a problem of how to balance mobility and loyalty, cost-flexibility and security, lack of clear career progression and enhancement. The interrelationship between mobility and loyalty is one that organisations need to address as recruitment, induction and training are not inexpensive items.

> If people walk out of the company they are walking out with a heck of a lot of knowledge and experience, and it takes a long time to build that up again with a new starter. It is not just a technical thing, not just the knowledge of our products, it's the knowledge of who the contacts are and how we deal with things, our standards, our working practices.
>
> (39B: team manager, medium-sized software services contractor)

To overcome the incompatibility of cost-flexibility and employee loyalty, some organisations have attempted to identify the appropriate extent of delayering that enables cost-flexibility while, at the same time, ensuring a sufficient level of incentive to encourage retention of staff:

> We are looking for empowerment – there will always be a central directorate. I see no reason why we should not be looking for a flatter organisation, a lot more empowerment out there... each region trying to operate as an independent company. So I would see us, certainly remaining as flat as we are. One of the dangers with going much flatter is that you do kill off incentives, as people will not see that there is anywhere to progress. A sideways move might be OK and indeed the money might be OK but a lot of people like the kudos of stepping up a rung. We are fairly flat now, you could probably drop out one level of management, probably in the future, but what would you do to the incentives?
>
> (22B: sales manager, multinational reprographic equipment manufacturer)

Fixed-term contracts bring into sharp relief the dilemma of flexibility and loyalty. People on fixed-term contracts may feel they have no obligation of loyalty, the very need for them to be mobile and flexible means that the organisation would dispense with their services whenever it suited. In that case, there needs to be a clearer contract of expectations from the outset that clarifies this relationship.

> Nobody has a job for life any more so why should you be loyal to your employer? Secondly, you have these big debts when you come out of college. So [graduate employees] are more likely to be thinking short term, to pay off their debts.
>
> (46B: project leader, multi-national computer service company)

Where a recruit is on a short-term contact (which may be renewable, or transformed into a permanent contract) then this implies a lack of loyalty by the organisation and considerable uncertainty for the employee, which, among other things, has a detrimental effect on efficiency.

> It's all going to short-term contracts, which are generally renewed but not necessarily. People don't stay in jobs for 20 years or more. Some do but it's becoming less and less like that. Obviously job security is not there. Because that's happening, people are less loyal to their companies than they used to be. They have this kind of "I am on a six-month contract, they could get rid of me in six months time, so why should I put in as much hard work into the company if they are not willing to give me more" attitude.
>
> (08C: graduate trainee, multi-national electrical products manufacturer)

At the other end of the continuum, an inclusive approach is more likely to encourage loyalty through involvement and commitment to the organisation. Prioritising transformation, through encouraging and developing a culture that supports facilitating leadership, risk-taking, entrepreneurialism (in the broadest sense) requires a bold stance. It is contingent on stakeholder empowerment and is likely to flourish in an inclusive organisational structure that is responsive to a range of stakeholder concerns and not just the financial bottom-line. Loyalty is likely to be higher in such a setting as the emphasis is not on profit- and pay-related performance indicators. However, there is a danger that loyalty transmutes, over time, into stagnation.

> What we have to confront is the idea that "it worked ten years ago, it will work now". With the pace of change, if it worked ten years ago, it probably *won't* work now, because people are different, the problems are different. So people have to unlearn old habits and to go through that rather painful experience of saying that what they learnt ten years ago may not be relevant, they may have to do something different. It's about freshness and the sheer resilience to keep on doing that. What the very high potential managers in [the company] have in common, is the self-confidence to go into that totally new, uncharted ground, to argue their point of view and to go into areas they don't know that much about, but knowing that no-one else does either.
>
> (66A: recruitment manager, multi-national petro-chemical company)

Recruitment

In many organisations, including some in the sample, recruitment procedures are, more often than not, designed to recruit people who will 'fit in' to an organisation and get on with things as quickly as possible – prioritising 'self-regulatory' or 'delegated' empowerment (Chapter 5). It is easier to identify a set of competencies and minimum paper qualifications that provide an indication of value-added potential than it is to design recruitment criteria that encapsulate transformative potential. The application of transformative attributes – synthesis, critique, analysis, decision-making, risk-taking, multi-layered communication and innovatory team-work facilitation – is much harder to identify in a decontextualised way than the evaluation of levels of narrowly defined competencies.

Transformative potential links the intellectual and philosophic to practice rather than seeing intellect (assessed by degree classification) as separate from a desired set of competencies. A lot of recruitment apparently ignores this inter-relationship at least in the early stages of the process. Recruitment policies and practices tend to identify 'safe' procedures that achieve value added as rapidly as possible but transformative potential is often sacrificed. Practices such as selection based on A-level grades of graduates or only looking at graduates from the 'top' universities, perpetuate the league table mentality that has developed in Britain's school system, irrespective of its validity in identifying potential change agents.

Emphasis on sets of competencies can be counterproductive when they are disengaged from the whole person, especially if no account is taken of the role the person is going to play, the context in which that role will be played out and the way it is likely to develop over time. The transformative agent is not a set of attributes but a person interacting with an environment, and that person is a complex of intellect and competencies that are not static (Chapter 6).

In large organisations, because of the number of applications, recruitment can become a fossilised, bureaucratic process.

> There was one happy year when we estimated that between a quarter and a third of all graduates applied to us because we were one of the few organisations that were taking them on, and we had to bring in very stringent paper restrictions, because we were just swamped, we did not know what to do with all these forms, just thousands and thousands of them.
>
> (62A: manager, large management consultants)

Bureaucratised procedures are likely to lead to an emphasis on 'safe' recruitment, bringing in people who perpetuate the organisation. Recruiting for 'safety' is not necessarily a problem in itself. People who fit in quickly tend to add value rapidly. However, people who fit in may be absorbed completely into the culture and, as such, merely reproduce it rather than push against the limits and help to take the organisation in new directions. After all, for some organisations, the whole point of recruiting graduates is to provide new ideas.

> There is a problem encompassed in 60% of our restaurant management workforce having worked up from being hourly paid employees, or working up from being crew. While it has its benefits as they know the business very, very well and can do the job very well, it also has disadvantages in that it almost becomes – incestuous is the wrong word – but we breed

> from ourselves and you don't get any fresh ideas. So I think that more and more we look to increase our graduate capacity or our graduate intake to ensure that we do get new ideas and new blood actually coming in. And we are very conscious of not having too many internal candidates.
>
> (61A: operations manager, international fast-food chain)

Recruiting graduates as a source of new ideas may be for operational innovation or to be nurtured as potential strategic managers. Rather less often is it guided by a rather more risky recruitment strategy seeking out potentially transformative employees.

> There is a problem because, on the premise that any process inspires conformance, the chances are that, if you have a recruitment process such as ours, you will end up by recruiting people who are going to be very capable in that first job, and the evidence shows that is what normally happens. You are less likely to identify the ability to learn, which in turn, can give you indications of the ability for people to grow and perhaps become future leaders. I sometimes have an urge to throw away all our recruitment processes and just see what would happen. I think we would probably have a higher number of failures in their first job, but we may well also have a high number of people who are prospective leaders. I am quite sure I wouldn't do that, but, I am seriously looking at ways to address this problem of recruiting people who have got that potential because I think we are running a high risk of squeezing that out of them, when they arrive, or even not recruiting them in the first place.
>
> (24A: senior executive, multi-national information systems company)

Safe adaptive-oriented recruitment tends to suggest a financial-oriented, conservative, organisation structure and culture that, out of policy or necessity, sees little need to engage other stakeholders. Thus, one might suggest that the degree of inclusiveness of the organisation is directly related to the level of risk in the recruitment process. This is explored further in Chapter 5.

Employee development

The approach taken by organisations towards the training and development of employees (discussed later in Chapter 10) reflects the value-added, enhancing and transformation continuum. At one end, there is the development of staff to meet the immediate needs of the organisation. This cost-flexible approach matches training to organisational needs. It is more about fulfilling immediate needs and improving job-relevant competencies than any investment in the wider development of the individual.

> We are looking at basic managerial skills at the moment, trying to put together a series of modules based around the competencies that we are looking for in our managers, it's almost like getting a passport, I have acquired those skills, I have got that experience and I feel competent in that area, so we are trying to put a whole training matrix together around that. It's very much about our culture.
>
> (29A: supply manager, medium-sized health product manufacturer)

However, in organisations that may historically have had a more focused, job-related approach, the idea of becoming a 'learning organisation'[2] is beginning to germinate:

---

[2] The notion of learning organisation is also somewhat ambiguous. In some uses it refers to an organisation that facilitates life-long learning for the employees, Ford's well-documented approach is an example. Alternatives are that it is an organisation that attempts to identify the learning requirements of employees so as to continuously improve the organisation. For example:

> In contrast to general education, company training is needs-driven. New graduate recruits are encouraged to develop the type of behaviour that will be required of them as managers and professionals to ensure the company's commitment to continuous improvement is achieved. New recruits must have the capacity to accept appraisal of the skills and capabilities required of them by the company and to help formulate plans to acquire these. This will ultimately enable them to manage BT's business in such a way as to develop a culture of continuous improvement amongst all staff and further develop the company as a learning organisation. (BT, 1993, p. 38)

A third usage is the notion of the organisation that continually learns about its role in a wider setting: something close to the 'inclusive' organisation (RSA, 1995).

> I would say we are a long way from being a learning culture, but I would say it is not unachievable. Five years ago, had we have had this conversation I might have said that I thought it was probably unachievable. I think we are moving very slowly towards it, but I think it is a bit like getting the stone rolling down the hill. When a few people begin to see the light we could really motor at a very fast pace.
>
> (79A: strategic manager, large, chartered accountants)

A more 'inclusive' approach aims at developing staff in more general ways, encouraging life-long learning and providing a wider commitment which recognises employees as important stakeholders in the organisation.

> …if someone wanted to do an Open University course, or a course which may not be a 100% relevant to their current job but it may well fit into a career path that they are thinking to develop, I am trying to be quite flexible there. (37A: deputy chief executive, small housing association)

Higher education–employer interface

The higher education-employer interface takes a variety of forms (Chapter 9) which also match the value-added to transformation continuum. For some organisations, the emphasis is on links that provide short-term enhancement of the organisation, through such things as commissioned research, work-related training courses and continuous professional development. In such cases, employers are customers looking for value-for-money for their investment. Higher education is a supplier of a product and values such links for the increase in income that is generated.

> The most stable and constructive type of relationship is one where we have a need and you can supply something, or indeed vice versa… you supply the best graduates and we have a need for them, and in the former case it is we have a need for say, some research to be done, you can do the research, so I think it is increasingly becoming almost a commercial or a market-driven relationship. (66A: recruitment manager, multinational petro-chemical company)

At the other end, the focus is on forging long-term links and partnership endeavours to ensure a continuous exchange of ideas of mutual benefit. Employers are participants rather than customers committed to spending time and effort as well as cash in building up relationships as a stakeholder in higher education. Academics are not merely providers of services but engage with and listen to the points of view of external organisations, including considering how these may feed into curricula, assessment procedures, and programme presentation.

> We have quite a lot of links. We have a post called a university liaison officer, and we route all our university work through him and he keeps in very close contact. We have a lot of contracts with university research department and he keeps an eye on those. And he deals with the recruitment links. We also sponsor chairs and research posts. We have a couple of professorships, and we have a number of Ph.D. studentships. Some of our people are invited to give guest lectures on courses. I am sometimes asked to give talks at [a university], I give talks in the management school. There is also a course that we jointly sponsor and approve. It is a special MBA course – a group of companies came together and worked with the university and approved this particular MBA course and we all send a number of students per year on to it. (82A: head of technology strategy, large power company)

Workplace profile

To help understand the relationship between graduate attributes and organisational change, it is helpful to build up a workplace profile. Such a profile identifies the characteristics of a number of interrelated elements including: organisational flexibility and ethos, the nature of employer empowerment, graduate attributes and approach to work, employee loyalty, recruitment practices, staff training and development, and higher education-employer links. For the sake of exposition, these elements, discussed above, can be seen as a set of parallel continua ranging from value-added through enhancing to transformative characteristics. (Figure 3.2).

Figure 3.2 Workplace profile

	Adding value	*Evolving*	*Transforming*
Flexible organisation Ethos and performance criteria	Cost-flexible. Short-term investments Success = profit, one-dimensional performance indicator, financial imperatives.	Response flexible. Cost conscious but attempting to develop partnerships with client groups to secure longer-term future.	Stakeholder flexible Long-term vision – 'inclusive' Multi-layered performance indicators, socially responsible: stakeholder criteria.
Empowerment	Self-regulatory empowerment	Delegated empowerment	Stakeholder empowerment
Graduate attributes and approach	Adaptive: knowledge and skills brought to the organisation. Ability to fit in to organisational culture. Takes no risks, does job competently 'Yes' people who have high expectations that if they please others they will succeed.	Adaptable: Ability to learn and add to knowledge and skill, ability to use knowledge and skills in face of change, to interact effectively, work in teams and communicate at a variety of levels. Demonstrates initiative within a pre-set framework.	Transformative: the use of transformative skills (analysis, critique, synthesis, multi-layered communication) to facilitate innovative teamwork. Inventive, knows boundaries but pushes them.
Employee loyalty	Loyalty dependent on cash and promotion.	Loyalty based on perception of future progress and commitment to principles of organisation.	Wider commitment to organisation through direct involvement as acknowledged stakeholder.
Staff development and training	Looking for enhancement of job-related competencies: return on investment.	Broader enhancement of staff, although still circumscribed by job relevance.	Learning organisation. Competencies plus: empower employees through broad development of staff.
Recruitment	Safe, conservative – prioritise those who will fit in.	Mixture of job-specific and speculative recruitment as senior management/ partner feedstock.	Risky – innovative, seeking those who will lead change.
Higher education–Employer interface	Employers as customers interested in value for money. HE as supplier of product, looking for additional cash.	Mutual involvement in mainly short-term projects for added-value.	Employers as participants, interested in spending time and effort as well as cash in building relationships. Academics listening. Development of partnership and exchange of ideas.

However, it is important to establish the following interpretative framework for the workplace profile.

- The profile is an orienting device to help clarify the relationship between graduate attributes and organisational change in the workplace.
- There is no 'ideal' profile, in the sense of desirable, optimum or stable state, to which individuals or organisations should strive. The position on the profile will, in part, be determined by external forces.
- There is no assumption that all individuals or all parts of a complex organisation will fit into a single point on any dimension of the profile. For example, some individuals may add value through directly applicable knowledge and being able to work effectively in a project team, others may have innovative ideas and be able to inspire teams to push boundaries. Some parts of an organisation may need to focus on adding-value while others may prioritise innovation.

What this schema offers is a means by which to understand the nature of the organisation and the graduate role within it. It is not to suggest that the transformation end of the continuum is intrinsically better than the value-added end. On the contrary, within every organisation there must be a balance between value-added and transformation:

> The company, I believe, is looking at the moment for people who will fit any number of roles, so they are looking for future managers. A future manager is somebody who can manage a finance department, marketing, sales, the all-round good person. Personally, at the moment, what I am looking for is somebody who will actually be able to do the job for me, that is, a finance person who doesn't necessarily fit in with a marketing profile, certainly doesn't fit in with a sales profile. To actually get people who will fit all of those profiles I think is very, very difficult. At the same time the company is looking for high flyers, you don't always want the highest flyers you can get, especially right at the moment we have got so many of them round the company that we are having problems getting the work done. People with great ideas, but actually accomplishing those ideas becomes a bit of a nightmare. So there is a slight difference between people who are looking strategically ahead and people like me who are just trying to operate tactically at the moment to deliver.
>
> (22B: sales manager, multinational reprographic equipment manufacturer)

If an organisation is to be flexible in terms of cost, and also take an inclusive approach – being responsive to a wider group of stakeholders – then there needs to be a balance of adaptive, adaptable and transformative people. That is, there is a need for people who can work in teams, who can relate quickly to an evolving structure and do not expect rigid lines of command and communication, but also people who are able to go beyond this and who take responsibility, inspire people to take forward ideas, who can take on various roles and grow the job, who lead rather than simply manage people.

Similarly, it is a mistake to assume that the traditional measurement of the 'best' or 'intellectually brightest' graduates are going to make an impact at the transformative end of the spectrum. Indeed, 'captains on the pitch' are unlikely to be 'boffins'. Intellect, while important, is not itself an indicator of transformative potential. Correspondingly, the transformative recruit is no more likely to be from a particular subject area or institution. It is a matter of a range of attributes and the ability to reflexively put them into practice.

The 'inclusivity' gap

Tomorrow's Company (RSA, 1995) claimed that most companies are 'convinced' by an 'inclusive' approach. Although not discussing the 'inclusive approach' directly, our research would lead us to agree with the impression gained in the RSA study. However, our research would confirm that there is a gap between what business leaders claim is important and the priorities that they set for their companies. To varying degrees, a significant number of survey respondents still appear, in practice, to reproduce aspects of the 1980s ethos, notably, top-down directive management and the over-reliance on financial performance indicators.

Although there are efforts to develop stronger client and customer relationships, and to empower employees, many of these are still initiated by financial imperatives. Senior management must, of necessity, be involved in developing and encouraging flexible structures if employees are to feel secure in developing transformative ideas. However, what appears to be occurring in most organisations is the 'imposition of empowerment' through organisational change and the increased expectations on the workforce to perform and respond to flexible work arrangements that suit the organisation. There appears to be little evidence of any democratic evolution of the 'inclusive' approach. The situation will undoubtedly change, but graduates need to be aware of the wider context and tension between flexibility for empowerment of stakeholders and flexibility driven by short-term financial imperatives. Most organisations, public as well as private, seem to be unsure whether, or how, to extricate themselves from the horns of that particular dilemma.

Summary

- Flexibility in organisational structures ranges from 'cost-flexibility' through 'response flexibility' to 'stakeholder flexibility'. Cost-flexibility prioritises responsiveness to costs while, at the other end, stakeholder-flexibility adopts an 'inclusive approach' to the concerns of a range of clients, customers and employees in addition to shareholders.

- Cost-flexible arrangements are primarily designed to enhance the responsiveness of the organisation rather than to empower the individual.

- The flexible organisation provides the potential to empower employees: empowerment takes a range of forms from self-regulatory through to stakeholder empowerment.

- Employers require transformative agents to deal with change. Transformation takes various forms, and can be seen to fall onto a continuum from added value through to evolutionary transformation.

- Employers also want people who can fit in and be effective as quickly as possible – the emphasis is on adaptive performers.

- There is a dilemma as transformative people, by definition, have ideas, cause friction, look ahead, take a 'helicopter view' and 'look outside the box'.

- Organisations are concerned that adaptive people are likely to have characteristics that would make them attractive to other employers, not least their flexibility and mobility.

- Furthermore, graduates are thought to have expectations of rapid advancement through a clearly-defined career path within an organisation leading to 'interesting' work and senior management positions.

- However, in a world where organisations are driven by financial concerns, and where a flexible organisation means one primarily designed to ensure the most rapid response to short-term cost considerations (i.e. cost-flexible), there is little opportunity to exhibit loyalty to employees. Thus there is no incentive for 'good' mobile, flexible employees to stay. The cost-flexible firm is in danger of losing its investment in adaptive people.

- The flexible organisation requires adaptive, adaptable and transformative people, those who can work in teams and relate quickly to an evolving structure, and not expect rigid lines of command and communication, but also people who can take responsibility who are able to develop ideas, take on various roles and grow the job – this conflicts among other things with the perceived expectations of graduates.

- Graduate status in itself is no guarantee of either adaptiveness or adaptability let alone transformative potential. In a sense, graduate status adds some immediate value through knowledge and some 'higher-level skills' such as analysis; however, there may be counter tendencies that reduce the value added, or at least delay it: viz. failure to understand organisational culture, commercial pressures or lack of prior opportunity to put theory into practice.

- What employers want are people who can get to the start of the transformation continuum quickly and have the potential to move up it rapidly, thus helping to continue to transform their flexible organisation.

- Recruitment policies and practices tend to identify 'safe' procedures that achieve 'value-added' as rapidly as possible, but transformative potential is often sacrificed.

- An 'inclusive approach' provides a framework to enhance and encourage a transformative process as it provides a context to support a broader flow of ideas from a wide range of stakeholders rather than the restriction and insecurity that comes from financially-dominated (cost-flexible) organisations.

- The degree of inclusiveness of the organisation can be seen as directly related to the level of risk in the recruitment process – safe, adaptive-oriented recruitment tends to suggest a financial-oriented organisational structure, with little attempt to engage other stakeholders.

- A workplace profile helps to understand how management organises the workplace to cope with change and how this relates to graduate attributes.

- Respondents appear, in principle, to endorse an 'inclusive', empowering approach to the development of the flexible organisation. In practice, financial requirements often override wider stakeholder concerns.

4 Changes in graduate careers: implications of flexibility

It often stated that the traditional graduate job has disappeared. Although downsizing and delayering result in fewer jobs overall, especially in large organisations, it is less clear that they result in fewer potential graduate jobs. Traditional 'fast-track' graduate recruitment may be declining (see Chapter 5) but the shifting nature of work, with an evident shift towards more ownership of the work process, opens up considerable potential for graduates, provided they step outside traditional preconceptions of a graduate career. Changing structures, associated with downsizing and delayering, increasingly emphasise empowerment, which in turn is seen to benefit from, or even require, a more educated workforce.

In short, a new set of graduate opportunities appears to have emerged, which graduates need to be aware of and be prepared to seize and develop:

> A lot of traditional jobs have disappeared, have been re-structured... So the jobs are changing and therefore the type of graduate we are looking for is changing as well to fit these different jobs... We have a production function and an engineering function and traditionally the production managers have managed the process, the engineers have maintained it. We are now looking in certain areas to amalgamate those roles so that you have, for example, an engineer as a production manager, and so again the requirements continue to change. And the one thing I can say that is going to be stable is the fact that we will be always changing.
>
> (40A: manager of training and development, large steel manufacturer)

Expanding graduate opportunities

The advent of the flexible organisation means that there are probably more opportunities for graduates although they are different from traditional graduate jobs. This concurs with recent data from the Institute of Employment Studies, which suggested that graduate recruiters expected an increase of 18% in the number of vacancies in 1995 compared to 1994 and that graduate unemployment was beginning to fall (DfEE, 1996a).

The development of the flexible organisation has created opportunities for graduates especially in 'symbolic-analytic services' (Reich, 1991). Rather than graduate opportunities disappearing, there is every indication that graduate opportunities are expanding, although outside the traditional ('high-flier') graduate career. There are organisations who are recruiting more graduates as a matter of policy or expediency, as a newspaper editorial training officer commented: 'When I started, graduate intake was about 10%, now its about 95%' (48A).

There are also indicators that expansion in small organisations, especially those providing symbolic-analytic services, will provide graduate opportunities. Indeed, more graduates are being employed by smaller companies, with about a quarter of all graduates employed by companies with less than 25 employees (DfEE, 1996a). There is some uncertainty as to whether this increase reflects a 'genuine increase in graduate demand' in small organisations or is merely a transient feature of the recession. However, it is certainly leading to a blurring of the distinction between graduate and non-graduate jobs (Flanders, 1995).

Restructuring, reorganisation and the development of a more client-oriented approach provide other opportunities for graduate work. Furthermore, graduates are tending to target areas that were previously staffed by non-graduates.

Indeed, there is a growing expectation, in some organisations that new recruits, particularly for management posts, will be graduates: 'In the UK, for better or for worse, it is now virtually impossible, in [the company], to get a management job without being a graduate' (11A). One small, specialist employment agency considered that graduates 'will eventually fulfil every role in the organisation' (17A).

Expansion, reorganisation and restructuring

An expanding source of graduate employment is small and medium enterprises, especially those providing symbolic-analytic services.

> There are so many different areas that you need to concentrate on when you are running the business that there are too many for two of us to do. So we are looking at passing some of those tasks off further down the line and graduates tend to be fairly capable people, with a reasonable level of commonsense when coming into the job. You tend to find that you can pass that type of work down to them and it gets done fairly responsibly. Graduates tend to come in with a different approach, a different angle on things, new ideas which perhaps we wouldn't consider ourselves. So we see that continuing over the next five to ten years.
>
> (15A: partner, small chartered accountants)

Some expansion in small and medium organisations is not specifically linked to increased graduate recruitment but it is likely that graduate-level recruits will be targeted:

> One thing I am certain is that we are going to grow, because we are a relatively young company, and in three years we have expanded significantly. We need to readjust our numbers, we are now looking at the marketplace to take more people on... The customer side of the business that will certainly grow so account managers and the like will start to come to the fore. (39B: team manager, medium-sized software services contractor)

Developments of information technology provides another potential expansion in graduate recruitment and these are far from confined to computer systems applications and development:

> We have had our existing [computer] system for about four years and there are now better systems available which could streamline some of our tasks. That could have an effect because certain tasks will maybe disappear or be automated whereas potentially other jobs may be created out of that... The business plan we have envisages an expansion over the next five to six years, albeit that there is no direct correlation between the number of units that we manage and own with the number of staff, but it may come to the stage, five to ten years ahead, when we might think about having additional resources just to cope with business growth. (37B: director of financial services, small housing association)

On the other hand, some smaller organisations, as they grow rapidly, sometimes actually require fewer graduates, as they move from research and product development into manufacturing. For example, a firm that specialises in medical laser technology needed graduate (or indeed, postgraduate) recruits in the early years of development, but now have a proportionately lower requirement for graduates with specialist skills as they move into production. Nonetheless, they are finding that the type of people they want 'tend to have put themselves through graduate education' (23A). This is also reflected in situations where expansion means taking on more support staff into an established graduate environment, so that jobs that might not appear as graduate jobs are filled by graduates:

> Probably all our finance department are graduates, probably all our personnel department are graduates. A substantial number of our secretaries are graduates. A substantial number of our IT function are graduates, so it is very much a graduate-orientated environment.
>
> (09A: head of personnel, large law firm)

Even in organisations where graduates have not traditionally played a major role, there is a growing trend to graduate recruitment, such as one international fast-food organisation who expect a significant increase in recruitment of graduates to management positions (61A). This growth in recruitment is often because of changing qualification routes or the need to 'professionalise' in a growth area:

> I'm not aware that the Group has deliberately targeted graduates for any post. I think its gratuitous if somebody has been a graduate. It might be seen as a useful part of a person's profile. The next five years or so the Group will be dominated by more and more people doing the social work-type role, and that will inevitably mean that we need to be looking at the organisational structure of care, and whereas we have been talking about a head of care who was qualified in some way or another, I think we will be talking about qualifications reaching much further down.
> (03A: head teacher, small private school for children with special needs)

In some areas there are new jobs as a result of a greater emphasis on a client orientation:

> …there are more jobs now that didn't exist five or six years ago, and I suppose a big one for us would be customer service. Customer service advisers need team leaders, which is a graduate job, quite a tough job. We've got a technical equivalent to that – field managers who look after teams of engineers who go onto customers' premises.
> (32B: recruitment and development manager, large telecommunications organisation)

Graduate targeting

In addition, there is a tendency for a wider range of jobs to be seen as target occupations by graduates, not least because of the 'exponential increase' (40B) in the number and range of degree courses now on offer.

> I would say graduates have had an increasing role [in this organisation]. When I first started a lot of journalists were recruited from papers, whereas now there are a lot of targeted postgraduate courses just for radio journalists. I would say over the last five years 90% of my recruits have been graduates.
> (13A: news manager, medium-sized private local radio station)

The increasing number of graduates on the labour market, irrespective of any flexibility-led reorganisation requiring graduate-level recruits, has encouraged some organisations to consider recruiting graduates, where perhaps they would not have done in the past. As Hugh Smith, of BT, commented in *Personnel Today*: 'There is no internal pressure at BT to take graduates into traditional school-leaver jobs but with the numbers of graduates growing it is almost inevitable.' This is a view reflected by respondents in the survey: 'It isn't something that I have looked at but now that you've actually asked, I think, "Oh yes", I say to people who recruit on my team, "have a look for a graduate."' (12A).

However, there are employers who do not see a larger number of available graduates leading to higher graduate recruitment as 'there just aren't the jobs available in the industry' (42A).

These increasing opportunities, within the flexible organisation, whether it incorporates cost-, response-, or stakeholder-flexibility, have implications for graduates. They have to be able to adjust to a less hierarchical and rigid structure; be prepared for a less clear career path and promotion ladder; accept that advancement will be based on effective contribution not seniority; be able to interact with a wide range of personnel, clients as well as colleagues at all levels; work in teams and expect to have a wide ranging, integrated job; expect to move between different areas rather than stay within a specialist field; and expect a substantial work load, considerable responsibility and be prepared to work flexible hours.

Furthermore, recruitment into 'graduate' careers is much more competitive and academia needs to prepare graduates to be able to hold their own in the graduate labour market. Furthermore, changes in organisational structure, and the increased numbers of graduates on the labour market mean that there is more and more expectation that graduates will enter organisations at all levels.

Degree as first base

A degree may once have been a passport into graduate employment, but with organisational changes and the expansion in the numbers of graduates, that is no longer the case. However, although having a first degree is no guarantee of a job, it does establish some credentials and provide some sort of guarantee of a particular level of ability and an indication of potential.

> ...the fact that they have that degree basically confirms they are people who think in a certain way and have certain abilities, so the next stage is a number of key competencies.
>
> (47A: personnel manager, multi-national food manufacturer)

A degree provides a basic benchmark for recruiters and by targeting graduates they are 'limiting the risk' associated with new employees (27D). However:

> When recruiting a graduate straight from university I want somebody who not only knows the square root of a jar of pickles but somebody who can get the lid off it as well.
>
> (84A: head of administration, emergency service)

Respondents from more than half the organisations in the sample indicated that having a degree was a necessary, but by no means a sufficient, criterion for getting a job, and that a degree is one 'building block' of many required from a graduate (09A). For many senior managers getting the job depends on such things as motivation and 'managerial potential' (08A):

> Everybody tends to put their academic qualifications on the first part of their CV – I'm not interested. I look: "Yes, degree. Fine!". Of far more importance to me is what was the last job they did and what did it entail and what do they say about it, because all that lot is the base, everything you did until you were 21, or whatever it is these days, is just preparing you for what is going to be the onslaught in the future.
>
> (60A: director commercial operations, large vehicle manufacturer)

> What plays a role in the final decision is, are we talking about people who have done something extra as well, whether it is extra-curricular activities or whether it is work experience, or climbing Mount Everest. Something that distinguishes them and therefore can give you some clue about drive, ambition, commercial awareness or whatever.
>
> (57A: senior executive, large brewing company)

However, it is incumbent on graduates to be aware that their learning is not over just because they have a degree:

> I think employers are realising and appreciating that a good graduate has more potential than a non-graduate, and will have better basic skills... But what graduates need to appreciate and understand is that it is only the beginning, they are only starting work, and there is still one hell of a lot to learn.
>
> (31A: managing director, medium-sized house builders and regenerators)

There is little evidence, from the sample, that there is any currency in the naive view that graduates will find employment simply because they have a degree. At best, as several respondents noted, 'the degree gets you the interview, when you are in the interview it's up to you to sell yourself' (01B), 'although I am not necessarily officially skilled in graphic design, the course gave me a broad enough spectrum of ability to get my foot in the door here' (14C). One respondent suggested that employers are no longer impressed by a degree as they see it as 'providing standard skills for an average job' (01C) and another thought that as degree education becomes the norm a degree will be:

> of mild interest, just like somebody might say, "well I'm interested in cycling". It'll be a part of the person's profile. Whereas at one time it was of overwhelming importance, what will happen is that the person as a person, will come to the fore.
>
> (03A: head teacher, small private school for children with special needs)

For some respondents the degree is necessary. This is clearly the case in postgraduate professions such as teaching and for advanced status in other areas such as becoming a health promotion specialist.[1] In law, for example:

> Graduates are pivotal. Graduate recruitment is our absolute lifeblood more than anywhere else I have ever worked. Even in accountancy you could recruit accountants after they have qualified. Here we see our future partners when we recruit our graduates, so it really is a long-term investment.
> (12A: personnel director, large law firm)

In other areas, recent graduates are convinced that, although they needed to exhibit a range of skills and abilities, they 'wouldn't have got the job without the degree' (15C), (20C):

> Well I wouldn't be able to work for the [company] now if I hadn't got a degree. I've got a lot of skills, certain skills such as analytical skills and confidence skills. The big thing is that I have a degree. It would have caused more problems if I didn't have one, people would have wanted to know why I didn't have a degree.
> (43C: news producer, large public broadcasting organisation)

Some respondents thought that a degree is necessary for promotion as it 'leapfrogs you to a position' (40C) and it provides more opportunities for training and development: 'A-level recruits don't seem to get the sort of lift and recognition that grads get' (47C). Some respondents were of the view that even if someone gets a job without a degree, future career prospects are blighted:

> I think the bulk of people that we recruit into the expectation for management positions should come from the graduate or graduate-equivalent population, for two reasons. One is that they have a number of skills, all this computer stuff they actually are going to need it now, and even more so in the future. The other reason is, if they haven't got a degree or a degree equivalent, then in management ranks they are at a disadvantage with their peers. I have forced one or two people through part-time degree courses to make sure that when they are in their thirties they can compete against the other graduates.
> (40D: chemical technician, large steel manufacturer)

For one respondent, employment opportunities are linked to spiralling credentialism:

> Obviously you need degrees to get anywhere and when you have got a degree you can't find anything so most employers are going to want you to get more pieces of paper.
> (29D: promotions buyer, medium-sized health product manufacturer)

This view was supported by one postgraduate who saw his M.Sc. as a 'foot in the door' opening up opportunities that were unavailable to him with just his first degree (39C).

Experience rather than graduate status

However, a few respondents claimed that graduate status is far less important than appropriate experience:

> Within our industry, fortunately, experience is the main thing that tends to be looked for, if there is somebody without experience we tend to not want to pay what a graduate would expect.
> (26C: salesman, multi-national business machines manufacturer)

> One of my colleagues is a graduate and has been in the business for a year and I am training her. It really does not matter, and I am two years younger than her and I have a very high

---

1 In such areas, the postgraduate professional qualification is often much more important, although a degree is often a pre-requisite of obtaining the professional recognition. However, even in areas that seem to be graduate strongholds, such as accountancy, there are experiments to expand non-graduate entry. For example, KPMG have started a policy of taking bright A-level students (*THES*, 6 September, 1996)

level of responsibility at an early age because I have demonstrated that I can cope with the responsibility and I am mature enough to handle it and it does not matter whether I've got a degree or A-levels.
(54D: assistant personnel manager, large international retailers)

At root, for many organisations, especially but not exclusively smaller ones, experience equates with being effective quickly, which is increasingly important and means experience becomes the 'prime consideration' (18A). For some organisations, professional qualification is also important:

The people we recruit are young, normally thirtyish, and they've had professional qualification plus, if we are lucky, two or three, or four years experience with an accountancy firm or with a major bank.
(27A: director, large public financial institution)

If someone had got ten years' relevant experience and a good track record the fact that they were not a graduate would not necessarily rule them out, especially if they had got a professional qualification.
(51B: research and information manager, medium-sized community health authority)

In the end, as a few respondents pointed out, it is the ability to persuade recruiters that the applicant could do the job, irrespective of graduate status:

It's ability that counts and whether or not you are a graduate makes not a lot of difference at the interview stage... You have got to able to convince us that you can do the work, so it makes not a jot of difference to us whether everybody who comes to us for a particular job that we advertise was a graduate or nobody is, as long as we can find the person among that pile who can do the job.
(41A: general manager, small registered charity)

Facing up to flexibility

Structural changes aimed at developing a more flexible organisation have implications for graduates. The changes suggest that graduates, whether they seize the new opportunities accorded by the increase in demand for symbolic-analytic services across all sectors, pursue traditional career routes or take on 'non-graduate' jobs, will need to accommodate five major outcomes of flatter, leaner structures:

- an unclear graduate promotion ladder;
- a need to be able to interact with a wide range of personnel;
- working in project-oriented teams rather than working as an individual in a traditional chain of responsibility;
- integrated job requirements;
- greater workload, longer working hours and more responsibility.

Unclear promotion ladder

Graduates need to be aware that promotion and career progression within delayered organisations are far less well defined than in traditional hierarchical organisations.

I think you can't come in any more and say you want to be a brand manager for the rest of your life, because it won't happen. Even since I have been here we have been through two restructures and my whole career plan, that I had when I came in, now does not exist.
(57C: category manager, large brewing company)

One of the problems, if you have a flatter structure, is that you can't always offer [graduates] a clear career path because there aren't the levels in the structure any more. Therefore, in terms of job satisfaction and career movement, they have got to be prepared to move sideways, to move around within the organisation a fair bit. What we are ultimately looking for is far more rounded people not specialists who can only do one thing. We need them to have exposure to a number of different area.
(76A: senior executive, multi-national motor component manufacturer)

GRADUATES' WORK: ORGANISATIONAL CHANGE AND STUDENTS' ATTRIBUTES

> Companies today, global companies, are moving towards flatter structures so you no longer have a very well defined progression from one level to the next in a structured process. The focus is going to be as much on developing people horizontally as it is vertically. Having said that, there still is a structure in place that does allow for upward growth and movement... But there is far less focus on the hierarchy and structure than has been the case in the past.
> (32A: development and training manager, large telecommunications organisation)

Not only are there fewer opportunities for promotion but more and more organisations, it seems, are moving towards a 'performance culture' (10B) for promotion rather than progression through grades based on time served. Even the civil service, which previously had 'quite a rigid careers frame with about eight or nine grades' (38A) that people worked through over time, is changing:

> All our systems are shifting to performance-based rather than on the basis of attainment, time serving or grading. Our whole pay system is going to performance-based. Hardly any element of pay in future will just be cost-of-living based. So the people who do better will get more pay. There is an education process for those who think they are very bright graduates, to understand that they are not born with a silver spoon in their mouth, that however good they may be in academic terms when they come to us, what we will be looking for is the ability to *do*. If they can't, they will be marked down. They will probably be on probation. They will be reverted. They will be given notice to quit. Whatever.
> (38B: director of personnel, civil service)

As flatter organisations have fewer grades, the emphasis is on advancement *within* grades and this involves looking at career progression 'in terms of responsibility and the role for which they are rewarded' (56A). For many graduates this means taking the initiative to develop their careers:

> There are fewer opportunities for people to start work at the lower end of the scale, and progress up a company and actually develop a career. People who start at the bottom now have to use their own initiative and take control of their own lives through looking at developing skills outside their work if they are going to progress... I don't see this changing in the next five years. The onus is very much more on the individual to take control if they are going to achieve anything through work.
> (45A: senior advisor, small public watchdog organisation)

Other organisations consider it their responsibility to assist this proactive process as employees run up against progression barriers:

> ... you are likely to be a salesperson or an admin. officer or a service technician for up to ten years, and in order to maintain a level of interest within that job you've got to be learning new approaches within the same job, and as a management team we have to keep coming up with new approaches to the same problems.
> (26B: area sales manager, multi-national business machines manufacturer)

In essence, if graduates join organisations with a 'traditional' notion that they are going to rise rapidly through the organisation, they are likely to be disappointed. Delayering has 'some implications for career progression for graduates coming in, but only if they see themselves in terms of management posts' (05A). Increasingly, graduates are likely to be part of the expanding symbolic-analytic area and should expect to 'build a career through a number of sideways moves' (63B):

> We have a research laboratory with 600 Ph.D.s working there, so there is certainly scope for a good career in that one area. But if they want to be the next chairman then they have got to put that behind them fairly soon in their career. From being head of lab., move across to be technical director, and then head of detergents regionally and the next thing you are a director. It sounds weird – you spent ten years doing your degree and then a doctorate to then find that you are going to turn your back on it all. You certainly need to get some experience in one area, enjoy it and then move out from that and get some general business awareness.
> (11D: graduate trainer, multi-national food manufacturers)

This shifting graduate role, linked to promotion, is not something confined to large organisations:

> A good example perhaps is our marketing manager. She started off as a secretary and [A's] personal assistant and she gravitated into marketing when she had done her Marketing Diploma. Now she's our marketing manager. (23B: general manager, small medical lasers manufacturer)

Interact with a wide range of personnel

The second major outcome of flatter, leaner organisational structures is the need to interact with a wider range of personnel, from shop-floor through to senior managers. Furthermore, interaction is not simply extending workers' horizons within old hierarchical frameworks; it involves more responsibility to engage with cross-functional teams:

> Within the formal structure nearly everybody is a member of a horizontal team and [graduates] have got to work well with that team... Then of course they can be in another situation where they are part of a cross-functional team, where there can be quite a range of seniority because of the different skills required for a project.
>
> (11B: head of management recruitment and training, multi-national food manufacturers)

One important aspect of delayered structures is a lack of formality and the ability to cross traditional hierarchical boundaries. This may be part of the normal working process, 'If I have a query, and my boss is out, I will go to his boss, no one is upset that you have gone over anybody's head, and their roles are far more mingled' (26C). Alternatively, it may be a means to resolve issues 'it is quite informal and I feel I can go to a senior manager if I'm not getting joy with my line manager' (19C).

However, a delayered organisation (irrespective of size) does not always embody an empowering structure:

> There isn't an apparent openness on the management's part and when there are issues that need to be addressed, they don't get addressed and it just gets shoved under the carpet and people feel frustrated, everyone talks behind closed doors.
>
> (19C: community worker, small publicly funded community health centre)

On a prosaic level, being able to successfully interact with a range of people, clients as well as colleagues, requires an appreciation of how one is perceived and ensuring that one achieves an appropriate impact – even when the preconception is rooted in sexism and ageism:

> If I am talking to someone very, very senior within an organisation, I don't feel threatened by that any more. You can find that intimidating. A very senior manager thinking – because of your age, because you are female – "We have got this young totty who walks in at 21 years of age. Should I take her seriously?" You've got to prove yourself the whole time. It is a challenge. The way you look, the way you speak, everything is so important. Clients wouldn't take me seriously unless I changed the way I looked and my whole approach. Instead of bouncing into a meeting, I was much more calm and it just gave a very different impression and it has made a huge difference to the way I work and how people look at me.
>
> (28D: project manager, small design and communications company)

Of course, one has to tread a careful path between clone-like absorption into a culture, effective challenging of stereotypes and the establishment of an individual identity. Awareness of other perspectives is also important as organisations develop an international perspective:

> I think we will see more and more senior managers and trainees within [the organisation] being encouraged, and left with little choice, to gain more and more international experience. This will become a requirement of any future important people within [the organisation]. I think you will see more moving around, you will probably see more corporate training programmes, involving international opportunities and a growth in that area.
>
> (47A: personnel manager, multi-national food manufacturer)

As Reich (1991, p. 171) points out, many companies are international even if they appear to be based in one country. Typically, a large company will have headquarters in one country, have production facilities on several continents, marketing and distribution centres on every continent, with lenders and investors in all major financial capitals and will be competing with similar companies: 'battle lines no longer correspond with national borders'.

Working in teams

Increasingly, organisations require less individualised modes of working and operate on the basis of project-oriented teams, which they see as the most efficient and most creative way to work.

> I think probably 30 years ago or so (I wasn't around then) teamworking was a matter of people who fitted in. They all came from a similar education, Oxbridge or Delft or something. Ten years ago it was much more individual – Thatcherism was all the individual, you fought for your individual bonus. Now, in the de-layered management of today, teamworking is increasingly important, particularly in the Asian cultures – bear in mind we are very international. And I think that will increasingly be reflected in the future.
>
> (66A: recruitment manager, multi-national petro-chemical company)

This has clear implications for graduates who come from a culture of individualised success.[2] Indeed, in some areas, notably the sciences, the university culture is almost diametrically opposed to that in a modern commercial science setting where people need to work in teams 'sharing there science' so they can 'understand each other's perspective and therefore contribute to the whole' (63A).

Graduates need to be aware that team working involves taking on a variety of roles:

> You can't have a team where every member of the team is a leader because you won't operate as a team. You need somebody who is the leader but you need someone who is the doer and someone who is the facilitator and so on.
>
> (28B: design manager, small design and communications company)

In some respects, teamworking is not just a personal challenge but an organisational one, dependent on enabling and encouraging teamworking through sufficiently well planned arrangements.

> It works as long as you have enough people to make it work. But if you have a team that's only got three people in it and one person's sick and one's on holiday... As long as you've got the numbers. It certainly empowers, if people are interested in responsibility but it's only as good or as strong as the bridge that controls it.
>
> (48A: editorial training officer, medium-sized newspaper publisher)

One recent graduate was of the view that teamworking was superficial:

> They tell me I'm working in a team but it's just words: I still feel like I am working in a hierarchy. I don't believe that will ever go away, not in British firms, because you have always got the managers and partners, who you are never going to treat as an equal because of the power they hold over you. If anything, I could see structures moving further back towards hierarchy. I guess I am supposed to be saying that it is all devolved and we are all team players but that's not the case.
>
> (71C: senior auditor, large international accountants)

---

2   Even where programmes of study provide students with opportunities for teamworking, assessment regimes frequently encourage the identification of individual contribution. The culture in higher education is one of individual success and failure, reflected in degree classification, and teamworking in an academic context often exhibits an element of artificiality. There is a need to explore more meaningful ways of encouraging and rewarding group working as a process. For most students, a placement experience provides the only real opportunity to develop meaningful teamworking skills.

Integrated job requirement

Across Europe, the requirements of flexibility have successfully challenged the boundaries of traditional job demarcation at lower levels but until recently resistance to flexibility has persisted at higher levels (Boyer, 1989). Managerial roles, while remaining specific in many European countries, are tending to become more flexible in Germany, Sweden, Ireland and the UK, where job roles are widening at all levels (Hutchinson and Brewster, 1994). Our respondents endorse this development: well over half the respondents indicated that delayering leads to less clearly demarcated job descriptions and a greater need for employees to undertake a wider range of jobs with less clerical or administrative support.

Flexible job roles require vertical integration such as using information technology to prepare reports or maintain databases, doing tasks that may formerly have been 'carried out by secretaries and administrative assistants' (54A):

> People are going to be more self-servicing. I don't think there are going to be secretaries and clerical assistants like there are now... People are going to be more highly qualified but at the same time they are going to be doing more for themselves because so many people have got degrees these days and more and more people are getting post-degree qualifications. So I just think there is going to be millions and trillions of graduates and that the secretary is going to be wiped out.
> (07C: executive officer, regional arts board)

However, the symbolic analyst's job does not just involve a degree of vertical integration; it also involves a considerable degree of horizontal adaptability and flexibility.

> I know we will have more and more development of people working bi-medially – telly and radio when necessary... There is no doubt that, although it will be a rocky path, within five years most of us will be filming our own stuff, editing it ourselves, that sort of thing – multi-skilled.
> (43A: specialist journalist manager, large public broadcasting organisation)

> I think graduate jobs have changed inasmuch as the organisation has changed. Jobs are less one-dimensional now. Everybody is expected to be able to do a little bit of everybody else's job.
> (41A: general manager, small registered charity)

Developing one's role horizontally also involves being more proactive in respect of client interaction:

> If you are a project manager and you are dealing with a client day-to-day you will probably have the best relationship of anybody with that particular client, so you should be able to get close to them and find out where there other needs are, what other things you might be able to do for them, or who else we should be contacting at the company.
> (04B: project director, small corporate literature specialists)

And this also applies to more traditional professions:

> The change for us is that people have to be much more market aware, understand the businesses more and therefore understand the client's needs. So in this profession – you might think that they have always had to do that, and to an extent they have – it is even more important to leave the 'being a lawyer' behind and really understand the clients.
> (12A: personnel director, large law firm)

Having a broader spread of roles is not only perceived as more efficient for the employer but also better for client relations. Respondents from one small design company (28B, 28D) suggested that clients like to interact with people in organisations who have a broad overview and are able to deal with all aspects of the work, rather than with an organisation that has a rather more fragmented client interface.

There is, therefore, little likelihood, in any sector, of an individual being able to specialise in a single area of work. Only a small minority of the respondents emphasised the specialist role while the majority talked explicitly of needing all-rounders to ensure greater flexibility and facilitate better communication and understanding within organisations.

> Traditionally people have become chartered quantity surveyors or a chartered building surveyors, but they have had to adapt and do tasks which are probably not within their original traditional training. They have had to get involved in things like project management, when possibly they are not formally trained as project managers.
>
> (16A: office director, medium-sized quantity and building surveyors)

Even in the most traditional of industries, there will be a change from simple functionary to a more integrated 'symbolic analyst' role, for example 'becoming as much accountants and bankers as engineers' (40C).

> The demarcation will go. People will be empowered and traditional railway roles will change. The individual will not deal with one aspect of the train and go and sit back for twenty minutes, he will actually process the train through the system, follow it through to source, monitor it, review it. They are going to give some sort of accountability to people.
>
> (50A: planning and analysis manager, large freight company)

Workload, working hours and responsibility

Many delayered, downsized organisations expect graduate-level employees to carry substantial workloads, work flexible hours and to take a good deal of responsibility. In the design area, for example, workloads appear to be increasing:

> They seem to have got rid of middle managers and they seem to be getting people to do more jobs than ever they used to. When I first started work, there used to be loads of designers and we'd all be doing one job a week, now there are about two people doing all those jobs nine people would do. It's quite frightening.
>
> (30D: graphic designer, small design consultancy)

> …we expect a lot from our staff, they work harder here than in most publishing companies… workload, taking on responsibility, and being answerable for what they do.
>
> (67B: marketing manager, small journal publishers)

Recent research has suggested that managers have a wider spread of responsibility (IM, 1996a) resulting in the majority of managers in a recent study suggesting that they needed, among other things, more broadly-based knowledge and that, hence, business or management qualifications would become more important (IM/AMC, 1996).

One aspect of the move to symbolic-analytic services might be the adoption of work patterns more normally associated with 'routine production services', such as shift working:

> I can certainly see us moving to seven-day a week working. We have got a pilot plant out there, this thing costs a lot of money. It is depreciating obviously, like any capital building does. Therefore, maximising the return means using it more. Using it more means working weekends or 24 hours a day to get the products to the market in the time that we have set ourselves. So I can see us moving to a shift-type system and the weekend concept vanishing.
>
> (63B: research manager, large pharmaceutical manufacturers)

> We have considered a two- or three-shift system and that may well come to pass… That would be a major shock for a company like this, which operates on a reasonably high intellectual plane. We are all people who like our weekends and social lives and it would be a reversion, almost a smokestack-type mentality, and that would be horrible. But it is something that we have to accept, it may actually come to pass, in fact it is almost certain to come to pass.
>
> (23B: general manager, small medical lasers manufacturer)

While this may, initially, appear an unwelcome development in an area of work traditionally conceived as having liberal working arrangements, it might serve to reduce the pressure of overwork that is currently rampant in Britain among symbolic-analytic workers, especially at higher levels, leading to considerable stress amongst managers (IM, 1996a) and a lack of time to analyse their personal development needs (IM, 1996b).

Although there are reduced layers of management, graduates are still likely to have a managerial role, but they have to learn what that embodies in flexible organisations. Close supervisory management of a small team is replaced by overview management of large numbers of people and with this comes the necessity to delegate control. The speed at which this managerial competence needs to be obtained varies from organisation to organisation:

> We've delayered over the last two years but there are associated problems. Who's doing the jobs, all the classic text book stuff of "if you take a layer out, does the job go down or up?". I'm sure you'll hear that it's gone up here rather than gone down. But that's almost like a training need: they've got to learn to delegate down but they've got to also learn to trust staff beneath them and whereas [managers] might trust a supervisor, they are finding it difficult to get to grips with trusting shop floor staff and they are looking for individuals to delegate to.
> (01A: training and safety officer, medium-sized private leisure and entertainment complex)

> Graduates need the ability to be able to manage the work and manage people, because within five to ten years they could find themselves heading up a branch or heading up a division. They could have as few as three people working for them or as many as 50 or 60... Usually they will be coming straight from university and they haven't got those skills. We have got to grow them in them. They are the underpinning competencies.
> (38B: director of personnel, civil service)

Uprating 'non-graduate' jobs

There is an issue about whether the new flexible graduate role involves an uprating of the traditional non-graduate job or a degrading of graduate abilities.

> My PA is a graduate management trainee; at one time we wouldn't have had that. We are tending to use graduates in sales doing business courses, and we take them for a year's training here. They are OK. We didn't do that before, we started that in the last couple of years.
> (49A: operations manager, computer-controlled systems manufacturer)

> In law I should think that more use will be made of non-qualified people. A lot of litigation, for example, is fairly paper-churning stuff and there is no reason why you should have to have done a degree, then your LPC, then your training contract, to be able to do these things and I think that there is going to be more use of [graduates as] clerks and legal executives because obviously they can be paid an awful lot less [than qualified solicitors].
> (06C: trainee solicitor, large law firm)

In the United States, many graduates are getting well paid jobs in 'non-traditional' blue-collar manufacturing jobs. Over 5% of blue-collar employees at the Ford Motor Company are graduates as were an unprecedented 20% of new assembly-plant recruits at Chrysler in Ontario (Flanders, 1995). This has led to debates about under-utilisation of graduates and a fifth of all graduates are classified by the U.S. Labor Bureau as under-utilised (unemployed or in very low-wage jobs). Under-utilisation of graduate attributes is also an issue in Britain:

> Graduates are not employed in non-graduate jobs, but we have found difficulty in giving graduates what we would think the right sort of training, and they have been doing menial tasks that we wouldn't wish them to do but somebody has to do them and it ends up being the most junior person and sometimes that is a graduate.
> (44B: line manager, large international highway design engineers)

Growing the job

However, in a recent *Skills and Enterprise Briefing*, it was suggested that 'the character of some of these jobs is changing and employers are responding to the influx of graduates into these non-traditional areas to more fully utilise their potential' (DfEE, 1996b, p. 2).

> You could do it without a degree but whether you would develop it into something more I don't know. My counterparts in other factories don't have degrees. I don't think it affects the job that they do. I don't think it means they do a good job or a bad job. It probably affects how they develop that job, whether they go looking to add responsibility to what they have already got. Or whether they are just happy to carry on and do a good job in what they are doing without looking to broaden it into a bigger job.
>
> (29C: buyer, medium-sized health product manufacturer)

However, the onus is as much on graduates to develop work roles as it is on employers to fully utilise graduate skills. As one line-manager pointed out, it is no use waiting and hoping for a more interesting role, it is incumbent on the employee to act: 'the reality is you can grow a position, you can grow your role within the company, even from the most mundane position' (26B).

The most remarkable example of growing the job in a delayered context was by a non-graduate, whose sheer dynamism and enthusiasm created a sub-industry within an organisation:

> In January 1995, when I first started doing the exports, we weren't doing any export business at all and this year we shall be set to turn over just under £1m in the export department. Exports are a lot more complicated so you need to be quite dedicated, you need to be there for your customers to understand, it is not like the UK where you have just got to understand one market. In export you have got to get round customs officials, you have got to get through customs procedures, duty boundaries and products analysis. You need to understand the marketplace before you can move. You need to know what your competitors are doing, what the other companies in that country are doing, so it is more than just a job. I enjoy doing it, so on the weekend I will quite happily, for a couple of hours, read a magazine on what is going on in the export world. I will surf on the Internet, which I have got at home, and see what is going on in the USA with competing products. So it almost becomes an obsession. One minute I can be speaking to Sweden, the next Finland – it makes the world seem a lot smaller. It is interesting.
>
> (80D: export manager, medium-sized brewing company)

'Growing the job' requires a willingness and confidence on the part of the graduate to develop the allocated role as well as a desire by managers to see the role grow and to facilitate and encourage the process:

> I would hope that organisations would be slightly more intelligent and they would look at the skills of the people they have got in the marketplace and develop the jobs and roles for them, rather than pushing out at the bottom level... what we ought to be able to do is expand the horizon of the graduates upwards and outwards and not push them down. I think the employment that we offer people is very much of a graduate content and at graduate level. So even our secretaries, who are graduates, take on a level of responsibility, client contact and organisation, which a lot of secretarial people would not necessarily do... There is a lot of job satisfaction and a lot of intellectual challenge in all those jobs.
>
> (09A: head of personnel, large law firm)

It would seem that graduates, given the opportunity, are not only capable but willing to 'grow' jobs. Out of frustration, boredom or opportunism, they add extra dimensions to one-dimensional jobs:

> It's only an administrative assistant job, it's like a clerical assistant really. It's a lot of photocopying and that's quite frustrating. But I have made the job my own. I have got involved with things that weren't in the job description just because I found the job as it stood quite boring... I am able to work on my own quite a lot because I was used to managing my time

at university and find it OK to manage different priorities here. I have taken on quite a lot of extra responsibilities, which I think I can handle because I had a good education and because I think I've got good writing skills and I've been able to use those a lot. I've taken over writing the bulletin which was something that I wouldn't have been given if I'd just been an admin. assistant without a university background.

(07C: executive officer, regional arts board)

Success in growing a job is related to the philosophy and rationale of the organisation. While some people will make the most of any situation, an 'inclusive' organisation, valuing and developing employee potential as one of a range of stakeholders, provides a more nourishing soil in which jobs can be grown than an organisation tightly constrained by financial concerns and offering only the insecurity of cost-flexibility and a one-dimensional, monetary evaluation of successful job growth. Although by no means at the polar ends of the 'flexibility continuum' (Figure 3.1), the following quotes provide an indication of the different emphases in 'growing' the job.

> I think they will need the guts to go forward with it and not to sit back and accept that their job role is a number puncher or a processor or something like that. They have got to have the will to want to learn, because if they don't then they will be out.
>
> (22C: car fleet manager, multinational reprographic equipment manufacturer)

> Graduates tend to be quite organised people, they tend to look at things in a different way, and usually we can give them a job function for that year, it is amazing the difference you get between one year and the next the way they perform that job or develop it.
>
> (49A: operations manager, computer-controlled systems manufacturer)

Summary

- The graduate career is not disappearing but it is changing with the emergence of flexible organisations, the growth of symbolic-analytic services and the movement of graduates into 'non-traditional' jobs.

- The advent of the flexible organisation means that there are probably more opportunities for graduates although they are different from traditional graduate jobs.

- There are indicators that expansion in small organisations, especially those providing symbolic-analytic services, will provide graduate opportunities. Indeed, more graduates are being employed by smaller companies.

- Restructuring, reorganisation and the development of a more client-oriented approach provide other opportunities for graduate work. Furthermore, graduates are tending to target areas that were previously staffed by non-graduates.

- The increasing number of graduates on the labour market, irrespective of any flexibility-led reorganisation requiring graduate-level recruits, has led organisations to consider recruiting graduates, where perhaps they would not have done in the past. However, there are employers who do not see a larger number of available graduates leading to higher graduate recruitment.

- Although graduate jobs are expanding, so is the supply of graduates. Many employers are also looking for various types of experience. Hence a degree is no guarantee of a job, let alone a career, and should only be seen as reaching 'first-base' in the recruitment process.

- Graduates need to be prepared for a less clear career path and promotion ladder in 'flexible' organisations.

- Graduates are likely to find that promotion and career advancement will be based on evaluation of performance rather than seniority or time-served.

- Working in a modern, delayered flexible organisation requires the ability, tact and confidence to interact with a wide range of personnel from senior managers, through colleagues to clients – some of whom may be overseas and operating in a different cultural context.
- Graduates will need to be able to work effectively in teams as there is little demand in a flexible organisation for introspective, individualised working.
- Working in the flexible organisation of the future will involve developing a horizontally and vertically integrated role – being self-servicing in respect of secretarial and administrative skills, using information technology, and developing a broad range of knowledge and ability.
- Graduates should expect to move between different areas within an organisation rather than stay within a specialist field.
- The flexible organisation of the near future is likely to impose substantial workloads and considerable responsibility on graduates from the outset, with an expectation that they will work flexible hours.
- Graduates may be in 'non-traditional' areas of work that are not 'graduate level'. Graduate expectations of their prospects, particularly in their first jobs, need to be realistic but positive. Much of their initial work may provide only a low level challenge. In which case graduates need to 'grow the job' and there is encouraging evidence that many do so.
- To maximise potential, employers should encourage and facilitate 'growing' jobs – a process more easily done in an inclusive 'response-flexible' organisation than a 'cost-flexible' organisation.

5 Recruitment policy and practices

Organisations that recruit graduates vary enormously in the degree of sophistication of their recruitment policies and procedures. Some large organisations have graduate recruitment departments, recruiting large numbers of graduates annually on an international scale, using highly-refined final assessment centres and with clear guidelines as to the target recruits.

> We are taking in something like 50 – 60 a year and that is simply to maintain a population of managers and middle managers of something like 2000 across the business.
>
> (40A: manager of training and development, large steel manufacturer)

On the other hand, many organisations adopt an *ad hoc*, often reactive, approach to recruitment (constrained by tight staffing budgets) rather than recruiting in anticipation of future needs. Recruitment criteria tend to be embodied in unique job-related, person specifications and procedures often hinge on 'subjective' evaluations based on face-to-face interviews. This means that employees are not specifically recruited because of their graduate status, which may be irrelevant. It is rather that they meet the job requirements. With the increase in graduates on the job market, it is likely that more graduates will be recruited into jobs where their degree is not a requirement.

Some organisations do not restrict their recruitment to graduates, they emphasise that they are looking for the right person for the job and that may, or may not, be a graduate.

Larger organisations tend to have more fully-developed recruitment polices than smaller organisations, not least because they can afford to invest in recruitment specialists. Furthermore, the recruitment budget of larger organisations are substantial and mistakes can prove very costly. However, it might be argued that it is a false economy for smaller organisations (other than the very small) to forego devising a seriously considered recruitment policy. Although they may have inadequate resources to establish a recruitment department, mistakes in recruitment are likely to be relatively more costly.

Recruitment procedures

The majority of organisations (large and small) employ graduates at a variety of levels and many employ a mixture of fresh graduates and those who have been in employment since graduation.

> There are two categories at this stage, we've got a pool of general researchers, these people who've come straight into this company from graduates, so very often it will be their first or second job... Then we have a category of staff, senior researchers... who have come in from other organisations... and they would have moved to us as a sort of second tier in their career development.
>
> (53A: chief executive, small private research organisation)

> Project managers are our main area of recruitment and they will always be people who have had experience of being project managers elsewhere, so they have to have had some experience, only about 10% fresh from university.
>
> (04A: owner, small corporate literature specialists)

Fast-track graduate recruitment

Graduates, particularly in large organisations, are still being recruited on graduate trainee schemes, with the aim that they will 'fast track' in the organisation to become the senior managers of the future.

> The management development programme for the fast-track recruits lasts for four years and they would be expected to take a general management role very early on, say, managing a team of representatives.
> (59B: line manager, large financial institution)

> ...it is the high flyers, it's the people who are going to be the future senior managers, the last three chairman have been trainees so it has a long culture of growing our own... by and large we don't want people who are going to stay in middle management jobs, we want high flyers moving through because the world is changing so fast.
> (11A: vice-president, multi-national food manufacturers)

> Fast-stream recruitment, as the name implies, the whole idea of that is to bring in very good graduates, to give them a full year training programme basically on arrival, and the objective of that is to get them promoted to middle-management positions in their late twenties, so that takes them on to a springboard so that they can then get into the senior ranks of the Civil Service in their thirties and forties.
> (38B: director of personnel, civil service)

Even when organisations do not specifically have a policy of fast-tracking, graduates are often expected to inevitably progress through the organisation faster than non-graduates, because they 'tend to be more able, more willing as well' (15A).

> At a local level, we don't have a specific policy but there's an inevitability. Well, almost certainly, when we take on somebody who's a graduate, then there is an expectation that those people will move quicker, but its not a stated policy as yet.
> (03A: head teacher, small private school for children with special needs)

Fast-track often, although not always, involves the organisation participating in recruitment events at universities. The bottom line for most 'fast-track' recruiters is that they are competing for the 'very best' graduates each year.

> We are likely to start running some assessment centres prior to the milk round as well, and it is really with the objective of getting in first. If we continue to rely on the milk round we will get what we deserve I suppose. We won't get the best. We have got to keep all options open and try to make sure that we recruit good people.
> (40A: manager of training and development, large steel manufacturer)

Several organisations say that although their fast-track recruitment is dominated by graduates, it is not solely for graduates and they would consider people entering from different routes such as A-level or from current employees (who may or may not be graduates).

In common with recent research on graduate engineers (Jones et al., 1994) our sample indicates that there is sometimes a conflict of interest between wanting to recruit the transformative leaders of the future, and wanting to employ people who will be capable of (and content with) doing the immediate, value-added job.

> I think the key thing to this, and I think it is an area we need to improve, is to understand what the ideal graduate is and for what level and to get a better understanding of the sort of mix of graduates that we want. Do we want the real high flyers? We do but we don't want them all to be real high flyers, because 90% of the jobs aren't top jobs.
> (40A: manager of training and development, large steel manufacturer)

Direct entry

Targeted, area-specific graduate recruitment, or 'direct entry graduates', again focuses on students fresh from university courses but 'they are brought in to do a particular job, not on development programmes' (39A).

> Graduates are recruited directly into a job. They start at a salary of about £20,000 a year in London, £17,000 outside and they are basically joining us as junior or trainee professionals.

> Within four to five years we would aim to get them to being a full technical professional, or financial professional, with the CIMA qualification or an IPD qualification or a Chartered Engineering qualification.
> (66A: recruitment manager, multi-national petro-chemical company)

This may be the only form of graduate recruitment used by an organisation or it may be in addition to fast-track recruitment. Where it parallels fast-track recruitment, direct entry may be a means of delegating control of job-specific recruitment to constituent companies (11A) or a means of recruiting specialist functions such as IT and personnel.

Some organisations (at the time of the study) were moving from general graduate recruitment to job-specific recruitment while others were planning to introduce a 'fast-track' approach to cope with anticipated expansion in the organisation. In some cases centralised international recruitment was being decentralised:

> We used to have a centralised graduate scheme, which was a European recruitment scheme focused very much on the UK and Ireland, And that was done highly professionally. The usual milk-round scheme, good contact building with some target universities, sending people out to the universities for presentations, getting 2,000 applications and screening applications, interviews, the whole rigmarole. The end result of that laborious process I think was probably not worth the effort, because you then recruit 30 people out of the whole lot. So we are changing that. We are going to be much more decentralised, we want every region – Continental Europe, UK and Ireland, Latin America, North America, Asia – to be responsible for their own graduate recruitment and every region has to define the proper channels for recruitment.
> (57A: senior executive, large brewing company)

Job-specific general recruitment

Organisations also use job-specific advertisements, usually wanting someone with some relevant experience, and which may also attract postgraduate or non-graduate applicants:

> We have in the past preferred graduates with previous experience mainly because the market has become more and more competitive. Training a graduate is an expense. If you can pick up a graduate with experience who can come in and do the job you want, she or he may cost a bit more but it is a better investment because you are saving on training.
> (44A: business development manager, large international highway design engineers)

This type of recruitment emphasises finding 'the best person for the job' (13A). This practice may well mean that the number of graduates employed in an organisation is hidden, that graduates who have been recruited to specific jobs are not necessarily seen as 'graduate employees' as their degree status may not be relevant to their job: "We had a chap on the shop floor who we found out by accident was a graduate" (73A). One public sector organisation said they would not know how many graduates were employed because employees are recruited to match job specifications. However:

> It is quite likely that people coming into my area of work will be graduates but this is not a requirement. In order to meet the skills of the researcher, that is, to undertake report writing, analysis of data and research methods, the person is usually a graduate.
> (35B: research and policy officer, local authority landlord)

Work-placement recruitment

A further form of recruitment is via work-placement experience (Chapter 8). Some organisations directly link recruitment to a placement period, others may recruit a placement student if they have a vacancy. Other forms of work experience, such as holiday working and short-term course-based project working may provide recruitment opportunities.

> At the end of that year, if the line manager feels that [the placement student's] performance has been good enough – we give them guidelines there – the person can be recommended for a place on a selection centre the following year. This means that they miss out the previous stages of the process and come straight in at selection-centre stage. Their experience in the year, and the fact that they have achieved that recommendation, should mean that they have a good chance of being successful.   (56A: graduate recruitment manager, large financial institution)

> I have done minor projects for them in the holidays. They had seen my results and they were quite happy with it. I also knew the system quite well, and usually when you come in it takes about six weeks to study the system, but I could go straight into it. I joined with another fellow student and while he was doing the induction I was straight on doing work. There was no formal recruitment procedure. Basically what happened was that on the summer before I graduated I made it known that I was interested in the position, and they thought about it. I gave them a ring early April, and they invited me in for a chat and they put an offer on the table.   (81C: software engineer, small, operator-systems design firm)

One respondent in a medium-sized manufacturing company said they found it difficult to recruit graduates who had been successful placement students with the organisation, because they were attracted to the benefits that larger organisations could offer, as 'other people had more attractive wage structures' (25A).

Some organisations have built up, or built upon, particular links with institutions (Chapter 9), through work placements, research projects or endowed chairs, which can then also be used as a way of recruiting graduates.

> ...we have approached [the local university] and indicated our willingness to take graduate people on and asked for CVs to be sent through, and then pick a short list of three or four, and then have formal interviews.   (81A: software development manager, small software design company)

> Our latest tactic is that we are trying to get friendly with a couple of universities and say "look we haven't got many jobs but they are interesting ones, give us your best people for placement, give us an option of interviewing your best people" so that we can get their help in selecting.   (25A: managing director, medium-sized shop-fitting manufacturer)

Targeting recruits

Targeting recruits is a sensible strategy when you are looking for subject specialists to undertake specific technical tasks. If a major food manufacturing company wants a food technologist and knows that a course at a particular university produces graduates equipped to do the job with minimal extra training, then it is sensible to target the course. Similarly, a specialist research and development department is wise to target particular postgraduate students with good theoretical understanding. However, many organisations target in particular ways in order to attract 'the best' graduates, whom they consider will be a 'success' within their organisation.

> The ideal candidate would probably have a 2:1 from an absolutely cracking university, who is the leader in their field, and they will have had a consistently excellent academic record. In addition they will probably have more than two languages, they will probably be captain of rugby or chairman of, say, the Rag Committee, and they will have run a Student Help-line and, I mean, its just terrifying, there *are* people like this around.
>   (09A: head of personnel, large law firm)

'Success', through such recruitment strategies, is more likely to be 'value-added' rather than 'transformative' (see Chapter 3).

Many organisations (especially larger ones) target young graduates, between 21 and 25 years of age, usually with a good degree, although initial selection could be on the basis of good A-level grades. Many fast-track recruiters target a small number of 'top' universities, although they rarely specify particular degree subjects. Some organisations have a preference for what they refer to as 'rigorous' courses, which tend to be single-honours courses in traditional subjects rather than 'new' subjects on 'pick-and-mix' modular schemes.

> Certainly the old established universities used to do pure degrees like chemistry, physics, maths, and when the polytechnics were created they started to offer these cross-subject, multi-subject degrees, like physics with geography. This was a deliberate policy and, of course, now what you find is that you get graduates coming out with these multi-disciplinary type degrees which tend to be more like 28 A-levels, rather than knowing one thing really well. Yet, in the kind of business we are in, we are really looking for people who are very knowledgeable in their technical area, so it suits us better to have someone who is a chemist with perhaps a business subject attached like a language or a commercial awareness type of module. You notice that in the interviews, the people who have done these very broad subjects cannot hack it technically against those who have done a very narrow subject.
>
> (82A: head of technology strategy, large power company)

> People do the wrong subject, I mean there are titles like Media Studies, some of the more modern titles that can make traditional employers look a little bit askance.
>
> (03A: head teacher, small private school for children with special needs)

This leads to two potential problems. First, the effective narrowing of the range of potential recruits. Second, the appointment of those who 'fit in' but may not be the most effective recruits in helping the organisation face the changes of the next century.

It is noticeable that a lot of large-scale recruitment involves traditional views, idiosyncratic prejudices and anecdotal evidence about appropriate targets. This is often based on good or bad experience with small numbers of recruits. Occasionally, there is some systematic research, but this is sometimes surrounded by pervasive myths that continue to inform the recruitment process, especially at the initial screening stage. Although many recruiters have broad images of what they are looking for at the final stages of recruitment, these are often set aside, as they are willing to admit, in the face of an exceptional candidate. The problem, which there appears to be some reluctance to face, is whether good candidates are being discarded too soon as a result of implementing tried-and-tested, traditional, and possibly outdated, criteria at the initial screening stage. In short, do procedures mitigate against adaptable, transformative graduates?

Often, the criteria used are very conservative and do not reflect the massive changes that have taken place in higher education. A major concern is that these traditional criteria do not account for the need for most students to support themselves through higher education by taking on paid employment of one sort or another. To still be looking for the 'Chairman of the Rag Committee' is to restrict potential recruits to those who have the time and leisure to undertake unpaid rather than paid work: in short it suggests a focus on upper-middle class students who do not need to work to subsist.

The same outcome results from an entirely different perception because of an emphasis on traditional recruiting targets. One law firm was open about its desire to recruit graduates who were not closeted and had a wider experience than holiday working in law firms. However, because they regarded the traditional universities as the home of 'intellectually able' students (with good A-level grades) they tended to recruit from a somewhat more privileged group and were, peculiarly in the current climate, of the view that 'students are just not having it tough enough' (12A). The effect is that:

> We don't get people who are the risk takers, who are the intrepid ones, to the extent that we would want... Over-indulgence by parents, I am pretty certain. We see people who might have worked for half dozen law firms. We don't care about that. Frankly, I would much rather them have been employed by a supermarket or been down on the factory floor, so that they learn a bit of understanding about the clients with whom they are going to have to deal.
>
> (12A: personnel director, large law firm)

Ironically, the narrowing of the field is operating to reduce the potential recruits who might be the kind of people they require (Chapter 6).

General selection criteria

A number of organisations have a set of criteria or a framework that they use in the selection of candidates through application forms, interviews and assessment centres. Some form of selection criteria is used by the vast majority of the organisations in the sample, whether for annual recruitment to graduate training schemes, or job-specific recruitment, which may or may not involve a graduate.

> We basically have a list of criteria for selection. The first thing we say is A-levels Grade C or above, which surprises people. For some areas we specify degree but not for that many. We have a set of 22 things which are defined as the skills or behaviours that are the most important to success within the organisation. Things like planning and organising ability, the ability to work as part of a team, results orientation, self-motivation, influencing skills and an awareness of their impact on other people. Problem solving, analytical ability – the ability to look at a problem in a logical way and come up with logical solutions. There are basically six-to-ten key competencies and either from the application form or a first interview or a second interview, we are designing those selection processes to give people the opportunity to show evidence of those kind of things.
>
> (47A: personnel manager, multi-national food manufacturer)

These organisational selection criteria have been devised in a number of ways, such as utilising the experience of the individual recruiter or interviewer, discussion between the selection panel, discussion assessing the qualities of successful graduates within the organisation, internal discussion with line managers and senior managers, and (typically for larger-scale recruitment) the use of external consultants (47A) and psychologists (38A). Criteria for selection is often closely linked to the person specification that has been drawn-up for a particular job (03A).

> We have a personnel sub-committee of the management committee which is just called together when it is time to do one of these, and we look at the job descriptions and change it if necessary and draw up new ones.   (20A: director, small publicly funded support and advice centre)

One organisation reported the opposite point of view, that in order to encourage diversity, they did not start off their selection with a pre-defined set of specific criteria:

> Particularly when you are working for TV, it is important to have a diverse and creative workforce so you want to attract people from all walks of life basically, and then you hope that it is reflected and comes out in your programme and everyone is contributing different ideas and has different ways of working, so I think that comes across, so I don't think there are many specific things.   (42A: training and personnel manager, medium-sized private broadcasting company)

The following criteria – age, qualification, institution and degree subject – that are taken into consideration by some organisations relate, in the majority of cases, to the recruitment of graduates straight from university. They are less of an issue when organisations are talking about recruiting graduates for whom this is not their first post-graduate job, as the relevant experience they have gained since completing their degree tends to outweigh other factors.

Age

Age is a contentious, and somewhat discriminatory, issue. For some graduate recruiters, 25 is the maximum age, and many others are nervous of recruiting people over 30, 'I personally would look towards the younger end, I know that is not politically correct, but that is just a personal preference' (51B). Most, but not all, 'fast-track' recruiters and some 'direct entry graduate' recruitment targets younger recruits. Age is much less often an issue for 'job-specific advertised' recruitment.

There are a lot of preconceptions and prejudices about the appropriate age of 'fast-track' and 'direct entry' graduate recruits.

> ...our experience shows that people who enter the law late [as mature students] do not usually make a success of it at the sort of level that we work. They might be absolutely cracking as a provincial solicitor or high street solicitor, or West End practice but in the City, generally, they are not a success... I don't think they have that absolute drive and determination to be a successful lawyer. Partly because they have done other things and they have actually discovered there's a whole world out there and it manages perfectly well without City lawyers. But that's not the business we are in. (09A: head of personnel, large law firm)

> ...they [mature graduates] probably would start with some barriers that they would have to overcome, because probably, at some stage they came off the rails a bit, because if they got the basic ability, as they have proved later in life, and had they sorted their minds out a bit better and got on with it at the right time, they would probably have never been mature students. (11B: head of management recruitment and training, multi-national food manufacturers)

> Somebody who is 30 plus probably had a career change and those sort of people I just think they might not be stable in the company, they might spend a couple of years with the company and move on. (14B: studio manager, small design and print agency)

However, some employers are willing to consider any suitable applicant regardless of how old they are: 'we have just recruited someone who is 52' (23A).

> If somebody is coming to us they have got a degree, they worked before they have been to university and they are about 28. That could be an ideal profile, they don't all have to be first-job people. Age doesn't matter, I think the only time it does matter is when the starting salary that we offer for graduates no longer becomes attractive if you are maybe mid-30s or whatever, but again if they want us then we want them. We would never discriminate on terms of age. (32B: recruitment and development manager, large telecommunications organisation)

Some organisations emphasise the benefits of employing mature graduates because they have gained particular skills and abilities from having their life experience. Indeed, if organisations want to employ people who already have experience and can be functional from the outset then they will have to consider older candidates.

> We are starting to see graduates of 28, 29, astonishingly 32. They, of course, bring the world with them, the communication skills, the ability to network that your standard graduate lacks. So they often win through in a situation like that. We are starting to recruit some people with wider experience who can provide more than just the intellectual qualification. (63A: human resources manager, large pharmaceutical manufacturers)

> We are not fussy about age, possibly older might be better though, I have to say, in terms of experience and the ability to demonstrate experience, a problem that anybody fresh out of college is always going to have is, can they demonstrate their ability and experience. (41A: general manager, small registered charity)

However, alongside these benefits there is still the slight reservation that mature graduates need to have a number of years left before retirement to make it viable for the organisation to invest in them.

> ...if you want to bring a graduate in and the graduate is going to be mid- to late-30s by the time they join, then you are cutting down their time-frame for career progression and you are perhaps not making the best of them. So the shrinking age profile of an organisation might actually be bad news as far as older graduate entry is concerned because the time to develop and mature your career will be decreased. (63B: research manager, large pharmaceutical manufacturers)

> Realistically, we have a rough cut-off that people must be qualified as solicitors by the age of 40. Only by that way can we say that they are going to have a reasonable career with us and end up being partners, so that roughly means 35–37 cut-off. (12A: personnel director, large law firm)

There is a fundamental dilemma that graduate recruiters often fail to address – mature graduates have many of the attributes required by employers but, for various reasons these are not seen to outweigh their age.

Qualification

Some graduate recruiters, especially 'fast-tack' recruiters, are looking for graduates with a first or upper-second class degree, or rather more ambiguously, the ability to have achieved one, even if they did not. With the high number of graduates now on the market, employers can specify high degree classifications and still be assured of a large pool of candidates. Some recruiters, as noted above, are looking at the candidates' A-level grades as well as their actual, or potential, degree classification.

> We are looking for As and Bs. If lower, they need other areas of their application that are stronger. We like people who let their hair down, gone out and done everything that their parents never let them do, but then they need a 2(i) or First. A couple of years ago we were bringing people in with 2(ii), who are still fantastic, but now we are getting about 3,000 applications for 50 positions, we have to put some sort of minimum criteria. We can ask for a 2(i) or First, as well as everything else, their character, their work experience, without making it too difficult for us to select them. (09B: graduate recruiter and training manager, large law firm)

> First of all we look for academic requirements. We look at their UCCA points and I think we demand at least three Bs, or the equivalent of 3 Bs at A-level. We look for a good degree result, either a 2(i) if they are a relevant graduate – relevant means that they have studied accountancy or something business related – or at least a 2(ii) in other subjects.
> (79B: line manager, large, chartered accountants)

Institution

Some employers recruiting graduates onto graduate training schemes tend to target what they call the 'top' universities (although they by no means have the same list), or target institutions which they feel have been successful in particular areas:

> We go for the universities which have the strongest legal departments and these are continually changing. We've just discovered that [University X] has some very good graduates coming out of there at the moment, law graduates, and so we are very alert to changes in the market… We often pay attention to *The Times* summary of who's got the best law faculties and we are quite pleased when it complements what we think. We have about 12 target universities, the majority of which are old universities, but then last year we recruited 54 trainees from 22 different establishments. (09B: graduate recruiter and training manager, large law firm)

> We target a number of universities and at those universities we will visit career fairs, we accept applications from any university but the fact that we have quite a small number of vacancies means we can't go everywhere. (47A: personnel manager, multi-national food manufacturer)

Several organisations refer to taking students from the older universities as they are sceptical about the reputation and standards of some of the new universities.

> I think that, in lots of people's minds, the fact that what used to be polys have now become universities has probably degraded the value of their qualification, which may be absolute nonsense. Of course, the types of courses that polys used to do were different from the traditional university courses. They are probably just as valuable as each other.
> (15A: partner, small chartered accountants)

Others take a broader view, drawing on a whole range of institutions.

> We get a fair number of people from [a new university] who are decently trained and therefore it tends to propagate. I personally have had about three or four, three of them were very bright and have gone on and are doing things now.
> (43A: specialist journalist manager, large public broadcasting organisation)

> We do not target and we try extremely hard to recruit from a broad range of universities… we have tried desperately hard in the fast stream to attract good people from everywhere, we certainly try very hard not to target.
> (38A: head of branch, civil service)

Part of the problem, as has been suggested, is that employers ascribe diversity to institutions and recruit from a limited range on the assumption that this will filter the kind of recruits they want, ignoring the fact that intellectually and in terms of all the other desirable attributes, there will be as much diversity within universities as between them. Recent American research has revealed this phenomenon even in the highly diverse US higher education system (Ratcliff and associates, 1995).

Degree subject

For some graduate jobs, a particular degree subject is necessary, and recruitment will take place on the basis of candidates having the relevant subject. For other jobs, certain subjects are preferred but not required.

> It is relatively easy for us to teach them management skills, supervisory skills, even communication skills to a degree, but we don't have the time, and I don't believe the company has the inclination either to say we are going to teach you science. The view here is, that is very much what universities are there for and that is one of the reasons we go on the milk round in universities to try and pick the best science-taught people.
> (63B: research manager, large pharmaceutical manufacturers)

Some employers say they do not specify the degree subject and it is rather the ability to have studied for a degree and the attributes acquired at university that are important: 'it is really the quality of the mind, which is the important thing' (27B).

> You can't tell whether somebody who has got a medieval English degree or a business degree is actually going to have more or less business awareness. It is really just in discussion with people, trying to understand whether they have read the papers that day, whether they understand how businesses make money, and how they function.
> (46B: project manager, multi-national computer service company)

> I don't care what you did your degree in, I really don't. If you want an engineer you want an engineer, if somebody is going to design a vehicle, then I don't want somebody who has got a degree in sociology. Even in areas like finance, I don't necessarily want a finance-trained human being. It is as much, if not more, about personal traits, personal drive and ambition. You could be managing director of this company with a degree in sociology.
> (60A: director commercial operations, large vehicle manufacturer)

> We have done some research, and in the long-term non-lawyers are more successful than lawyers. We take about a third non-law and two-thirds law, because for a whole variety of reasons we have to train non-lawyers for a year more, so it costs us significantly more. We don't care where they come from or what their discipline is as long as they are the best.
> (09A: head of personnel, large law firm)

On the other hand, this openness can sometimes be mediated by preconceptions of the kinds of attributes that are associated with particular degrees. The same open law firm, despite wanting graduates with linguistic skills, was of the view that:

> Linguists do not generally make good lawyers. So, in our ideal candidate, we are looking for somebody who has an innate language ability, perhaps they have got a parent who is of that language and they have been brought up as bilingual. They have spent a lot of time in that country and that has developed their language skills. If we have somebody who comes to us with a degree in Russian, very often they are not going to make a good lawyer because they think differently. You get a guy with a degree in maths, they make extraordinarily successful lawyers because they think in the same way and think in an analytical, factual way that lawyers need to think, whereas a linguist will not. That is not to say we exclude linguists, but we look at them quite sceptically.
> (09A: head of personnel, large law firm)

Another respondent, who identified a range of general attributes of all graduates implying them to be open, empathetic and responsive, qualified his remarks, as follows:

> If I was appointing graduates for a care post I would be happier if I saw that a graduate did psychology, sociology or one or two of the sciences. If somebody was a graduate in a 'structured' discipline such as electrical engineering then I would be quizzing them about flexibility of thought.
> (03A: head teacher, small private school for children with special needs)

Practices

Respondents report a variety of ways of actually selecting their graduate employees, the main process being using application forms and interviews, with larger recruiters often combining these methods with assessment centres and various forms of tests. Large organisations also target graduates through the 'milk round'. However, there are reservations about its effectiveness:

> The main change has been the almost abolition of the milk round, where companies that wait until the final year, have missed very often the best of the graduates. The best graduates, even by the first year, are looking to see which employers are right for them, and increasingly they have the self-confidence to lay down some very strict criteria on what they are looking for in an employer.
> (66A: recruitment manager, multi-national petro-chemical company)

For smaller organisations, targeting institutions in this structured, expensive way is often not a reasonable approach to recruiting graduates:

> We have quite a small turnover of more senior staff or jobs where we would be looking at the graduates or the need for a degree so we don't have a recruitment drive through the universities' career services.
> (37A: deputy chief executive, small housing association)

However, as discussed later in Chapter 9, the links between SMEs and university career services may be of increasing importance as graduate employment in these kinds of organisations increases.

Assessment centres and tests

Many of the major graduate recruiters use assessment centres. A major function of the centres is to explore how well potential recruits interact and successfully solve problems, particularly those which are relevant to their future work role (AGR, 1993).

Many respondents who use (or were recruited through) assessment centres outlined what they are designed to test: 'Ability to lead, ability to work with others, solve problems, focus on what has been asked of them, maturity' (22A).

> ...your ability to work with other people, team building, fit into a team, work with a team, show not necessarily leadership, but enough self-confidence to be able to put your point across when appropriate. How you communicated, and whether you got to the point or not. Whether you could make a decision based on information. Whether you could read and understand the information in the first place. Whether you could stand up and present

> that competently, so communication, presentation, how you interact with other people. Whether you can make a decision and plan things. Then there were aptitude tests, mathematical ability, and the interview was interesting, they are also looking for some degree of individuality as well.
>
> (47C: process engineer, multi-national food manufacturer)

> It wasn't your knowledge, it was all the other aspects, your personality side, whether you could work within a team, whether you were a loner, what made you tick, how you could be motivated and what demotivated you. What it is supposed to show is whether the person who is going to be employed will fit within the existing framework.
>
> (31C: senior quantity surveyor, medium-sized house builders and regenerators)

Various kinds of tests are used by recruiters, such as psychometric tests, aptitude tests, numeracy and literacy tests and so on, which may or may not be part of an assessment centre programme. These tests are intended to provide 'objective' measurement of a candidate's abilities, disposition, and attitudes against a set of pre-defined recruitment criteria. In some circumstances, the tests are misused to provide some sort of overall profile of potential recruits, independent of criteria. Selection of candidates can also involve tests based on work-based problems, which can be combined with a presentation of suggestions and solutions.

> We used to recruit simply on the basis of interview looking very much at the art form knowledge of the people we are appointing... now we make everybody go through a test where they have to assess three grant applications, write a report, make recommendations against those applications and justifying them... because there is no point however brilliant somebody is in terms of their expertise, if they can't communicate that quickly and efficiently then they are of limited use to us.
>
> (07A: deputy chief executive, regional arts board)

> We give them just a very basic piece of work that we get thrown at us every day and really we are trying to find out what abilities they have got on the computer.
>
> (30A: owner, small design consultancy)

There is some scepticism about the use of assessment centres and tests by those who are using them, and more particularly by those who do not use them: 'It is good for battery testing but at the end of the day we are looking for individuals' (63A). There is some concern that they are relied upon too heavily.

> I think it is a benefit and is a good way of testing people, but I think too much emphasis is placed on it. I agree I think it does form part of the scenario but certainly not to the extent that it seems to have placed on it at this moment in time. I think it presupposes that you are telling the truth or that you don't know what you are doing when you do these tests. If you know what these tests are about, you can manipulate the results to make you fit the profile. It's not foolproof.
>
> (31C: senior quantity surveyor, medium-sized house builders and regenerators)

Some organisations, often smaller ones, are hostile to the use of testing and prefer to rely on intuitive judgement.

> We positively don't use them. I see them as an excuse. I have worked in organisations that have used them and really it's a crutch, in many cases, for not wanting to exercise personal judgement and intuition. We trust our judgement here and we have made very few mistakes, there have been a minimal number, only one in the history of the company. We avoid testing like the plague. I put most of those tests in the same category as having handwriting analysis done. I rely very much on personal judgement and we have no formal interview process. The interview process is quite informal, it's all about talking.
>
> (23A: chief executive, small medical lasers manufacturer)

Interviews

Interviews can be used as a form of recruitment on their own, or in conjunction with assessment centres and tests. Types outlined by respondents range from formalised interviews, often a series with different people within the organisation, to informal conversational interviews on a one-to-one basis. In the sample, selection based on interviews is the practice employed by the majority of smaller organisations.

> Two people interview the candidate, myself and one of the senior team leaders. We also usually have a technical questionnaire that they are asked to fill in so we not only believe what they say, they basically prove it through the questionnaire. I use my experience. There is no formal procedure.   (81A: software development manager, small, operator-systems design firm)

> We have changed our recruiting technique over the last couple of years, we used to do it on a one-to-one basis and we found it very hit and miss. Now we have three people interview everybody for about 15 minutes. They have certain areas they need to talk to them about… They all mark them and we look at them at lunch time and then we get rid of about half the people at that stage. The best ones we take into an afternoon session, and then we talk in depth about the way they interface to people, generally to see if they can work in teams.
> (49A: operations manager, computer-controlled systems manufacturer)

> …eventually a position came up and I was told they wanted me. I had a quick informal chat with the station controller and news manager. It wasn't like a board interview.
> (13C: news co-ordinator, medium-sized private local radio station)

As with selection from application forms and attributes being tested at assessment centres, employers often formulate a set of core competencies or specific criteria for use in the interview process. Alongside these there are also less definable assessments based on the general personality of the candidate and whether they will 'fit' into the workplace, if they will be able to 'get along with their colleagues' (30C) and work in a team.

> And that's something that is very important in such a small company and in a company where you need to work in teams and you switch from working with one group of people to another… And I think they needed to be convinced that I would fit in.
> (28C: project manager, small design and communications company)

> The things that I look for are interpersonal skills, their manner towards me – this is a dreadful thing to say but I am going to say it anyway – particularly with men, who have been to a boys' school – they have gone into a male-dominated faculty at university, perhaps played rugby or snooker or done something very male dominated – to be confronted with a woman interviewer, they either patronise me horribly, which doesn't go down very well, or do not take me seriously, which doesn't take very well either. So I am looking for an ability to interact with me in a way that I would be happy for them to interact with my clients. I am looking for them to demonstrate logical thought and lateral thought, and to have done their research.   (62A: manager, large management consultants)

In the end, though, the interview provides a forum for the candidate to make an impression and be convincing:

> I would be looking for somebody who had a smart appearance, who would be coming in to us with a confident persona, who communicates very well, and has the ability to convince you that they are the person you want for the job.
> (61A: operations manager, international fast-food chain)

Summary

- Graduate recruitment can range from large-scale annual recruitment policies (typically in larger organisations) to job-specific recruitment to meet immediate needs.

- Organisations may recruit graduates through a variety of procedures, including: fast-track recruitment, aimed at fulfilling future (often management) roles; direct-entry job-specific recruitment, aimed at recruiting new graduates into specific roles; more generalised job-specific recruitment which may attract graduates, non-graduates or post-graduates; recruitment based on graduates' successful completion of work-based placements within the organisation; and, through close links built up with particular higher education institutions or departments.

- Targeting recruits from particular subjects, or from universities from which organisations have, in the past, found candidates to be strong in particular areas, can be a sensible strategy for organisations wanting graduates to undertake specific technical roles. However, general targeting by organisations to attract 'the best' graduates can narrow the range of potential recruits and could exclude graduates who might be the people they are looking for.

- Selection criteria are used at all stages of recruitment: for selection from application forms, during interviews and for assessment centres and tests. These selection criteria are devised in a number of ways, by those immediately involved in the selection, through consultation with graduates and managers within the organisation, and through outside agencies such as recruitment consultants and psychologists.

- When recruiting newly graduated employees, many organisations still concentrate on recruiting 21-year-olds, although some do consider mature graduates as, potentially, they have the combination of a formal qualification and experience.

- A first or upper-second degree classification is seen by some organisations as the minimum requirement in a climate where organisations can choose from a large pool of graduates.

- Some of the larger organisations target what they consider to be the 'top' higher education institutions, while others aim to reach a broader range of graduates in their recruitment.

- A particular degree subject is essential for some professions, whilst for others it is the ability to have studied for a degree and the experience gained from being at university that is important.

- A range of practices are also used to recruit graduates. Interviews are the most common form of recruitment practice, as a selection method on their own and in combination with various tests and assessment centres. Assessment centres are often used for fast-track recruitment.

6 Attributes of graduates

There are large numbers of graduates looking for jobs and employers, as we have seen, no longer recruit simply on the basis of degree status. A degree might be necessary or desirable but employers are looking for a range of other attributes when employing and retaining graduates. This will continue to be the case in the foreseeable future. Graduates will need to develop a profile of attributes: knowledge, skills, abilities and personal attributes that suit them to work in the organisation of the future.

Employers want graduates with a range of *personal attributes* including:

- intellect, including a range of attributes such as analysis, critique, synthesis and an ability to think things through in order to solve problems;
- knowledge, especially understanding the basic principles of a subject discipline, general knowledge, knowledge of the organisation and commercial awareness, although in many organisations knowledge *of* something is much less important than the ability to acquire knowledge;
- willingness and ability to learn and continue learning, to appreciate that learning continues throughout life;
- flexibility and adaptablity to respond to change, to pre-empt change and ultimately to lead change;
- self-regulatory skills, such as self-discipline, time-keeping, ability to deal with stress, prioritisation, planning and an ability to 'juggle' several things at once;
- self-motivation, ranging from being a self-starter to seeing things through to a conclusion, including such 'characteristics' as resilience, tenacity and determination;
- self-assurance, including self-confidence, self-awareness, self-belief, self-sufficiency, self-direction and self-promotion.

These personal attributes are seen as playing an important role in the ability of graduates to be able to fit into the work culture, do the job, develop ideas, take initiative and responsibility and ultimately help organisations deal with change.

However, these personal attributes, while important, are not sufficient as the flexible workplace requires *interactive attributes*, such as interpersonal skills, teamworking, and communication skills. The delayered, project-focused organisation requires the ability to:

- communicate, formally and informally, with a wide range of people both internal and external to the organisation;
- relate to, and feel comfortable with, people at all levels in the organisation as well as a range of external stakeholders, to be able to make and maintain relationships as circumstances change;
- work effectively in teams, often more than one team at once, and to be able to re-adjust roles from one project situation to another in an ever-shifting work situation.

In this chapter, the different personal and interactive attributes will be explored in actual work situations. The chapter will attempt to explore what employers mean by personal attributes, such things as willingness to learn, self-confidence and commercial awareness, and by interactive attributes such as communication, teamworking and interpersonal skills. For many employers the interactive attributes are closely interrelated in practice, especially in project-working, and this interrelationship will be explored to see how they are used to add value, to enable evolution and to effect transformation.

Lists of attributes

There are innumerable studies that have produced lists of graduate attributes desired by employers. Some of these studies are sophisticated in attempting to prioritise these attributes in terms of their importance to employers. Some go further and explore how satisfied employers are with the attributes of graduates in their employ.[1]

In this research we have avoided placing any emphasis on the listing and ranking of graduate attributes. The various studies have produced useful indicators of the kinds of skills and abilities that graduates need in addition to knowledge and, increasingly, they are showing enormous similarities across discipline boundaries, employment sectors and international boundaries. We know that a set of 'transferable skills' or 'competencies' including communication, teamworking, problem-solving, leadership, numeracy, self-confidence, willingness to learn and flexibility, are widely required (Harvey with Green, 1994).

Furthermore these lists of attributes are changing little over time, which begs the question: 'Is anybody listening?' (Harvey, Burrows, and Green, 1992). There has been some slight shift in emphasis, reflecting preferred ways of working in commerce and industry, such as increased desire for flexibility, interpersonal skills and team-working but essentially 'there has been very little change in the last 20–30 years in the sorts of attributes we want' (11A).

> I do not see management competencies changing significantly, what I see is that in some circumstances, in some stage of development, some of them will be more important than others, but things like commercial awareness, some basic intellectual capabilities, results orientation, interpersonal skills, will always be important. In my former company we did some research 25 years ago about successful managers and unsuccessful managers and what behavioural characteristics distinguished one from the other, and we came to the conclusion that there were four main headings: conceptual effectiveness, operational effectiveness, interpersonal effectiveness, and achievement motivation. And when you look back, conceptual effectiveness has strategic ability, intellect. Operational effectiveness has to do with how good are you at doing your job, functional competence or whatever you want to call it. Interpersonal effectiveness – you find that they go one-to-one. Achievement motivation, that is results orientation, drive, ambition. It has not changed in 25 years, fundamentally.
>
> (57A: senior executive, large brewing company)

Although employers and researchers have identified a number of attributes, which are in particular demand, there are enormous variations in emphasis. This makes it impossible to identify a universal set as the following comments suggest:

> We are looking for everything that every other high profile employer is looking for: intellectual excellence, team-working skills, professional ability, ability to relate to clients, all the things that you must have heard a hundred times.
>
> (09A: head of personnel, large law firm)

> Someone who is not totally dominated by work but is a hard worker, and is willing to put extra time in. Somebody who is interested in what he is doing, somebody who can talk to other people and work in a group. Our ideal person is somebody who will eventually become married and have two children. Somebody who feels responsible for what they are doing, and wants to take on responsibility.
>
> (49A: operations manager, computer-controlled systems manufacturer)

In practice, the list of desirable attributes is getting longer. Employers, if asked, want everything. While this ever-growing list may serve to alert educationalists and represent employer views, it does not necessarily help graduates. As lists get longer they become unachievable, which leaves some graduates regarding themselves as inadequate and they may become demoralised.

---

1 Gordon (1983), TA (1988), PSU (1989), UDACE (1991), NBEET (1992), Harvey with Green (1994), AGR (1995).

Lists are reductionist: they fragment the whole person into a set of isolated attributes. They do not 'add up' to an holistic whole, to somebody with a set of interrelated characteristics and abilities within a workplace context. To be a success at work, graduates need to be 'whole people', not a collection of disconnected attributes.

The wide range of attributes required by employers makes it impossible to describe the 'ideal graduate'. The relative balance of attributes is unique in each setting, and indeed, takes a variety of combinations appropriate to a number of different roles within a single setting.

> I don't think there's an ideal graduate. Graduates come in all shapes and sizes. For us an ideal graduate would be – it would be a different series of people actually. We could have the ideal graduate who could be a 21-year-old who has gone straight to university, just completed a psychology degree, is absolutely burning with motivation, really up-to-date in terms of knowledge, and is coming to us with other expectations, that are going to work for us for a year and then go off to change to clinical psychology. That could be absolutely ideal. It could equally be the woman who has brought up her children at home, completed a distance-learning degree, has really good life experience, plus a bit of structured thinking acquired from the degree – that would be ideal. I mean it could be the teacher who has got good experience, just finished an M.Ed., up-to-date in terms of knowledge about severe learning difficulties, autism, that could be ideal.
>
> (03A: head teacher, small private school for children with special needs)

What we know less about is what is meant by the terms in these ever-expanding lists. How do they relate to the world of work? This chapter will analyse the meanings attached to some of the key attributes and the next chapter will explore whether or not graduates and their employers feel that their undergraduate experience equips them with the attributes that make them effective in the world of work.

Personal attributes

Knowledge

A small number of employers consider subject-based knowledge as important in their graduate employees. In such cases the emphasis is on the understanding of 'first principles' rather than the accumulation of large stocks of specialist knowledge.

In addition, employers refer to general knowledge, knowledge of the organisation and commercial awareness. 'Business acumen' (77B) is now and will continue to be as important in the public sector as it has been in the commercial world.

> I think that the way GPs have fund-holding practices is going to happen in the hospital system… they [doctors] will need to be more aware of things in the business world, financially and economically.
>
> (75C2: doctor, medium-sized public hospital)

Intellect

A major reason for employing graduates is to get bright, intelligent recruits (CUCD, 1990). For many employers, intellect is more important than degree subject knowledge.

> We do not care about degree discipline… when I joined we had linguists, classicists, somebody with a music degree joined my intake as well as economics, maths, the sort of things you would normally expect, so demonstration of intellect is key.
>
> (62A: manager, large management consultants)

Many employers report that they 'take for granted' graduates' intellectual ability. However, there are caveats related to this implicit assumption of degree-based intellect. First, where once a degree holder would have been automatically assumed to be of an appropriate intellectual ability, and have some appropriate discipline knowledge (that may or may not have been relevant) the current situation is, as we have seen, that this merely gets a graduate to first base (Chapter 4). To go beyond this, graduates need to able to demonstrate their intellectual ability to solve problems using 'higher-level' skills such as analysis, critique and synthesis.

Second, when recruiting, some organisations differentiate between graduates and the 'cream' or 'very best' graduates and determine this by reference to degree classification, university or course, or even A-level score (Chapter 5). While this may have been the case for many years in some organisations, the massification of higher education has acted as a stimulus to this differentiation on a wider front. Several employers are of the view that a degree no longer has the currency it once had.

A third caveat is the relative importance of intelligence and experience. For some employers, graduate status is no substitute for experience (Chapter 4).

Willingness to learn

Willingness to learn was identified as an important attribute in the *Employer Satisfaction* research (Harvey with Green, 1994) and crucial in a situation of constant change. This is reflected in the current research:

> …being prepared to adapt to a changing employment structure, that's the other thing, not only is a job not for life but an area of work can disappear because it becomes unprofitable in this country and is taken over by a developing country or is mechanised, so people need to be prepared to learn new skills right throughout their careers now… Breaking down cultural barriers of associating types of people with types of jobs and being prepared to learn skills in different areas.
> (45A: senior advisor, small public watchdog organisation)

Respondents' attitudes to continuous learning and development are discussed further in Chapter 10.

Self-skills

Self-skills include self-regulatory skills, self-motivation and self-assurance. In a delayered, flexible organisation these self-skills are important if a graduate recruit is going to add value rapidly to the organisation.

> I actually expect them to self-start and get on with it… I don't want somebody who is extremely bright, who I give a job to, and he does the job and sits and waits for me to give him something else to do. I need self-starters, streetwise, mature-for-their-age people who recognise that the purpose of the degree in industry is to achieve an improvement or a success. It isn't purely an exercise for the academic.
> (40B: production manager, large steel manufacturer)

> I need somebody who is single-minded enough to overcome rejection and be able to bounce back and make the next telephone call in the belief that somebody is going to accept them and accept their product. That combined with a desire to succeed, which overcomes the inevitable disappointments that you get with this kind of job.
> (26B: area sales manager, multi-national business machines manufacturer)

> In a research environment a lot of what we do fails, and it can be quite depressing when that happens, especially when you have put a lot of effort into it. We want somebody who has a certain tenacity to see a job through, take a few setbacks to be able to make the final progress forward.
> (63B: research manager, large pharmaceutical manufacturers)

In many delayered, flexible organisations it is important that graduate-level employees take on responsibility, use initiative, identify their own work agendas (within overall parameters) in order to add value with the minimum of supervision. Self-skills are also a necessary component of a transformative skills profile. Pushing boundaries and motivating others to be innovative requires a degree of self-belief and self-confidence, and ability to deliver a contribution in a team-work setting. Resilience and tenacity are important but take on different emphasis: less a determination to complete, more the self-motivation to constantly re-engage and relearn as well as the patience, drive and enthusiasm to encourage others to reflect, change and innovate.

> You need people to be very conscientious and to be constantly striving to develop things, constantly looking at things in a creative way and pushing themselves to do work that nobody is demanding of them. (41A: general manager, small registered charity)

However, there is a need for a balance of 'self-skills' within an organisation to facilitate effective working and development.

> You don't want people coming in and using initiative 100% because you can never operate your business they would be questioning everything you did. You have to have some sort of core to your business, ways of doing things, systems, whatever. You don't want people constantly questioning them, but you do want people to question things, to think for themselves, but they just have to have the sort of maturity and the nous to realise when – it's judgement isn't it, to know when to its appropriate to work within boundaries. (04A: owner, small corporate literature specialists)

Interactive attributes

Employers and graduates indicate a wide range of desirable attributes but the key ones, emphasised across all sectors, are summed up by a recent graduate: 'You have got to be of a level of intelligence, be able to get on with people, be able to communicate – all this working in a team' (40C). These central interactive attributes are now discussed in more detail.

Communication

In study after study, communication skills emerge as one of the most important, if not *the* most important quality that employers require of graduates.[2] Possessing good communication skills is often seen by employers as an indicator of potential success (Harvey with Green, 1994). There are several reasons why communication skills are a valued requirement:

- to communicate ideas with others, including senior managers and non-graduates;
- to influence people within the organisation and affect action;
- to communicate with clients or customers.

Guirdham (1995) suggests that to communicate is simply to transmit meaning. However, 'communication skills' covers an enormous range of attributes, and to help students towards success at work, it is necessary to explore exactly what meanings employers attach to them, perhaps more importantly how employees will be expected to use them in the changing workplace.

> …it is something we have thought about over the years and we've tried to develop the meaning and establish really what are we looking for when we say that we want someone with communication skills, because it has so many ramifications and permutations that not all communication skills necessarily are relevant to what we do. (06A: partner, large law firm)

Communication it is by no means a simple concept, embracing both written and oral communication. 'Written communication skills' includes a vast array of abilities such as the ability to spell, writing bullet-point reports, drafting letters, sending e-mails, networking via the Internet, producing press releases, summarising published documents, setting down in concise form recommendations and reasons for action, and writing manuals. 'Oral communication' includes, among other things, the ability to undertake formal presentations, the ability to intervene effectively in meetings and participate in group discussions, informal exchange of ideas with colleagues, and the ability to persuade others (clients and colleagues).

---

2 SCOEG (1985), Greenwood, Edge and Hodgetts (1987), IMS/AGR (1991), Allen and Scrams (1991) Banta (1991) CBI (1991) Harvey, Burrows and Green (1992), NBEET (1992), Binks, Grant and Exley (1993), Harvey (1993), Business–Higher Education Round Table (1992).

The ways in which employees are expected to use their communication skills are many and varied. The advent of integrated job requirements means that employees are taking on increasingly complex roles and need to engage with people at various levels to be effective.

> An ability to communicate at all different levels and to do so clearly and effectively, meaning that internally they are very good at dealing with different members of the team that make a brochure actually happen, and externally they are good at dealing potentially with suppliers that we use, photographers, printers whatever, but also good at dealing with different people in the client organisation, who could be anything from the chairman down, so communication skills would be absolutely key.
> (04B: project director, small corporate literature specialists)

Fundamentals: spelling, grammar, vocabulary

Various studies have noted that a small proportion of employers indicate that some graduates (and even postgraduates) showed a grasp of fundamentals that fell below their expectation of graduate standards (a point that seemed particularly acute in engineering)[3]. In the current study, this was not a major issue. The majority of employers were satisfied that graduates know 'the basic tenets' (50A).

Only a small number of organisations expressed reservations or warned against sloppiness on application forms:

> It would be helpful if they could spell. One of the things I notice is that the quality of written work is certainly not of the standard, even among graduates. Knowing where to put apostrophes... I am not only talking of reports to trustees and internal documents, but the way we communicate to the outside world, letters to residents, tenants handbooks, the kind of public images that people have of the [organisation]. It is very important the way things are presented and they should be well expressed.
> (37A: deputy chief executive, small housing association)

> People here are very quick to judge you if they get a piece of work that is ill-spelt and badly punctuated. These sort of things are important. And it needs to be well presented so that it looks inviting to read. People in this company are under pressure and anything that comes in which is a mess just won't even get read. That's what I mean by communication skills.
> (32B: recruitment and development manager, large telecommunications organisation)

These fundamentals are increasingly important in modern organisations in which employees can no longer rely on administrative support and will increasingly have to prepare their own letters, reports and communicate via direct electronic links.

Writing for a variety of audiences

Although there was some concern about fundamentals of grammar and spelling, a more often-voiced concern is the limited writing style of graduates and the corresponding inability to judge the receptivity of their audience. This corresponds with the outcome of the *Employer Satisfaction* study, which noted that while graduates may be proficient at producing essays, laboratory reports, academic projects and dissertations, they are seen as 'relatively poor at producing other forms of written communication'. It was also noted that graduates tend to lack report-writing skills, a point also made in *Matching Skills* (BT, 1993, p. 33).

> I expect people to be able to write a reasonable standard of letters and documentation. I expect them to be reasonably confident in terms of dealing with clients of our company, and other professional disciplines. I would like to think that they know when to stop in terms of coming back and asking for advice and basically to cover the risk of our firm.
> (16A: office director, medium-sized quantity and building surveyors)

---

3   Quibble (1991), James (1992), Torrance, Thomas and Robinson (1992), Harvey with Green (1994).

> Written communication skills are clearly important. Being concise is important, being accurate and writing in a manner which is free from ambiguity is important... Effectively we are looking for people who can write in almost a bullet-point form. We are no longer really looking for people who can write wonderfully flowing 25-page documents, which take two hours to read.
> (27B: manager, large public financial institution)

Using information technology

In increasingly delayered organisational structures, the basic use of IT, for such things as word-processing and data-processing, is becoming more of a fundamental requirement of graduates. As discussed in Chapter 4, the traditional layer of administrative support is disappearing and graduates will be expected to be self-servicing.

> It is increasingly important to have basic experience with either a word processor or computer. Training is available but I think there is a certain basic standard expected. Not that there has to be a qualification, just basic experience, but it is becoming more and more important.
> (58A: development co-ordinator, small publicly funded arts publishers)

> We don't expect our graduates to write programmes, but as a matter of course they can all turn the computer on and knock a spreadsheet out.
> (16A: office director, medium-sized quantity and building surveyors)

IT is increasingly important in terms of communicating internally and externally, through faxing and e-mailing and also in facilitating 'networking'.

> ...they need to be able to access both internal and external databases and network around the world to gain the latest ideas from the Internet, from academic institutions. They need to be able to build networks, and that requires give and take, communication skills again and IT skills, and, slightly to our surprise, we find that a lot of graduates do not have the IT skills that we might now expect of today's generation.
> (63A: human resources manager, large pharmaceutical manufacturers)

> Communication used to be all paper – instructions, rule books and so on. Communication now is both through IT – e-mail, Internet, in-house notice boards on the computer – but also inter-communication skills within the office. It's more important now just to wander down the corridor and talk to people, get things done faster and off the cuff rather than the formality of minutes and that sort of thing.
> (38B: director of personnel, civil service)

Oral communication

The importance of oral communication has been highlighted in studies of job advertisements in Britain (Green, 1990) and Australia (NBEET, 1992), which have shown that oral communication was the most frequently required 'transferable personal skill'. There is a growing emphasis on the need to have good oral communication skills as there is considerable expectation that employees will interact on a personal level with a range of people within a company, 'so communication skills at all levels have to be very good, very presentable, a mixture of being serious and conscientious' (26B).

Oral communication ranges from one-to-one interactions at an operational level to selling oneself and one's work to a well-informed peer group or to management:

> The ability to tell someone or describe to someone exactly what you want them to do. Or the ability to take instructions from someone as to what they want you to do. It is making people understand as easily as possible certain procedures or certain things on a professional basis.
> (13D: broadcast journalist, medium-sized private local radio station)

> Verbal and scientific communication skills have become even more important. Most of our review of projects is done in open meetings, so researchers need to be able to communicate verbally. We have to train them to present well, and to present tough stuff. This isn't a nice easy subject, they have got to present their science in a structured, interesting way to a peer group audience and to be able to do so with the right facts and not to get lost in the detail. That is how projects are continued or stopped, or moved forward in the development programme. Work is now presented via verbal skills, rather than by written report. It is a much more open and selling environment and so the graduates become sales people for their projects.
>
> (63A: human resources manager, large pharmaceutical manufacturers)

The other important side of communication is listening (James, 1992; Binks, Exley and Grant, 1993). An often underrated skill, it is important in many contexts to be a 'good' or *active* listener. It was suggested by one employer that:

> People will need to be better communicators and have better communication skills, not just written, but in terms of listening and being able to modify what you are saying to the audience that you are delivering that communication to.
>
> (59D: business change manager, large financial institution)

Language ability

'Communication skills' is sometimes taken to include the ability to communicate in a second language. Somewhat surprisingly, given the international perspective of many organisations, only a few mentioned second languages. Among those who commented on the desirability of a language other than English, there seems to be a reliance on other countries to make the running:

> …although we are an international company and largely French owned, the actual language of communication is English. But naturally if somebody was working abroad on an assignment, then if they are working for a client, then obviously if they have languages it would help but it is not something we are looking for.
>
> (46A: senior consultant, multi-national computer service company)

> …in the context of this organisation we have quite a few dealings with people in Sweden, so we are lucky that they can speak English quite well. If they didn't we would be in serious difficulties when it actually came to developing partnerships.
>
> (50C: performance analyst, large freight company)

However, in view of the anticipated increase of trade in the Far East, one organisation could foresee problems ahead:

> The biggest issue for us would be Japanese and Chinese clearly – most of the European languages, either we can speak sufficient of their language or they can speak sufficient of ours to muddle through, but Japanese and Chinese would be difficult. The degree of interaction between ourselves and the Japanese and Chinese is likely to increase, especially the Chinese, as the pharmaceutical market of China opens up.
>
> (63B: research manager, large pharmaceutical manufacturers)

Teamworking

Teamworking is another attribute that is emphasised by employers. It is valued as it enables employees to:
- develop ideas with others, including senior managers and non-graduates;
- engage effectively with others to affect action in a mutually interdependent situation;
- build up a network of contacts inside the organisation;
- play an appropriate role in the organisation client interface.

Virtually all respondents suggested that teamworking is an integral part of working in a modern organisation: 'at some point during their career they will need an ability to work as part of a team' (47A). There is very little scope or encouragement to work outside teams.

> Teamwork is extremely important to our business, and we can accept one or two introverts but we are looking for fairly 'normal' people. Sometimes we get brilliant people but we don't employ them because they are loners – very difficult. Unless we find that they can mix with other people and work with them it is extremely difficult.
>
> (49A: operations manager, computer-controlled systems manufacturer)

Team-working can be defined as working collectively to achieve a common goal, with a clear 'understanding of what your roles and responsibilities are within that team' (50C). The team situation requires a high level of mutual trust and co-operation. Several organisations refer to the importance of teamworking in terms of problem solving, and suggest this may be a more creative way of working as '…each member has some pieces of a jigsaw, which cannot be completed until all members' pieces are brought together' (Guirdham, 1995).

> The projects that we are working on require a combination of skills that not one individual can bring to bear. If it's one person they can sometimes become a little bit stale, which is true of a lot of businesses. If you can involve other people and get different creative inputs to your problems, you will get different approaches to problem solving, different attitudes, different ways of looking at issues. That must be of benefit so long as you can control that process, and it just doesn't run away with itself.
>
> (04B: project director, small corporate literature specialists)

Many employers consider the ability to work in teams, not just one team but the ability to 'team hop' from one to another according to a particular function, as a crucial attribute.

> Most tasks that I give them have got some element of teamwork and it is always different teams. One person can have four pieces of work and each piece of work involves liaison with a completely different team. The person is either leading it or is a member of the team.
>
> (70B: line manager, multi-national petro-chemical company)

> We have client service teams and they are ever-changing. The day a new graduate has finished one job as the junior member of a team, he or she will move on to another client and join a different team… What one is talking about is this skill of being able to fit in with an ever-changing group of teams and feed off them, and into them, and interact with other teams.
>
> (79A: partner, large international accountants)

Effective teamworking includes leadership. However, it is important that employees are able to adopt a range of teamworking roles and not always strive to lead teams.

> There is leadership capabilities, abilities to lead a team, lead through vision and values which are pretty difficult to test out at a selection, but they are certainly things we are looking at for the future.
>
> (47A: personnel manager, multi-national food manufacturer)

> Obviously you can't have a team where every member of the team is a leader because you won't operate as a team. To have teams working together you need somebody who is the leader but you need someone who is the doer and someone who is the facilitator and so on. If they need a team leader and a motivator and a driver, they are going to look for somebody with those skills. If the hole in that team is a facilitator then the emphasis will be on those skills.
>
> (28B: design manager, small design and communications company)

Furthermore, leading teams is not about commanding, but persuading people to do things and develop ideas. It is about encouraging involvement and ideas at all levels.

> Team-working skills are without doubt, important. The way it works here is everyone has an input and we are looking for ideas and it doesn't matter whether it comes from a technician, a student or the project manager. So communication skills are extremely important.
>
> (82D: senior technician and safety officer, large power company)

> As we all become increasingly specialised, no one individual knows sufficient normally to take a decision so increasingly you need multi-disciplined teams. We need people who can lead in situations where they don't have hierarchical control, it's just a team of equals. Somebody may be called team leader but nevertheless you can't actually fire the person on your team. Increasingly people are less inclined – the decline of deference I think its been called – to say well he's the boss, he knows best, then arguably they will need to be persuaded.
>
> (11A: vice-president, multi-national food manufacturers)

Interpersonal skills

Employers identified interpersonal skills as an essential attribute of prospective graduate employees. Indeed, the importance of interpersonal skills has been identified as a vital element in relating and interacting with clients and customers, and clearly represents an issue high on the agenda of many organisations (Harvey & Knight, 1996). In a sense, interpersonal skill is the 'glue' that combines all the other attributes together. Good interpersonal skills are valued because they:

- facilitate communication of ideas with others at all levels within flatter organisations;
- are necessary to influence people within the organisation and thereby effect action;
- facilitate appropriate interaction with clients or customers.

However, as there are different types of 'glue' for different circumstances, there are different notions of what interpersonal skills involve in practice. For some it is about being friendly and approachable:

> When you are working with people the first thing is that you have got to be approachable, come across to people as approachable, sincere, knowledgeable on your subject, warm, caring, those sort of things, they are interpersonal skills.
>
> (41A: general manager, small registered charity)

More often than not, interpersonal skills relate directly to fitting into the workplace culture. For some this primarily means being aware that the workplace embodies a different culture to university:

> Their experience of studying leads some [graduates] to be quite insular and what I would like to see is more emphasis on interpersonal skills and their importance in the workplace. Potentially, they have quite a hard job coming into a group as a new graduate. They are going to be received differently by people and if they have some skills that they can draw on, it might help make that transition into the workplace easier.
>
> (32D: programme manager, large telecommunications organisation)

For most 'fitting-in' is about being able to work with others in a team situation; indeed, interpersonal skills is sometimes seen as synonymous with teamworking:

> Interpersonal skills are important. It is so valuable when students say they have learned about working in a team, contributing as part of a team, it improves their self-confidence and gives them an idea of what it is like to work in a company.
>
> (42A: training and personnel manager, medium private broadcasting organisation)

Sometimes employees are expected to complement effective working with involvement in a wider work-based social culture:

> There are two sorts of personality aspects that we look for. The social level – getting on with people, being a reasonably personable individual. There is a teamworking side to that – can you actually fit into a team, work constructively with other people?
>
> (71A: strategic manager, large international accountants)

> You are in an environment that is quite pressured anyway, you don't want people who are not going to come forward with ideas, who are not going to be able to contribute, not just to the working environment but to the social environment as well. So it is very important that the person that we take on fits in. You have got to have somebody who has a sense of humour... If they don't appear as if they will fit in socially then we have got a problem. It isn't just somebody who is really good at doing debits and credits, I need somebody who can work with the people out there.
>
> (22B: sales manager, multinational reprographic equipment manufacturer)

Some employers seem to have difficulty in applying specific meaning to interpersonal skills, further demonstrating the problems associated with attempts to deconstruct such terms. Interpersonal skills, people skills, interaction skills are all terms for a similar array of attributes to do with how employees relate to other people within and outside the organisation. Exactly what is covered varies from one 'definition' to another, but broadly it involves being effective in any interactive situation, be it in a work, business or social setting.

Interpersonal skills are somewhat less tangible than communication or teamworking skills and some employers regard them as rather more difficult to develop through training programmes. This view is based on a notion that interpersonal skills are rooted in personal attributes; that individuals' personal development or early socialisation influences their capacity to interact with and relate to others (Guirdham, 1995). This has led some employers to place a lot of emphasis on graduates' personal attributes when recruiting. Sir Charles Darby, chief executive of Bass Taverns, for example, is clear that 'when recruiting we are more interested in personal qualities' (Harvey, 1993, p. 37).

The work placement was highlighted by respondents as major means of developing these personal attributes as it was recognised that academic courses are not necessarily the most appropriate or best place for interpersonal skills to be developed:

> I do believe that four-year degrees with a year out in industry is a good way of building some of the other skills in the ideal graduate, some of the interpersonal stuff. And I don't see any other way to do that, you can't expect the degree to do everything. So development as individuals is something I don't think you can expect, but to have the year placement is a good way of starting that process.
>
> (82B: line manager, large international manufacturer/service organisation)

In light of the problems associated with identifying particular aspects that conjoin to develop and/or produce good interpersonal skills, employers highlighted the potential risk of employing graduates who, although they have the necessary 'paper qualifications' and demonstrate the technical knowledge required for the post, may not 'make the grade' in terms of their interpersonal skills. Even where highly technical or academic ability is the overriding emphasis, employers are increasingly eager to see that knowledge and skill supported with more interactive attributes:

> The future for us is less about brute force and more about intellectual power and responsiveness of the organisation and in our case we are about solving problems in the nuclear area, and we need people who can think cleverly technically, and then in addition they need all the interpersonal skills.
>
> (82A: head of technology strategy, large power company)

Interrelationship of interactive attributes

Teamworking, communication and interpersonal skills are inextricably linked in the delayered organisation. For instance, it is highly unlikely that someone with underdeveloped interpersonal skills would be able to engage effectively with colleagues and clients, let alone inspire a team.

> Communication skills are always vital, so is the way that you deal with people. So, interpersonal skills are important, which was something that was looked at pretty closely when I joined the bank. It was looked at the assessment centre, how you dealt with people from different cultures, and so on.
>
> (36C: branch manager, large financial institution)

> You could put two different teams on an identical project and they could have exactly the same problems put in front of them, but depending on how the two teams gel together and the personalities involved, one project could run smoothly and one I believe could go horrendously wrong if you go in with a defensive attitude, you don't want to co-operate, you are going to do your contract, you are going to do no more.
>
> (55B: associate, small quantity surveyors)

Employers want people who will be effective in a future changing world. As we have seen in Chapters 2 and 3, the extent to which organisations have dared to 'ride the wave of change' covers a broad spectrum ranging from cost flexible to stakeholder flexible.

These interrelated attributes come together at one end of the adaptive-adaptable-transformative continuum to facilitate maximum value-added by enabling people to fit in to the workplace culture. Being a good communicator, with well-developed interpersonal skills, an effective team player and an understanding of the culture enables the graduate to 'fit in' to the organisation.

They are also necessary for effective organisational adaptation as good teamworking, communication and interpersonal skills are vital to persuade people to innovative courses of action. The development of ideas in an organisational setting is also contingent on the coming together of these interactive skills.

At another level still, communication, teamworking and interpersonal skills are fundamental to any transformation of the organisation. People who have highly developed interpersonal skills and multi-layered communication abilities and who can combine these with their higher level intellectual skill are required to help transform organisations to enable them to stay ahead of their competitors.

This interrelationship (Figure 6.1) operates both internally to the organisation and externally in terms of its dealings with stakeholders. The following section explores how employers envisage the interrelationship of these interactive skills and suggests that the predominant view revolves around the persuasive, motivating impact of mutually developmental teamwork.

Fitting in

A majority of employers expressed the need for graduates who could 'fit in', 'get on' and generally work with other people both within, and external to, the employing organisation:

> You have to feel quite confident talking to clients and inspiring trust and confidence and communicating. You are representing [the company] – a sort of corporate communication. And then you have to talk to your suppliers because if you are project manager here you are buying in a lot of different people. You talk to writers, designers, printers. It is quite a range so it is being able to give them clear views about what you want and when. And then, obviously, there are people within the building here that it is very much a team-based approach and it is reporting to people but it's also asking for jobs to be done because people will have various knowledge and experience that you need them to input into your project. Generally, I would say, that working in a building like this, you have to get on. And being out here as well, there's even more pressure on personal relationships to work. Because it is really quite a pressurised job and you can't really afford to have people not getting on.
>
> (28C: project manager, small design and communications company)

Some employers expressed an increasing need for graduates who can come into the organisation and be immediately effective and make a positive contribution. This requires graduates to be able to rapidly integrate and immerse themselves into the culture and operation of the organisation.

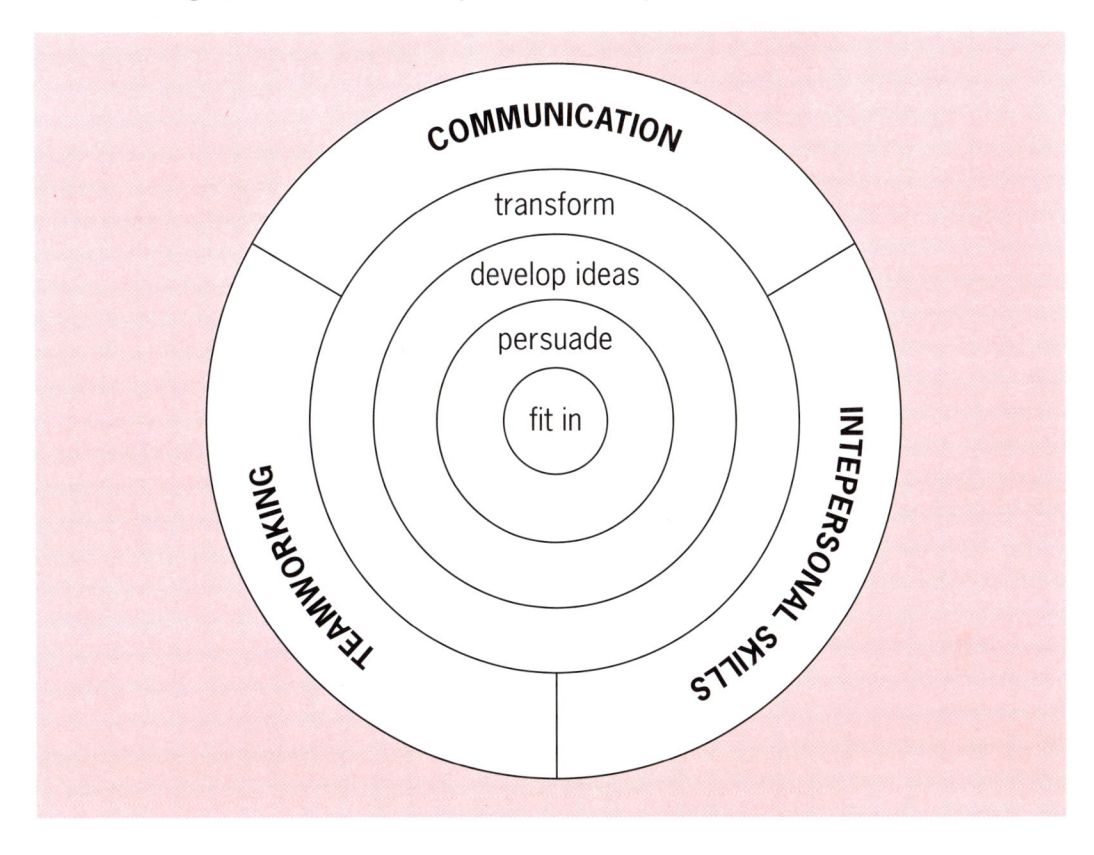

Figure 6.1 Interrelationship and levels of impact of interactive attributes

[Diagram: concentric circles with outer ring divided into COMMUNICATION, INTERPERSONAL SKILLS, TEAMWORKING; inner rings labelled (from outer to inner): transform, develop ideas, persuade, fit in]

Fitting-in is one end of the continuum, it is about adding value quickly rather than 'rocking the boat'. At its extreme, it is about conformity and uniformity:

> In a team you need to be more or less all the same, look similar and do similar things, if you are very different you have to be better than everyone else to get away with it, if you aren't then you can get picked on. Normally it is easier if you are samey as far as team work is concerned. Everybody can pull together, and everybody knows what everybody else is doing, the team work is much more coherent. If you take it too far it becomes too sterile and everybody is exactly the same. (46B: project leader, multi-national computer service company)

> It is being aware of other people you are working with and what their needs are – almost trying to read body signals. Yes, that's a good time to speak to somebody, that's a bad time or I feel about this but I need to say about it this way.
> (28B: design manager, small design and communications company)

Persuading

There is a substantial element of *persuasion* necessary in the commercial and industrial sphere. Employees need to make a persuasive case to support their ideas and influence others in one-to-one and team situations, at all levels, internally and externally.

> Well it's no good being very bright and having the best idea if you can't actually persuade certain doubters, and you need different sorts of influencing skills for different sorts of situations and different sorts of people, so it is not just one technique.
> (11A: vice-president, multi-national food manufacturers)

Persuading others moves beyond having ideas and views and sharing them. It means being able to convince others that your ideas have worth and to persuade them to take them on board. This involves clear expression through communication such as presentation, 'people who are more able to present ideas clearly and fluently and advocate and persuade' (07A). It also means being able to think on your feet, coping with critical questions by answering in such a way that will convince 'doubters' that your argument is sound.

> The ability to express yourself in a clear manner, I guess, the ideas you have in your head to get across to somebody in a way which is going to influence them to do what you want them to do.
> (17A: office manager, small private specialist employment agency)

> There's a lot more project work. There's a lot more giving presentations to people. Presenting what your work is or what you hope its going to be, to get management to buy it.
> (38A: head of branch, civil service)

> Our job is to get the best deal possible for our client, therefore we have to put across our client's side of the argument as persuasively and effectively as possible and that is a fairly skilled process. You simply can't go into a meeting and say "This is what happened therefore our client is entitled to compensation". It's a much more sophisticated process than that. To be able to convert the position into something tangible for the client takes a lot more.
> (06A: partner, large law firm)

In a teamwork situation, persuasion can mean moving beyond all team members fitting in and conforming to one model, to a situation where team members persuade others of their ideas and also take on board the ideas of other team members.

> In general you want people who you believe could be influential amongst their peer group, although not necessarily put in any position of greater seniority, and get the respect of them and is ready to adapt to the way the discussion and conclusions are coming out of the group... Someone who has certain influential skills, has thought things through soundly and got their own good ideas but at the same time is ready to trade those in and be ready to accept that the conclusion of the whole group might be better.
> (11B: head of management recruitment and training, multi-national food manufacturers)

Developing ideas

Organisations have not just experienced organisational change, but also change in the way they develop ideas and tackle problems. Where this was perhaps once done within tightly circumscribed departments, the delayered, downsized organisation is more fluid:

> In the West we tend to tackle problems in a hard, academic, fact-finding way, analysing it, arguing it through. I think, though, there is a move towards greater creativity, which can be demonstrated by more diverse teamwork, by people of different backgrounds, working on particular problems and actually working them through in a more organic, holistic approach rather than analysing the hell out of everything... Increasingly you solve problems by who you know and not what you know. What you know is almost certainly out of date by now. Because the organisation is de-layered, there is no longer a resident expert, and so the most amazing sort of problems get thrown at me and I have to solve them somehow. And you are then networking to find who you know, via the Internet or the libraries, to somehow get a lead on what to do and where to get it. I think that is particularly important.
> (66A: recruitment manager, multi-national petro-chemical company)

Developing ideas involves analysing situations rather than merely responding to what is there.

> ...we need people who can think and contribute to change processes and where graduates are really very helpful and where they really make the biggest impact is coming in and developing things. You can give them a new project or you can ask them to look at something and they will come at it with a fresh pair of eyes and they have some knowledge about how to think their way logically through things. A lot of our managers do not logically think through problem solving, they will identify a problem look for a quick solution then

they will spend all their time trying to force it to work, whereas in fact what we are looking for are people who can spend more time understanding the problem then developing options, testing out how they will work, picking the one that will work and then making it work.

(77A: director of human resources: health service contractors)

There is recognition that developing ideas involves interaction. Different people can bring different ideas. Networking and group fusion are an important element in taking things forward, embracing new ways of solving problems and thus enhancing the organisation:

Graduates can solve difficult problems and persuade people to begin to think about different things when nobody wants to, they can deal with the general public when they are screaming and shouting at them, etc. Those are important tasks, if you can add those skills on to critical thinking then you have somebody who is going to be very useful to the organisation.

(77A: director of human resources: health service contractors)

Other employers may require graduates to be independent, able to work on their own initiative in the field, and to take on a more innovative or representative role with clients and customers away from the operational base. Such requirements rely heavily on well developed interpersonal skills and ability to communicate:

People that can stand on their own two feet, people who can interact with others well and not take offence, when we send people overseas we need people who can represent the firm well in a smaller environment because overseas it is a lot harder. 1100 people work in London so there is support there, but when you go to overseas offices, for instance, New York there are five people there, so we need people who have good interpersonal skills, good communication skills, who present themselves well. We are looking for people who have eye for detail, people who can convey themselves precisely and accurately.

(78A: recruitment manager, large international law firm)

Transforming

People who have the ability to transform organisations have all the qualities already outlined together with the ability to apply their intellectual skills; analysis, critique and synthesis to steer change. Such people can see new possibilities and are prepared to take risks and push the boundaries to effect change, people who can 'lead their teams, develop their teams, motivate their teams, inspire their teams' (40A), who, in addition, can reflect and never stop learning.

My understanding of teamworking skills is breaking down the organisational structure and making it work more effectively. People tend to see organisational structures as being a bit of a barrier, it is there, it's an artificial barrier because there is a hierarchy in place and people don't feel themselves as being all working together towards a common goal… I think that is a common problem within this industry that we tend to think that we have an exclusive right on good ideas and we don't. I think that is one thing that came out of university courses, that you don't know everything and you can't possibly know everything, you have got to rely on other people.

(50C: performance analyst, large freight company)

There is a difference acknowledged between innovative leadership, where someone motivates themselves and others to strive for shared goals, and directive management where decision-making and action are imposed. It has been suggested that 'change creates the need for leadership and leaders are, or are perceived to be, innovators and drivers of change' (Middlehurst, 1995). Thus successful leadership is crucial to organisations in a state of flux.

I work for a very good leader and he is recognised for his leadership skills, his ability to enthuse, to motivate and to provide sound objects and clarity of purpose. To have clear, strong leaders is important. Not an authoritative, dictatorial one – that's a thing of the past. Empowering people who work for you, but leading them forward, I think, is the cue for business success.

(11C: marketing officer, multi-national food manufacturers)

> We don't generally go for the loud brash type, if there is one thing that really gets up people's noses here and that's people who do that. We look for people who have got a forceful style about them but who can really work with others. It is a difficult balance. There are a few people who, because of their intellect and because of the way they get on with people, can get you to do anything.
>
> (70B: line manager, multi-national petro-chemical company)

Summary

- There are large numbers of graduates looking for jobs and employers are looking for a range of knowledge, skills, abilities and personal attributes in addition to degree status. Graduates will need to develop a profile of attributes applicable to the workplace of the future.

- Among the *personal attributes* employers look for are: intellect (including analysis, critique, synthesis and problem-solving ability), knowledge (especially understanding basic principles), willingness and ability to learn, flexibility and adaptability to respond to change, self-regulatory skills, (such as self-discipline, time-keeping, and planning) self-motivation and self-assurance.

- These personal attributes are seen as playing an important role in the ability of graduates to be able to fit into the work culture, do the job, develop ideas, take initiative and responsibility and ultimately help organisations deal with change.

- Employers also require *interactive attributes*, such as interpersonal skills, teamworking, and communication skills. These are pivotal for delayered, project-focused organisations.

- The research has avoided placing any emphasis on the listing and ranking of graduate attributes. There are many studies that address employer requirements of graduates, which reveal similarities over time and across discipline boundaries, employment sectors and international boundaries.

- Although employers and researchers have identified a number of attributes that are in particular demand, there are enormous variations in emphasis, which make it impossible to identify a universal set. In practice, the list of desirable attributes is getting longer.

- For most employers, intellect and willingness to learn are more important than degree subject knowledge.

- In a delayered, flexible organisation a range of self-skills – self-regulation, self-motivation and self-assurance – are important if a graduate recruit is going to add value rapidly to the organisation. Self-skills are also a necessary component of a transformative skills profile. Pushing boundaries and motivating others to be innovative requires a degree of self-belief and self-confidence, and ability to deliver a contribution in a team-work setting.

- In study after study, written and oral communication skills emerge as one of the most important, if not *the* most important, quality that employers require of graduates. However, 'communication skills' covers a range of attributes including: the ability to spell, write bullet-point reports, draft letters, send e-mails, network via the Internet, produce press releases, make formal presentations, intervene effectively in meetings, and persuade others.

- Teamworking is attribute that is emphasised by respondents who suggested that it is an integral part of working in a modern organisation. Teamworking includes taking a variety of roles and the ability to 'hop' from one team to another.

- Employers identified interpersonal skills as an essential attribute of prospective graduate employees. They are the 'glue' that combines all the other attributes together. However, there are different notions of what interpersonal skills involves, ranging from being friendly and approachable to being aware of workplace culture and operating within it.

- Teamworking, communication and interpersonal skills are inextricably linked in the delayered organisation. For instance, it is highly unlikely that someone with underdeveloped interpersonal skills would be able to engage effectively with colleagues and clients, let alone inspire a team.

- These interrelated interactive attributes come together at one end of the adaptive-adaptable-transformative continuum to facilitate maximum value added by enabling people to fit in to the workplace culture. Being a good communicator, with well-developed interpersonal skills, an effective team player and an understanding of the culture enables the graduate to 'fit in' to the organisation.
- They also combine at the transformative end of the continuum: people who have highly developed interpersonal skills and multi-layered communication abilities and who can combine these with their higher level intellectual skill are required to help transform organisations to enable them to stay ahead of their competitors.

7 Benefits of a degree

Respondents to the survey were of the view that an undergraduate degree is a worthwhile experience and equips graduates with a range of abilities and skills in addition to knowledge. However, despite being intellectually equipped for the world of work, graduates are often ill-equipped to fit into the culture of the work-place.

Cost-effectiveness of graduates

Half the managers in the sample attempted to directly address the issue of the cost effectiveness of employing graduates. Of these, approximately three-quarters indicated that graduates are *definitely* cost effective. Some respondents offered a value-for-money appraisal:

> Yes, they certainly are. It is easy to make that glib statement, I mean this is a mega-bucks industry and value for money, with a successful compound behind us, can be measured in hundreds of millions of pounds, but they are good value for money. We are able to get a lot out of them.
> (63A: human resources manager, large pharmaceutical manufacturers)

> At the moment we are just riding on the fact that we get graduates for the same rate of pay that we previously paid people who weren't graduates. It's a field day for employers. It's frightening when I look at the applications that we get, we have staggeringly qualified people applying for posts. There are just phenomenal skills that are out there, so we have been able to make some really good appointments.
> (07A: deputy chief executive, regional arts board)

> We have roughly worked out it will cost us about £100,000 for each trainee, because from the day we recruit them to the day they qualify it is normally three or four years. We would like to think we get a return on our investment, although we have also calculated that that doesn't happen until they are two years qualified, that is post-qualification. We encourage everyone that we recruit to stay with the firm, sometimes it happens, sometimes it doesn't. We have a fairly good retention rate, it stands around 80 – 90%.
> (78A: trainee recruiter, large, international law firm)

Ironically, this advantageous climate leads a few respondents, mainly in small organisations, to be cautious in their concurrence with the view that employing graduates is cost-effective. They feared that should the tide turn and it become a seller's market, then they would find graduate recruitment difficult or prohibitively expensive, which would be a retrograde step as far as the development of their organisation was concerned.

> I think if the economy picked up dramatically and the bigger companies offered more money and opportunities to graduates, there would come a point where the availability of graduates would reduce. They would possibly become less cost effective and less of an investment for the future, because there would be more opportunities open to them and they would be skipping off, having been trained. But the main reason we recruit graduates at the moment isn't because you have to be a graduate to do the job, its because they are good value for money, they are cheap and they are good calibre people.
> (17A: partner, small private specialist employment agency)

Others implied that, while cost-effective, the value of employing graduates might not be so easily converted into cash terms:

> Graduates come in with a level of education and intellect, and the level of work and commitment that is involved in passing a degree. So, in a sense, there are certain hoops that have been jumped through in quite a short space of time. They have been trained to an extent in broad skills rather than just a specific academic qualification. They are usually people who are willing to train further and to take further courses. They are not frightened by that and they are usually quite alert in terms of what is happening in employment in their specific field.
>
> (58A: development co-ordinator, small publicly funded arts publishers)

> I don't think we have ever done any hard-core analysis on it, but certainly it is felt very strongly in this company, and our new CE has made the point several times, that the graduate recruitment programme is absolutely crucial to our future. It is that sense of new ideas, new ways of thinking, challenging the status quo, that is absolutely crucial – and I don't know how you put a value on that.
>
> (32A: development and training manager, large telecommunications organisation)

For some respondents, the cost-effectiveness of graduates is contingent as much on the effort the employer puts in to initial orientation and training as it is on the abilities of graduates 'if I have a graduate that has no computer literacy skills then it is my responsibility to bring them up to the point where they can type their own letters' (19B). A small number of managers see graduate recruitment as their lifeblood and, rather than assess whether graduates are a good investment, suggest that graduates recruitment has to be made to be cost-effective (44A).

> The fact that we continue to take ever larger numbers of graduates seems to indicate that there are no real concerns about their cost effectiveness. So, in that way, we make them cost-effective. In terms of retention, they stay, generally we have about 75% after three or four years which isn't bad.
>
> (32B: recruitment and development manager, large telecommunications organisation)

A handful of managers from small and medium organisations thought graduates to be cost effective but were somewhat more guarded in their endorsement. For some, the cost-effectiveness of graduate recruitment depended on the individuals recruited:

> Whether graduates are cost-effective depends very much on the sort of post we are talking about. The danger is that highly qualified graduates are not going to find some of the jobs stretching enough. There is a risk that you can spend a lot of money on recruitment selection, and then end up with somebody who may have superb qualifications and high intellect but who is not suitable for the sort of job that we have available.
>
> (37A: deputy chief executive, small housing association)

Only two respondents tended towards a negative view of the cost-effectiveness of graduate recruitment as they need people who can 'hit the deck running' and were more inclined to pay the extra for experienced people (04A).

Worthwhile doing a degree?

All the recent graduates in the sample confirmed that their undergraduate degree experience had been worthwhile. Approximately four-fifths, in organisations from all sectors and sizes, were unconditionally positive about the experience:

> Absolutely yes. Personally I think everyone should go on to some form of higher education where possible.
>
> (18C: junior design engineer, small private design consultancy)

> Definitely. I strongly recommend that everyone should get a degree or get to a point where they think I would like to learn about this for my own reasons. The more knowledge you get it gives you a larger view of the world.
>
> (14C: project manager, small design and print agency)

> Definitely, because it gave me certain experiences. One was living away from home, gaining my own independence and all that experience, having the opportunity to be with the people I probably wouldn't have met if I'd have stayed in Birmingham. Getting to know another part of the country. There is a discipline at university around meeting deadlines, working within a time-scale and, because it is over a four-year period, actually seeing something through – being able to show a commitment.
>
> (19C: community worker, small publicly funded community health centre)

A few recent graduates were positive but somewhat more sceptical:

> Think twice about it, if you have got a specific career in mind, then look at other ways... By the time somebody has come out of university and they go in at the bottom, they probably wouldn't do anything any quicker. But having said that, then you would miss all the other side of it. The things that you gain personally from it, which I know I did, and I wouldn't want to have missed out on that.
>
> (15C: computing supervisor, small chartered accountants)

Apart from a degree being the first step for many kinds of job (see Chapter 4), respondents identified three other types of benefit from doing a degree:

- personal development;
- usefulness whilst in the job;
- general benefits to employers.

Personal development

Many strategic and line managers see an undergraduate experience as having a major positive impact on the personal development of graduates. They regarded the personal development aspect of a degree course as at least as important as the intellectual benefits and often more important than the development of a specific knowledge base.

> The advantages to me of a graduate would be that he or she would probably have a broader range of thinking, rather than someone who has not been a graduate. He or she ought to be able to assimilate things quicker and, in many cases, that is the case. Of course, that peters out as people get a bit older. Wider and more strategically thinking from time-to-time as well. And I'm not sure there are any downsides.
>
> (36B: area manager, large financial institution)

Graduates saw themselves as 'growing' into more mature, rounded people with a broader perspective on the world as a result of their undergraduate experience.

> I think it is just the sense of independence, I think it is because you have been thrown into this place where you don't know anyone and you have to get along, and I think for the work environment it is very, very important.
>
> (60C: finance controller, large vehicle manufacturer)

> Apart from the obvious qualifications I think it has developed me as a person and the independence of having to fund myself while living away, paying the bills and making sure you organise your time so that you are putting enough aside for your work, so I think generally it has rounded me off at the same time
>
> (78C1: recent graduate, large, international law firm)

For some graduates the intellectual milieu itself was the main stimulus for personal development, and some respondents clearly miss the 'ability to feed off each other', which is seen as unique to a university environment (14C). Some new graduates emphasised the importance of balancing vocational potential from a degree course with the equally important personal benefits of undergraduate education:

> I wouldn't want do a course so specific that if would only take you into one job. I think it is important that you do the degree for itself. You go away and you learn various sort of people skills and independence skills, because at that age they are very formative years... I don't

think higher education should become so specialised that if you want to be a journalist you have to do one particular degree, because then there would be dangers in that and everyone would be just clones and wouldn't be very rounded.

(43C: news producer, large public broadcasting organisation)

It would have been easier to do a degree that was working me towards a well paid job that I was qualified to do. But that's not why I did my degree. I did it because I was interested in the subject, I wanted to go through the process of doing a degree.

(03C: teacher, small private school for children with special needs)

Only one graduate considered he had gained little or nothing at all from his undergraduate experience (despite regarding it as beneficial overall), commenting that he 'used it as a way of getting into civil engineering and it hasn't changed me in any way' (44C). In a slightly different vein, a non-graduate thought that the personal development attributable to an undergraduate education was possibly overstated, or at least equally achievable without doing a degree.

It does give you a guideline to someone's intelligence. I just think they shouldn't shut the door necessarily to someone with good O-levels or A-levels because that is also a measure of intelligence, ability and potential. There is vague talk that going to university makes you a rounder person but there are other ways of spending those three years. I'm not sure it does necessarily make you a better person than someone who has been working for three years.

(27D: equity markets analyst, large public financial institution)

Benefits for work

Respondents identified three sorts of direct benefit of their undergraduate experience in their current workplace. First, specific elements of their course were acknowledged as of direct use in the job they are undertaking, such as organisational psychology, statistics, economics and information technology, or specialist knowledge in technical areas. Second, the degree experience developed specific job-relevant skills. Third, the degree was seen as providing a general level of ability, skill and self-development from which the work situation benefited.

Many recent graduates considered that their degree experience had considerably enhanced their communication and organisational skills:

All the extended essays that I had to do have been good because they are a real good test of your writing skills and your organisational skills. Also most of the time you have a heavy workload at university so I have been able to prioritise now in this job.

(07C: executive officer, regional arts board)

The project writing that we did at university is useful. I have been having to write up things while I have been here and I am having to give talks quite frequently as well, and that sort of thing. Those are the sort of skills that you do pick up at university.

(63C: assistant research scientist, large pharmaceutical manufacturers)

In general, the ability to communicate was seen as a positive outcome, although most acknowledged the limits of their communicative style as a result of a narrow lecturer-oriented audience. Some graduates feel that they did not perhaps have the opportunity they would have liked to develop aspects of communication skills. This missing element was also raised by respondents in a study of language students from one university of whom 60% needed oral presentation skills for their job but only 25% actually acquired them from their course (Phillips-Kerr, 1991). Similarly, only 38% of finalists at old universities in 1993 thought they had acquired public speaking skills (MORI, 1993). Occasionally, respondents pointed to wider opportunities:

…throughout the five years you had to do a group presentation each year for the first three, there was about three presentations done in the fourth year, and the fifth year the majority of the work was on group presentation, it was group-orientated and your results had to be

> communicated in a group situation and it wasn't just fellow classmates either, it was a group of local businessmen and representatives of trade and industry who were given the opportunity to ask questions.
>
> (31C: senior quantity surveyor, medium-sized house builders and regenerators)

In *Matching Skills*, BT managers describe finding 'difficulty persuading new graduate recruits to redefine their sense of achievement from the highly individual academic mode, to achievement based on teamwork and co-operation' (BT, 1993, p. 33). The *Employer Satisfaction* study similarly showed that some employers regarded graduates as sometimes incapable of working in teams and often preferred to act alone to solve problems. However, overall, employers were quite satisfied with the teamworking ability of graduate recruits (Harvey with Green, 1994). Anecdotal evidence also suggests that programmes of study in higher education institutions in Britain place increasing emphasis on teamworking.

In the sample, there were several graduates who felt they had developed teamworking skills during their undergraduate experience:

> During my time at [University X] we used to give mock presentations and we worked in a team, it was like a mock courtroom presentation and you worked in a group of two and one of you gave a presentation on behalf of the other on a certain point of law, almost like a debate really, and the other person followed that up. We had that sort of team experience.
>
> (09C: graduate trainee, large law firm)

However, some graduates and managers thought that the culture of individual performance results in the underdevelopment of teamwork in university programmes:

> My degree was an awful lot of solo work with very little opportunity for teamworking. I had friends who did business studies and they were always doing group work, they were always doing group presentations on something or another. My teamwork came from team sports and being involved in setting up the Student Advice Centre.
>
> (80C: sales co-ordinator, medium-sized brewing company)

One respondent made the point that although graduates may not have developed teamworking, this is not a shortfall particular to graduates.

> Everyone takes time to acclimatise to teamworking. I know it is very fashionable to say that graduates come without teamworking skills but I deliberately did not say that, I said they were no worse than anyone else and, as far as we are concerned, it is not a serious problem.
>
> (25A: managing director, medium-sized shop-fitting manufacturer)

The majority of new graduates thought that little of the specific academic content of their course was particularly relevant to the job, much more important were a broader range of skills, abilities and dispositions:

> I think when you are at university you have to plan and organise and prioritise your time to actually get your studies done as well as enjoying yourself. So I think that's one of the things you learn which is useful in the workplace. Actually it is essential here. You have to be able to do that.
>
> (28C: project manager, small design and communications company)

> I suppose to a certain extent working under pressure is one that you gain at university, the habit of working outside of hours because of studying outside of lecture time, when you are working commissioning a big plant just because it is five o'clock you don't necessarily want to down tools if you have deadlines to meet.
>
> (47C: process engineer, multi-national food manufacturer)

Many recent graduates thought that much of what they could offer as a graduate was underutilised in their current job. For some respondents, the technical material in their course goes way beyond that required in the workplace while others never intended their degree subject to be linked to future work:

> Most of the work I did at university would probably be useful in the research and development field rather than in the common workplace. I think also some of my friends from university also haven't used what they have learned because they have gone into information technology.
> (49C: project designer, computer-controlled systems manufacturer)

> I never actually thought that the subject matter of my history degree would be useful in my job. It was the skills it was going to teach me that I was particularly interested in.
> (67C: recent graduate, small journal publishers)

Prepared for work

Although many graduates considered that their degree was enormously beneficial both in personal and work-related terms, a large number considered that the undergraduate experience did not adequately prepare them for the world of work. About one in ten confirmed that their university experience had prepared them. Rather more suggested that the degree equipped them for *getting* a job rather than performing in the work place.

> Graduates are better equipped to get jobs, this is very much my perspective from having done the interviewing over the years. I cheated a little bit and asked my brother who's a senior lecturer, how they prepare students [for job applications] these days. It was quite impressive. They are putting a lot more thought and work into it with the students these days. I think in my early days of interviewing there was a bit of complacency from students who felt that, in some ways, they were owed a job. Now I see people targeting as opposed to spraying all over the place, which wastes less of everyone's time.
> (54A: assistant to deputy chairman, large international retailers)

There was a feeling that direct practical application of techniques was missing from most undergraduate experience, with the exception of those who had a placement element (Chapter 8). Advice on how to present and sell oneself in the employment situation was also lacking. For some, the undergraduate course created unreal expectations of the world of work:

> It was a very unrealistic view of what life would be like when you had finished from college, a much rosier view than it actually is. We had a lot of visiting lecturers, tutors who have all worked freelance, and you were very much given the impression that when you left you could set up by yourself and be a freelance designer or you would write to people and they would be begging you to come and work for them. Not until you actually get out there do you realise it was all lies, the impression you were given was wrong.
> (18C: junior design engineer, small private design consultancy)

Many respondents thought their undergraduate course lacked any real meaningful engagement with the world of work:

> I don't think my undergraduate degree, other than my legal skills, really taught me a great deal about being in the workplace. It didn't teach me a lot about making presentations, all the practical skills that you're expected to use at work. But I went to quite a an academic course. I know people who have been to the old polys who have come out with a far more hands-on experience. They have helped run law centres, they've made lots of presentations, they've done telephone advice on Nightline or whatever, but some of these things weren't available to me.
> (06C: trainee solicitor, large law firm)

One graduate considered that this lack of engagement was due to academic staff having no current involvement in industry:

> My experience of higher education institutions is that a lot of the lecturing staff that are in the establishments haven't got the experience of working in outside industry, and I think that is a significant drawback, for the simple reason that they don't understand what is

actually needed out there in the working environment. It helps to have been in an office, or to have been outside to see what is going on rather than reading journals. They tend to get too involved in the theoretical side of things rather than becoming practically involved, and I don't think the current lecturing staff that there is in higher education, is going to be actually flexible enough to meet the demands of people in the future, or provide them with the necessary level of understanding to actually get on in a modern working environment.

(50C: performance analyst, large freight company)

However, some graduates suggested that it would be difficult to prepare undergraduates in a rapidly changing world 'other than to make sure you appreciate that there are going to be changes' (36C). Most just found that the expectations in the work situation were tantamount to a culture shock:

Although I have worked for people before during vacations, suddenly being thrust into the work place I didn't know what to expect... Here they tend to throw you in with a customer and you get on with it. I don't suppose when you leave university you really know how to deal with other people let alone a customer where you have to behave in a certain manner.

(49C: project designer, computer-controlled systems manufacturer)

No, it was a right shock coming here, a big adjustment... I had to get used to the boundaries and get used to commitment as well, just being organised when it matters to other people as well as yourself. Also I didn't know anything about pensions, or wages or tax, and what you should expect from your employer, like decent holidays and stuff like that.

(20C: photographic adviser, small publicly funded support and advice centre)

The view of recent graduates are, in part, matched by the strategic and line-managers who expressed views about the preparedness of graduates for the world of work. Over half thought them not well prepared in general:

When you take a graduate on, they are very good conceptually. The negative side of that is that they can be too thorough and it can take far too long, they know everything there is to know about design but when it comes to practicalities like printing it, they are on another planet. So you take a graduate who is a good designer and then you have to teach them about processing that design. For example, if somebody wants a brochure designed they will come up with a brilliant concept, but by the time they have finished with their design the client can't afford it, it's gone way over budget, there is no practical way it can be used, and they will think in three to six months schedule whereas we think in three to six days.

(14A: owner, small design and print agency)

I look for is a lively open communicative, interesting personality that will actually take them through the realities of what they have been trained for, what they are actually going to do, and this is where I get very critical about the colleges because they don't prepare them for anything, they don't prepare the personalities, the presentation abilities, they don't prepare them for the real world because they tell them a pack of lies about going into industry.

(69A: strategic manager, small design agency)

However, there were a small number of senior managers who are not necessarily expecting graduates to be well prepared: 'The reality is that graduates haven't got a world-of-work experience, they can't relate directly to work scenarios because they have never been there' (52A). On the other hand, some managers considered that some graduates were better prepared than they used to be:

The vast majority that we take on are frighteningly qualified. I mean you see their applications and you see what they have done, it can be sort of wind surfing in Egypt – I know that sounds ridiculous but we are finding that the kind of grads that we take on are actually quite sophisticated in what they have done... A lot of the universities do very realistic project work... I am not saying that there couldn't be more done to prepare them for the workforce but I think many more degrees now have an element of "what use will this be to you when you are in the world of work?", whereas a few years ago it was very much education for education's sake. I think we have drifted away from that now.

(46A: senior consultant, multi-national computer service company)

When I joined the job market it was a lot easier than it is now. I graduated in '88, so it is not that long ago really, I wasn't anywhere near as prepared as I would expect graduates to be today. I would probably not pass the screening, because I had very bad A-level results. I think graduates take it much more seriously now. The polarisation between well prepared candidates and poor candidates has become more explicit, and I don't know whether that is just the individuals that I have personally interviewed, or whether I have just become harder at interviewing, but I find it easier now to decide which way I am going to go. To make a sweeping generalisation, women are often better prepared than men. Like for like, women have often done their research better, I think it is the confidence thing, because I think men think they can wing it and girls don't. I also wonder whether it is because women perceive that they are trying to move into a very male-dominated environments which, despite our best efforts to get our female intake up, we are still very male dominated.

(62A: manager, large management consultants)

Graduates versus non-graduates

Graduates' view

Most of the recent graduates in the sample were of the view that they were better equipped for the workplace than if they had completed their education at A-levels and tended to compare themselves favourably with non-graduates:

I think I do a better job because I've got a degree. I've been through the process of going to university and working in groups, working to deadlines, writing quality reports, thinking about what I have written. It sounds awful, but some people here don't think about what they have written. I think those things have been to my advantage. I have learnt to work, to think about things in much greater detail. Particularly my written work, I think really does show, not necessarily that I'm a graduate but that I've studied further than the sixth form.

(03C: teacher, small private school for children with special needs)

Yes. I've been to school and gone straight to doing a degree, but when I speak to [someone] who hasn't done a degree, you do notice differences in just the scope of the things you see and the things you are aware of. It does make you more aware of various aspects of work and life.

(14C: project manager, small design and print agency)

Generally, recent graduates thought they had, in broad terms, more to offer including being more 'academic', 'stretchable', 'multi-tasking', ambitious, flexible and rounded, being quicker to grasp things, having a wider view and being more suitable 'as management material'. In general, these self-analyses were modest and self-deprecating while nonetheless clear in identifying advantages of graduates over non-graduates:

A graduate will tend to be far more dedicated or willing to put time and effort into doing a job as well, whereas a school-leaver will look to get something done as quick as possible and for that sacrifice quality sometimes. Often a graduate will be more self-motivated, I suppose that is what is at the core of it. That's probably the reason why they went to university in the first place. They saw it as a way forward. They have higher aspirations, whereas a school-leaver would have stumbled in looking for a job.

(26C: salesman, multi-national business machines manufacturer)

A handful of respondents were of the opinion that, in respect of their current job, their undergraduate experience provided them with no particular advantage over finishing at A-level:

> Those who have been through the ranks know the job a lot more fully than me and they know everyone so they probably can relate to people but having said that I can come in and hopefully bring a lot of new ideas. We're talking at the moment about budgeting and because they have come in and maybe worked as cleaner and then as a leisure operator or whatever, they are not going to know about budgeting or anything like that. So although I haven't got specific knowledge of all the jobs, I can add other knowledge such as the budgeting. (01C: duty manager, medium-sized private leisure and entertainment complex)

> When it came to getting a job at the end of it, I thought that there were a lot of jobs that interested me and I did not need a degree to apply for them. Various jobs which interested me seemed to be the sort of position where you would start at the bottom and work your way up, which did not need a degree. A-Levels, or some kind of vocational course would have sufficed for these positions. (51C: information analyst, medium-sized community health authority)

However, virtually all respondents considered that their career prospects were much better having taken a degree than if they had finished at A-level.

> I have got to my position in under four years – it has taken others about fifteen, if not longer. So it has accelerated my prospects quite a lot. (50C: performance analyst, large freight company)

One respondent was somewhat more ambiguous about the benefit of going on to do a degree and only one respondent seriously doubted that his prospects were enhanced by doing a degree.

Managers' views

Strategic and line managers in the sample were overwhelmingly of the view that graduates had advantages over non-graduates. Most strategic managers thought graduates were basically brighter, sharper and more analytic than non-graduates.

> Those that stand out are not only those who can learn the technical side quickly but they can pick up an issue apply the technical training quickly; they can get to the heart of the issue. They can find out what matters and they can then present advice to say me as a senior manager which presents the relevant facts in a very concise form but then focuses on what the answer is. The less good ones clearly learn a bit more slowly but they are much less able to get to the heart of an issue, much more inclined to present you with the facts but not the analysis. And that's more likely to be somebody that hasn't had a graduate background. (27B: manager, large public financial institution)

> The advantage of a graduate over a non-graduate is probably they are more self-assured and usually they have a much better idea of how to think things through. So posed with a problem, most of them usually approach it working it through from a to b, whereas a non-graduate will usually go on experience of what happened in the past and solve it that way. (29A: supply manager, medium-sized health product manufacturer)

The fact that graduates were perceived as able to go back to first principles and work things out was seen as important in some settings.

> Good graduates are cost-effective because they can understand technical issues and solve them, take all factors into account, and increasingly solve them from theoretical principles. More and more in industry, the science and technology is developed by computer modelling rather than through sucking it and see. We don't have places for the person who can wield a 28-pound sledgehammer or who does experiment after experiment until he gets the right one. We need the graduate who thinks: "If I do this one experiment I'm absolutely confident that is all I need to do." (82A: head of technology strategy, large power company)

Graduates were seen as more adaptable and flexible and able to develop new ideas:

> I think the good thing about people who come off good dynamic courses is they have got new ideas and they are very open to new things and often got new skills which are probably harder to acquire outside a university. (20A: director, small publicly funded support and advice centre)

> I think that the skill in graduates is the ability to be flexible, to have a broad knowledge base with a number of different subjects, but to have a level of intellectual ability, and I think that is particularly in terms of problem solving, through doing a degree and going through that discipline. (65B: contract manager, large gas suppliers)

Graduates were also seen as more mature, with a broader outlook, as more self-motivated, committed, tenacious, enthusiastic, energised or ambitious:

> There is a certain level of maturity there which you wouldn't get in an 18-year-old school leaver. Because they have actually been away from home, existed on their own and had to look after themselves. They're a little bit more streetwise. Disadvantages: I can't think of any to be honest. (15A: partner, small chartered accountants)

For some strategic managers, there is hardly any reason these days why a bright person should not be a graduate:

> Because the opportunities are much wider now, it is hardly an excuse not to go to university now. In the past people have said to me it was much harder to get into university, there were jobs at 18, the money was tempting and so on, but today there has to be something wrong with somebody's judgement – I suspect that our world is going towards saying, if you haven't got a degree there's something wrong with you. Which I think is a pity, and I can't say that in the company there isn't anybody in the company who doesn't think like that. I think that as a company we say we must guard against that temptation. (11A: vice-president, multi-national food manufacturers)

Non-graduates were seen as having an advantage in a limited number of areas. For example, a few managers suggested that as they recruited non-graduates from other organisations, they tended to have more experience than graduates. A couple of managers thought that non-graduates are less likely to get bored, have lower expectations and are prepared to do mundane tasks although suggested that they sometimes 'get bitter as a result of getting stuck in a rut' (11A). On the other hand, graduates are sometimes perceived as having inflated expectations, which leads them to get bored, frustrated and to seek alternative employment (03A).

Only one respondent considered that non-graduates had an advantage over graduates because they were cheaper, while three line managers considered that graduates showed no clear advantages over non-graduates.

Non-graduates' view

Most of the non-graduates who compared themselves with graduates thought, on balance, they matched or outshone comparable graduates, mainly because they had more years' experience. Given that one of the criteria for inclusion in the survey was that a non-graduate should be doing a similar job to a graduate, this self-assessment was probably well founded. In almost all cases the non-graduate had been in a comparable post for a longer period of time.

> There are two sides to it. In my case now I think I have much more on-the-job experience whereas I might not be as intellectually strong as a graduate who has spent four to five years at university. In this kind of industry you get further on merit rather than qualifications on paper. (13D: broadcast journalist, medium-sized private local radio station)

Sometimes non-graduates feel resentful of the emphasis placed on graduates despite the fact that they do not appear to be as well equipped to do the job:

> I think in some instances I'm better. Not academically but with regards to work experience, man management, problem solving, everything that involves the day-to-day process in the work place... You'll be watching graduates being sent on these week-long courses to do with this and that, running around like headless chickens, knowing full well in five years time you will be reporting to them. It's demoralising. As far as I can see, if they can groom a graduate they can groom a non-graduate, because a non-graduate could have a lot more to offer.
>
> (29D: promotions buyer, medium-sized health product manufacturer)

A few non-graduates felt that they were not as good as graduates, or at least felt that other people held that view of them, because they lacked confidence, drive, ambition, management and research skills:

> I work with graduates here. I do feel that sometimes perhaps I am not as good as them. And it is silly really, but it is something that is there and there is nothing I can do about it except go out there and do part-time courses – constantly showing that I am keen and enthusiastic to learn.
>
> (28D: project manager, small design and communications company)

> My ten years work experience is worth the three years at university. I am learning things now doing my degree, that would have been so valuable to me if I had done them straight after school, or even done it as a part-time person at age 18. When I keep thinking about what would be the ideal world I think it would be joining the company at age 18 and doing a distance-education degree at age 18, so that you are working and you are studying, that would be perfect.
>
> (11D: graduate trainer, multi-national food manufacturers)

On balance, one experienced non-graduate noted:

> It depends on the individual. I'll be better than a lot of people at certain things and I'll be worse at other things. Communication skills of graduates are usually good and their initiative seems to be very lively. They will get up and do things whereas other members of staff take a while to build up to things. A graduate tends to be more of a self-starter and self-motivated. Whether it's because they are bit more mature I don't know... By the mere fact of being a graduate they are regarded as much more intelligent and, because of the nature of the bank's system, they will have so much more attention put on them... Therefore, if they have got anything about them and the work is reasonable they will get on a lot better than a 'normal' member of staff.
>
> (36D: branch manager, large financial institution)

Half the non-graduates discussed whether or not they felt they missed out by not doing a degree. Two respondents cautioned against the assumption that one needs to get a degree to get on, but feared that this would increasingly be seen to be the case by employers.

> I think it depends on the person, because each individual is different. I didn't want to go to university, I didn't think it would benefit me in any way whatsoever. For some people, I think it helps them mature. But, now a degree is more of a requirement, which I think is a shame really, because I think some people are capable of doing what I have done without getting a degree.
>
> (22D: pricing manager, multinational reprographic equipment manufacturer)

The other non-graduates regretted not doing a degree for various reasons. For one it would have been an easier option than 'working in the coal mines', for another it was a feeling of having missed the opportunity to study an area of interest. For most of the others, not having a degree has meant that they had to work much harder than graduate colleagues to demonstrate ability and they felt that they needed to have a degree to prove themselves, at least to themselves:

> Doing a degree part-time was worth it I think in the end. It was a personal thing really. I just wanted to prove I could do it. I wanted to prove to myself. I always believed I was just as intelligent as the rest of them. I needed, I wanted something on paper that would show that I was.
>
> (27D: equity markets analyst, large public financial institution)

The length and nature of degree course

Various ideas have been mooted about the length of degree courses and where they might best be pursued. Two different options that have been suggested were discussed by respondents.

First, the idea of two years at university followed by a final year or years in the workplace. The respondents who discussed it ruled it out as lacking any feasibility at all. Typical comments include:

> I don't know that they would finish their degree quite honestly. To be quite honest with you, the first year you are here, if you intend to have a career with [the firm] you are going to be struggling to complete a degree as well. You could pass your degree and probably at the end of the year I doubt if you would have put enough into the company to be recognised as potential for the future. Why anybody would think there's some benefit in putting people under further pressure by doing their degree and work, particularly in their first year of work, beats me.
> (22B: sales manager, multinational reprographic equipment manufacturer)

> I suspect practically that would be very difficult. Not least because the pressures on the staff here are pretty great. Even the new entrants. So if they were having to produce work up to [the organisation's] standards plus learn or study in relation to a degree course as well for a full year, I think that would be a pretty big strain... Thinking back to the three years that I spent in university in the UK I can't see any obvious way in which that could have been contracted down to two years because I would have missed out on quite a lot of the breadth of the subject. I suspect I might have ended up with quite a narrow focus in economics. Also, you grow up quite a bit in three years and you mature a little bit in a way that you might not necessarily after only two years.
> (27B: manager, large public financial institution)

The second suggestion is the 'two-plus-two' degree, with two years in an equivalent of a 'community college' (in the further education sector) taking students to the equivalent of the end of first year degree standard, followed by two years at university to complete a degree.

Respondents, rather than endorse a reduction in time spent in a university setting away from home, thought that it important that as much time as possible developing independence and maturity was essential.

> They have usually left home and I think if they have done that, that has matured them to a certain degree. They have also had a level of learning that gives them a platform of coping with additional learning. It is the motor industry philosophy that learning is something that we all have to do all the time, and one of the things a graduate will have had to have done is go through a process of learning, which isn't necessarily there with other people.
> (76A: senior executive, multi-national motor component manufacturer)

The nearest anyone got to endorsing a 'two-plus-two' approach was a respondent from an engineering company who proposed the equivalent of a two-year national curriculum at undergraduate level followed by autonomously determined specialisms:

> There is a huge variation – I might want to appoint somebody with a manufacturing systems engineering degree but beyond the fact that they will have studied vaguely the same topics, the content of one manufacturing systems engineering course is very different from what's in another. That's why we tend to work with particular departments, which have provided us with what we want, rather than recruit broadly. At foundation level (the first two years of a degree programme), why don't we teach standard courses in our universities? In the final stages of their degree, where you want the student to develop capability to think at a deeper level, fine, have specialisation, have difference between university degree courses. What you mostly want from a graduate is what they have learned in their foundation years. You will probably have to train them in the specialism you want within your business, anyway. Having specialised just proves that they have got that ability to think deeply. There are

probably 200 different basic macro-economic courses being taught in this country, it's a nonsense. Far too much time is wasted re-inventing the wheel.

(74B: human resource manager, multi-national engineering company)

A key element of any change for respondents is, if anything, to increase the length of the conventional undergraduate degree:

When I was actually at university I felt that it was very intensive. I would have preferred the same amount of material spread over four years, instead of three. It was always a hell of a pressure to try and get things done. Although I think if they had stretched it over four years they would have crammed even more in, which would have defeated the object.

(23C: electrical engineer, small medical lasers manufacturer)

Rather than add more content or provide more space to deal with the same amount of content, most respondents considered that lengthening the course to include a work placement would be very beneficial (this is discussed further in Chapter 8).

I'm not convinced about two-year degree programmes, I think it is too short. I would push for more four-year degrees, or a three-year degree with a follow-up year of some description. It allows people, if they have done a very pure degree subject, to build on in that extra year via work experience, or studying IT, or management course, or languages. I think that would be beneficial.

(04B: project director, small corporate literature specialists)

A concomitant part of the 'two-plus-two' degree is the award of an interim qualification after the first two years. While few respondents directly addressed the validity of this potential interim award there appears to be little enthusiasm for anything short of a full degree. This was evident in the comments related to the possibility of an NVQ or GNVQ alternative to graduate recruitment or as general qualification route: 'It is not accepted by any means, it is not seen as equal, it is not seen as anything' (42A).

About a quarter of the managers in the sample commented on (G)NVQs. A third had no intention of pursuing a (G)NVQ recruitment route. Most of the rest were unsure about them and were awaiting developments, as they were of the opinion that (G)NVQs were running into too many difficulties:

I don't think the position of NVQ is secure, and I don't think it gives the kind of confidence that it's going to replace approved qualifications... We are on the cusp. It's either going to be implemented as projected with external degrees and things like that will linked into it, or else its going to wither on the vine. We're just in a period where it's hard to predict.

(03A: head teacher, small private school for children with special needs)

One manager indicated that he had no need to bother with (G)NVQ as the organisation had plenty of graduates to recruit from, another thought it would be applicable to non-professional people. Several managers admitted not knowing enough about (G)NVQs. Only one manager was intending to actively develop a procedure and another was prepared to consider (G)NVQ qualifications if the individual merits of an applicant fitted other criteria.

Summary

- The overwhelming majority of strategic and line-managers regarded investing in graduates as a cost-effective activity.

- All the graduates interviewed confirmed that it had been worthwhile doing their degree and the vast majority were unconditionally positive.

- Employers and recent graduates agree overwhelmingly that an undergraduate degree experience has a major positive impact on personal development.

- Recent graduates indicated that their undergraduate experience had direct benefit for their current workplace. Some of the course was relevant but, in the main, it was skills and abilities developed as a degree student that were most pertinent.
- Some recent graduates reported that much of the content of their course and some of the skills and abilities they had acquired on an undergraduate degree were not utilised in their current work.
- Graduates and managers, in the main, thought that although their degree experience was beneficial, graduates were not well prepared for the world of work.
- In particular, some graduates considered that the degree, especially if it lacked a placement element, failed to provide sufficient opportunities to develop the basic skills, such as oral presentation skills and teamworking.
- Overall, graduates felt that their abilities and their prospects were far more enhanced than if they had stopped their education at A-level and the vast majority of graduates felt they are more effective at work than non-graduates.
- Strategic and line-managers overwhelmingly considered graduates as having advantages over non-graduates.
- Most non-graduates interviewed thought that the additional experience they had accrued made them as good, if not better, than comparable graduates. However, many wished they had done a degree and most thought that they would have reached their current position quicker if they had. Several had undertaken a degree on a part-time basis while at work.
- There is no discernible support from any of the respondents for a shorter length degree course.
- Graduates and their employers are overwhelmingly of the view that a substantial part of the benefit of a degree course for young graduates is the extended experience of living away from home.
- There is little evidence of graduate employers seriously considering (G)NVQ as an alternative recruitment qualification.

8 Work placements

Employers were eager to suggest means by which higher education could improve, although there was a reluctance to interfere in the way the academic community runs its affairs. There is a diminishing demand for 'boffins' in a rapidly changing world, where knowledge has a short shelf-life, and where the world is no longer head-over-heels in love with higher education. There is a sense, therefore, that academics in universities, should move away from prescribing the exact nature of the perfect, highly cultivated, *knowledge* variety of graduate and instead provide graduates who have a broader range of attributes, which enable them to 'do the job'.

Work placements were one of the most regularly mentioned suggestions by the respondents for helping students towards success at work, improving links and bridging the 'skills gap'. Both employers and graduate employees identify the workplace experience as beneficial for developing an awareness of organisational culture. Work experience would help develop a culture of adaptation to 'the real world of work'.

The role of work placements in student development is not new and its value has been well documented. A number of benefits can be identified for all stakeholders; indeed, practical work experience is a statutory requirement in much of the education sector. In addition, some professional bodies require a period of supervised experience in the workplace, as part of the curriculum, in order to qualify and practise (Harvey and Mason, 1995). This is particularly the case in medicine and health-related courses that are regulated by statute. Furthermore, government-funded research findings justified the 20% additional cost of sandwich programmes on the grounds that they could generate much additional value (RISE, 1985).

Harvey with Green (1994) found 'an unqualified endorsement of work experience' among employers. Employers consider that work experience through placements is a valuable part of undergraduate education generally, in terms of preparing them for employment and, more specifically, enhancing skills development relevant to the workplace. Students are made aware of current work practices, can relate what has been learned theoretically in the classroom to a workplace situation, and can develop personally in terms of greater self-confidence and maturity (Duckenfield and Stirner, 1992).

Placement provision

Many employers provide placements and were enthusiastic about the benefits to be gained and were fully aware of their responsibility to provide students with a meaningful experience. However, the nature of provision and the extent to which employers have specific policies on placement provision varies from organisation to organisation.

Some organisations take placement students on an *ad hoc* basis:

> We do take undergraduates on work placements, we don't advertise but if people write in we do try and place them. (31A: managing director, medium-sized house builders and regenerators)

> We have one or two placements in the summer but I would not say we have an organised scheme… every now and again we get a student. I can't see it increasing unfortunately, because of the squeeze there is on resources here, so I see that as a struggle to keep anything in place. (38A: head of branch, civil service)

Other organisations are attempting to develop a placement culture:

> We have, in the last couple of years, taken people on as thick-sandwich students, so that has been new, but there are only two or three universities who actually have placements as part of their degrees, anyway.
> (12A: personnel director, large law firm)

Some organisations already have an established tradition of providing placements:

> We've got a guy here now from university, we've had quite a lot of placement people. We can get some value out of them, but we've got a bit of responsibility to help young people if we can, and I have always had work-experience, and work-shadow people from either schools or universities.
> (04A: owner, small corporate literature specialists)

> We offer undergraduate placements throughout the summer, Christmas and Easter: work placements for students in the City who are studying law. They have to apply. If anything the competition for a work placement is even more ferocious than the competition for a training contract… We also take other graduates or undergraduates in other areas as well.
> (09A: head of personnel, large law firm)

Some organisations clearly feel the need to accept students on placements as a form of reciprocation with higher education institutions with whom they would like to develop closer and stronger links, especially where the subject matter is specific rather than general.

> I think it works pretty well, probably the strongest links are with the one-year placements at the University post-graduate course. It is probably the strongest in terms of our commitment and the students are paid a salary while they work with us and clearly their practical experience with us is a crucial part of their qualification. I am sure anything like this can be improved; you are never totally satisfied, but by and large I think it works pretty well.
> (37A: deputy chief executive, small housing association)

Through work placements, employers and higher education institutions can establish more meaningful relationships with each other, enabling a mutual understanding between 'cultures'. Through such links higher education institutions are able to make the curriculum more relevant to the demands of the workplace (Knapper and Cropley, 1985).

> I think it's a little bit of both, employers and universities. If employers come to universities and say we would like students to have these skills, we appreciate that you cannot teach these skills, these skills can only be acquired by people doing work experience or getting involved in societies etc., then somebody needs to be saying that to students when they begin their university courses… It needs the universities to be able to have the flexibility. So if a student comes to them and says "in between my second and third years I want to take six months or a year out so I can go and work in industry or business" then they need to accommodate that. But then the employers obviously need to have these opportunities available, so it's both sides need to make it work.
> (04B: project director, small corporate literature specialists)

Length of placement and investment of effort

The length of the placement also varies from organisation to organisation and according to the students' degree programme: placements range from two weeks to a whole year. Longer placements are seen as preferable to short placements mainly because employers are looking for a return on their investment in training and staff time.

> Four weeks work experience is not enough, you need to get into a company for at least 12 months and work very closely with that company. I think the government should fund companies to take on and help people. We can't afford to do it because we are only a small company.
> (14B: studio manager, small design and print agency)

> We've offered anything from two weeks to nine weeks work experience and it can be specific to a department or they can do the whole tour working with a range of managers. The plan in the future is to bring in a one-year sandwich course person into some areas.
>
> (01A: training and safety officer, medium-sized private leisure and entertainment complex)

Recent graduates with experience of short-term placements felt that a longer period would have been beneficial.

> The work experience we did was only four weeks, we could maybe have done more of that, and it was in the second year of a three-year course. So, probably the work experience needed to be expanded.   (01C: duty manager, medium-sized private leisure and entertainment complex)

> It was only for about two weeks. It wasn't really long enough, you can't get any depth of experience or knowledge… if I did it again I would definitely do a sandwich course, or something a bit more vocational.   (61C: assistant manager, international fast-food chain)

For some organisations, the length of the placement is linked to the investment of time and energy necessary to make the experience effective for both the student and the organisation:

> They need to be of about six months' duration. If I have somebody in here over the summer for three months, I never treat them as part of the department. I just haven't got the time to get them integrated into the department. I will have a specific job I want doing, which is probably a pretty boring job and at the end of three months we shake hands and say goodbye. If somebody is here for about six months then they actually get treated as part of the department, they get integrated and they get exposed to much more of the business culture as well.   (74B: human resource manager, multi-national engineering company)

> …a six-month placement is hardly worth it, I don't think, for the person to get something out of it. It depends what the objective is – if the objective is just to get a rough idea as to how companies operate, then six months might be sufficient, may be six weeks in one of four areas for instance. But I think, as a company, we have to invest some time in that person so they gain something from it.   (39C: programmer, medium-sized software services contractor)

Several respondents emphasised the need for the placement experience to be worthwhile. This places a considerable onus on the organisation.

> From an employer's point of view they are not really going to want to give someone a lot of responsibility who is only going to be there and then go back to their course, so that is easier said than done.   (17B: office manager, small private specialist employment agency)

> It would be very difficult unless we have something specific we can work on, and so it is getting the actual plan of what they would be doing, what training would they need to have and where would they go it is something we are looking at very seriously…
>
> (46A: senior consultant, multi-national computer service company)

However, the responsibility for making the placement a success also falls on the student, and that they have to adopt an appropriate attitude to the workplace experience:

> We had one in particular, who, I think, came in and treated it like lectures – got up late, rolled in late, really mucked around a bit during the day and rolled off home. And really for him, I think, the degree was something he had drifted into as the next thing to do, rather than going to work.   (23A: chief executive, small medical lasers manufacturer)

Options

Several graduate employees who had not undertaken a work placement felt that they had missed out and would have appreciated such opportunities had they been available.

> Had there been relevant work experience available, like had you been able to work in the Civil Service for six months as part of an option on your degree – I would have bitten their arm off. But that wasn't available.
>
> (10C: supervisor, large financial institution)

> I certainly think I would have enjoyed a placement. It would have been good for me... And I suppose you could have just expanded the course by having a placement year out.
>
> (27C: recent graduate, large public financial institution)

> I think I chose a very academic course. There was no industrial placement facility. I did a foundation year which covered every topic under the sun from astrophysics to medieval history just because I wanted to try every subject on offer and see what I really liked. Which was brilliant experience but it didn't actually do a lot for career prospects because it wasn't very tailored to business studies or that sort of thing... But I think courses are now much more tailored towards giving you a bit more business knowledge and experience. When I did it, three years ago, you could pick up a really straight academic degree and never go near an industrial placement and never have any clue what work was like.
>
> (28C: project manager, small design and communications company)

For some respondents, a placement would have given them a window into the 'real world' of work.

> I think we were quite lacking in a realisation of how a real company operates in the real world. I have got friends who did a year's placement and that was a great benefit.
>
> (18C: junior design engineer, small private design consultancy)

> It would be very useful to have a placement just so that people have got an idea of what sort of jobs they are going into. That sort of thing would give people a much better choice.
>
> (79C: auditor, large, chartered accountants)

Career focus

The placement experience is seen by both employers and graduate employees as enabling students to have a taste of a career, which helps them to decide what they want (or do not want) to do after graduation:

> I deal with work-based placements with a number of colleges. I think what would be ideal is for them to spend time with the service. You see life in its truest sense, it can be very earthy and cut and thrust. You are in the middle of social problems and fights and trauma and I think that people need to see that before they take the line that that's what they want to come into, because it can look very glamorous from the outside. The bottom line is that as a paramedic they are on their own, they are accountable and responsible.
>
> (77B: line manager: health service contractors)

> We are doing a lot more of that here, we have a French student here doing some work on statistics. She has done a customer-satisfaction survey. She has done some great work and I am sure it has helped her focus on where she wants to go in the future.
>
> (26B: area sales manager, multi-national business machines manufacturer)

Indeed, many graduates admitted that they were not sure of what they wanted after graduation:

> If I had known at the time what I wanted to do. If some teacher had asked me what I was considering and suggested that I do a work placement at a relevant company or field, then yes, it would have been useful.
>
> (12C: trainee solicitor, large law firm)

> I think a lot of people leave university, apply for accountancy and are not sure what accountancy is... you never know until you actually do it, and I think that people who do have summer placements here actually benefit quite a lot. Some of them realise it is not for them, and that is the right time to do it rather than starting a three-year contract.
>
> (79C: auditor, large, chartered accountants)

Recruitment

In addition to giving students a taste of a potential career, placements can be used as a recruitment tool (Chapter 5). Indeed, one of the main advantages of work placements for employers is the opportunity to screen students as potential recruits. Hogg (1995) has stated that placements are an 'ideal way for companies and graduates to get to know each other...'.

> I worked for 11 weeks with the firm on a summer vacation scheme. Two weeks of training and then seven weeks on a client site, working with real consultants and real clients. The clients didn't know that I was a student so I had to fulfil the role of a consultant. They didn't know any difference and that was really good experience for me. I classed it as the longest second interview ever, where they got a chance to see how I worked under pressure in a real client environment and I had a good taste of what life with the firm would be like, if I did decide to join.
> (62C: new graduate, large management consultants)

The use of placements is also an ideal way for small and medium businesses to recruit graduates as it cuts down on the risk of recruiting an inexperienced, unknown graduate:

> Two of the graduates we have employed in the past have come through placements, and one was sponsored through his final year as well. Those were done on an *ad hoc* basis, we don't have a permanent link with [the university] to say we will take one student every year on placement.
> (81A: software development manager, small, operator-systems design firm)

Experience in the workplace provides opportunities for students to make contacts for their future career and in some cases there may be the prospect of carving out a job with their placement provider in the future.

> ...he came here on work experience, went off and did some other things, contacted us and, based on the work experience he had here, we didn't have a vacancy... but we created one for him. We have benefited in that he got very specific training relevant to us during that part of his course and has come back now and we have someone who could step in without requiring any additional training.
> (23A: chief executive, small medical lasers manufacturer)

> At the end of his year with me he applied for a job as a training officer and he is now a training officer, and yet when he started that wasn't what he wanted to do he wanted to be an operations manager. So it's that kind of thing that hopefully we can develop people to their strengths, while at the same time we are taking strengths away from them that help to progress the business.
> (01A: training and safety officer, medium-sized private leisure and entertainment complex)

Advantages at interviews

Graduates who had undertaken a work placement felt that they had an advantage over other applicants when applying for jobs. For some, the advantage was simply that they had work experience that employers so often want:

> I suppose without being a graduate with that industrial placement and being on a degree course that allowed me to do that I wouldn't have got a job, because from what I know, a lot of the people that are employed here have done industrial placement years, and that is what they prefer, so that is one benefit that I have had.
> (22C: car fleet manager, multinational reprographic equipment manufacturer)

Other recent graduates thought that the placement experience gave them an insight into the kinds of attitudes and abilities that employers sought in the recruitment process:

> I think that it is going to be harder for people with a non-vocational degree to come into a business environment. As I did a placement I was at a significant advantage, because I knew

what employers were looking for when they took people on, and I had experience. You are either going to have to work before you go to university or get some low-paid experience while you are at university if you don't do a placement.

(22B: sales manager, multinational reprographic equipment manufacturer)

I had lots of jobs while I was at college but it's nothing like having this kind of job, it would help in interview as well when you are trying to get the jobs, and you had no clear idea when you saw a job advertised what it actually meant and what they were looking for.

(20C: photographic adviser, small publicly funded support and advice centre)

Attributes derived from a placement experience

The placement experience provides a wealth of opportunities to develop attributes that can help students to be successful in the future world of work, ranging from the development of personal skills, through the application in a commercial setting of theoretical knowledge to an appreciation of the culture and practices of the workplace.

In terms of the benefits of placements, their order would be (1) money, (2) a real insight into how a lot of the theory they learn is actually applied (3) access to a lot of equipment that we are privileged to have and a lot of universities don't have; we have probably more modern, faster, better equipment than a lot of universities are able to afford, and (4) the business of working in teams and seeing what it is like to actually contribute to a group scientific development, rather than being asked to work independently on their own, so they become social. (63A: human resources manager, large pharmaceutical manufacturers)

Several respondents talked about the general skills development that derived from their placement experience:

I think perhaps everyone should have the opportunity to take a year out to do a sandwich course. I know that some people go to certain institutions because that's the only institution that offers them a sandwich course that does, say, Law and Business Studies. I think it should be more widely available… I didn't really have any problem with my undergraduate degree, but it was coupled with a postgraduate degree where I was taught a lot of practical skills, so the two of them fitted together very well. Perhaps if I did a purely academic degree and then went straight in to the workplace I would be lacking an awful lot of skills.

(06C: trainee solicitor, large law firm)

Tuned into work culture

When recruiting, employers have witnessed in their recruits who have undertaken a work placement, more mature attitudes to work and a better appreciation of industry (Harvey, 1994). There is, therefore, a sense in which the risks involved in recruitment are reduced.

Probably, thinking about it, those that have done the year placement do come over better. They fit into the organisation a lot better, they are not so overawed by having managers around and stuff like that, they are much easier with themselves… Usually students who have been out for a year are a bit more confident, they are a bit easier with their surroundings and not as tentative. (22B: sales manager, multinational reprographic equipment manufacturer)

Business awareness and maturity… are significantly improved by work placements, either through a sandwich course and maybe a year before they go to university. We are looking for people who are relatively streetwise in the organisation, so that is a major benefit. Also when we undertake graduate assessment centres (where we are looking for leadership and management skills)… Those people who have worked in organisations previously have a host of examples of experiences that they are able to share with us. That makes them

stronger candidates than those who have just gone from school to higher education and then come straight to us. So it is an advantage to the individual concerned to have done a placement.
(36A: senior manager, large financial institution)

We try to look at people who are mature in their views and I would think somebody who had just been at university for three years hasn't had the same experience as somebody on a sandwich course and has spent a year on the shop floor and understands the ways of the world a little bit more.
(76A: senior executive, multi-national motor component manufacturer)

Recent graduates also consider their placement experience, which provided insights into work culture, enabled them to be more rapidly effective:

> We have got a lot of students in here and I think they learn quite a bit from being on placement. They are thrown in at the deep end but by the end of it they are a lot more acclimatised to industry. And when they come out I think they will be of more immediate use rather than having to struggle through.
> (49C: project designer, computer-controlled systems manufacturer)

> I think every student should go on some sort of work placement, because I think being a student doesn't prepare you for going to work. I had never been in a full-time job… I've done a lot of voluntary work throughout my degree but, even so, it doesn't prepare you for different personalities in a team. I know it's difficult to prepare someone for that, but at least if you've had three months block experience of working with the same people every day, no matter if you hate them or you love them, it is really good experience.
> (05C: youth worker, publicly funded youth service)

Specific attributes developed in the placement situation include teamworking, time-management, prioritisation and management skills.

> Things like trying to manage my time, making lists of things I needed to do, keeping track of what work I was doing, getting back to my manager frequently for update and touch base to find out what was important. That's something that I have brought with me [from placement]. It was definitely helpful just being in a work environment, where you are being pushed to complete stuff on time, having to co-ordinate things you do with a lot of other people, going to people, asking for help, co-ordinating shifts. The beginnings of management experience.
> (47C: process engineer, multi-national food manufacturer)

> Most of the stuff I learnt when I was at university was through my placements. I picked up management skills by being on placement and seeing how the managers of those placements ran things. The whole time you're on placement you're developing your skills in terms of basic youth work and community work and some research skills. In terms of the course itself, a lot of it was boring and pretty uninformative.
> (05D: senior community worker, publicly funded youth service)

Enhancing understanding

The use of a workplace situation can provide a valuable resource for institutions and ideal opportunities, not just for students to develop the skills they need for employment, but, given the necessary conditions, can enhance students' theoretical understanding and help them to become independent learners (Duckenfield and Stirner 1992).

> I mean, it's all well and good somebody being able to write an essay on "Marx and labour", or whatever, but if they can relate it to work much more, then they are going to be much better workers. So I think the ties have got to increase. Had I been able to come to a place like this and somebody had said, "right, this is sociology in practice. Can you see the structure here, can you see the working relationships?", it would have been immensely beneficial.
> (03C: teacher, small private school for children with special needs)

> Those that went on the industrial year tended, overall, to get better degree results than those that hadn't. I think it is because they had a real-world experience and most of the jobs were economics-related and in lectures and discussions you could see things come out of people's experience. That's because they had been out in the environment for a year: reading the press, experiencing what actually goes on in day-to-day firms that deal with the sort of things that you want to do.
>
> (27C: recent graduate, large public financial institution)

However, two recent graduates decided against embarking on a course with a placement element on the grounds that a protracted period out of an academic culture would have made it difficult to continue their studies:

> A placement is probably quite a good idea. Well, certainly over the summer vacation, that sort of time. I don't think I would want to take a year out, because of the learning thing. Coming to work you are learning different things, it is not academic, and I think you would lose the academic momentum. Same reason for not having a break between A-levels and university.
>
> (23C: electrical engineer, small medical lasers manufacturer)

> I think a placement would have proved useful. But I think some people see it as a year out, and it can be difficult to get back to study because of the different life-style. I felt if I took time off I wouldn't want to carry on studying.
>
> (49C: project designer, computer-controlled systems manufacturer)

Conclusion

Overall, there is a consensus among different stakeholders that placement experience has a positive value for students. However, it cannot be assumed that work placements are beneficial per se. A number of factors can influence the success or otherwise of the placement. Such a venture is not feasible without partnership – collaboration between all parties involved. It also needs to be 'adequately funded' (63B). Attention has been drawn to the possible pitfalls and the ways in which these can be avoided so that students have a quality learning experience in the workplace, one that empowers them and inspires them to continue to learn.

A recent report suggests that 'organisational cultures in work-based learning host organisations have a substantial influence on what the student learns' and as a result, students may experience 'the same hazards encountered by many employees: ignorance of procedures to be followed, lack of confidence in their own judgement, fear of criticism or rebuff, pressure to speed up, multiple demands, isolation, boredom' (QSC 1995, p. 7).

> It is very different being a graduate, being at school all your life, and suddenly being thrown into the work environment. It's a totally different situation and that year got me used to it and to the fact that people view graduates in a different light... On my placement they seemed to think. "Oh a student, think they know it all", and then they realised that I wasn't like that and it was okay. But there was a definite hostility there to start. I think it is fear as well. They maybe see people on graduate training schemes ending up on a higher level than themselves.
>
> (17C: graduate recruitment consultant, small private specialist employment agency)

> I think one of the main problems that I had with the whole placement was that the guy who was actually in charge of me didn't have a great deal of experience of working with graduates and couldn't really give me a great deal of guidance or consistency of work.
>
> (50C: performance analyst, large freight company)

In other circumstances, a placement student can end up as a replacement for a regular employee. In one sense that provides a 'real' experience but it can lead to a student having a rather restricted experience of the organisation:

> The danger is that when you get very tight on the head-count restraints, you tend to use them [placement students] for regular production work… That's not really what we should be using students for. It should be project-type work so they get a view of various different aspects of the company, not just one particular type of job. They get a good view of the company but maybe it is not in their, or our, benefit in the long term to actually approach it like that.
>
> (22B: sales manager, multinational reprographic equipment manufacturer)

Overall, though, despite the caveats about providing a meaningful experience, the respondents in the study, both managers and recent graduates endorsed placements and were of the view that they greatly enhanced the student experience.

Summary

- Placements are seen by employers and graduate employees as the single most significant missing element of the majority of degree programmes.

- Placements provide opportunities for employers and higher education institutions to 'talk to each other'. Such opportunities are recognised and appreciated by employers.

- There is overwhelming support for work placements in order to provide students with opportunities to develop an awareness of organisational culture and opportunities for skills development.

- Many placements, by involving students in the practical application of theories learnt in higher education, provide a context that helps develop students' understanding of academic matters.

- Students who have experienced a work placement are in the main better prepared for work.

- A year-long placement is considered preferable to a short placement both in terms of employers getting a return on their investment and students gaining a worthwhile experience.

- Placements can offer real opportunities for students to decide on a future career path.

- Employers use the placement as an opportunity to screen potential recruits. This method is thought less risky than other recruitment practices. In some cases, placements may lead directly to employment.

- Students on placement may get paid and thereby have their financial burden eased.

- There is a danger that students can be used as cheap labour and their skills under-utilised. This inhibits development and is not good practice.

- There would appear to be the potential for many more placements. Employers are committed to the idea but are constrained by limited resources. Some small firms have reservations because of the substantial investment required to give students a meaningful experience.

HE – Employer links

Collaboration between employers and higher education is recognised by all stakeholders as beneficial. Many employers recognise that they have a responsibility to raise awareness of the need to build and maintain such relationships. The world of work, industry and commerce has a great deal of experience to contribute to higher education and this can be done in numerous ways: involvement in course content, lecturing, seminars, workshops, work shadowing, and commissioning research as well as providing work placements (AGR, 1995, DTI/CIHE, 1990, CBI, 1994, 1995, DE, 1992).

The majority of respondents recognised the need for collaboration in order to gain understanding between higher education and employers and thus to enable students to succeed in the workplace. There is clear indication that a good deal of collaborative activity already exists. Among the organisations in the sample, a number of models of good practice were identified. This is exemplified by one organisation that had invested considerable time and effort into establishing a strong 'symbiotic' link with their local HE institution:

> When I came here I found there were virtually no links anywhere. It was just like a desert, nobody was thinking forward, nobody was developing ideas. The only way we are going to do that and keep abreast of things that are actually developing and changing, particularly when it comes to research and development, is to be working alongside higher and further education. I cannot envisage that they can be separate.
>
> (77A: director of human resources, medium-sized health service contractor)

Benefits of links

Many respondents from a range of organisations indicated a strong desire for closer, more informed links with higher education, now and in the future. Broadly speaking, five reasons were given:

- to enable colleges to run courses which are relevant to the processes in the workplace;
- to provide students with practical experience and tuition;
- to involve members of organisations with universities in situations that are economically viable or rewarding to the organisation;
- to increase feedback from higher education;
- to ensure students (especially on part-time courses) are learning in a way that meets their needs and the needs of the employer.

Views expressed regarding such links were, in the main, positive. Some respondents clearly felt that it was very important for employers to be involved with higher education and to develop and maintain links wherever possible. Respondents agreed that links with higher education enhanced understanding from both parties:

> We maintain a very, very close link with tutors, with directors of studies, with the career service, that probably is half of our job... We want to make sure that tutors and directors of studies are aware of our needs as an employer. We want the best candidates to apply to us, so it is very much a two-way thing. We are able to talk to the people who are creating the curricula, they are able to find out what we want as an employer, which is partly why

> [University X] has such an excellent law faculty. It is very much commercial based. They came and spoke to us, not just us, other major city firms and said… "What do you want?", and it works extraordinarily well.
>
> (09A: head of personnel, large law firm)

One area where links with higher education have been identified as particularly useful is the development of practical, rather than the theoretical skills. In smaller organisations, the cost of training employees to use expensive or hi-tech machinery precludes on-the-job training as it 'ties up a particular piece of equipment' (42A). Linking up with colleges that can both provide access to the equipment and practical experience is an attractive proposition to employers.

Making the links

Forging links with higher education is not easy, according to some respondents, as it can be very expensive, time consuming and not all colleges or universities are prepared to enter into such relationships with 'strangers', preferring instead to stick with the employers they know.

> We also like to build up strong links with the law faculty themselves, that is under way, it takes a huge investment and also they are quite wary, especially if we have gone somewhere like Oxbridge, they have their favourite firms and it is still quite an old-school-tie network, which is quite interesting. It is very difficult to get in there. So in terms of our links with higher education we would try and take advantage of any invitation we were given to go to a lunch or go to a talk or whatever. It is one area we are looking at improving, but the contact that we have is very strong.
>
> (09B: graduate recruiter and training manager, large law firm)

Given the pressure on costs in all areas of organisational enterprise, it is all too easy for employers to suggest that they cannot afford to spend time and money approaching colleges, developing or contributing to courses, or releasing staff for teaching. At a time when many organisations are cutting back on staff in attempts to streamline their operations, fewer people within the organisation have the time to get involved with higher education.

> We are a very streamlined organisation, for example in personnel there is just the two of us to look after 180… You find that you don't have as much time to be involved as you would like to. Having said that, like many other TV broadcasters, we are very keen and do take an active interest in these sort of areas. It is really only the time constraints that prevent us getting more involved.
>
> (42A: training and personnel manager, medium-sized private broadcasting company)

The onus could equally be on higher education institutions to approach employers with ideas for closer links. Respondents differed on the scale and extent of the effort put into fostering or maintaining links, even when there was a clear understanding of the benefits involved.

> In the business that we are in, *real* information exchange is vital, and not just reading papers and stuff like that. That is often not real information, it's packaged information. Actually going down, seeing people and talking to them and getting a real feeling for what is going on, so we tend to do quite a bit of that where possible.
>
> (23B: general manager, small medical lasers manufacturer)

> At one stage I did teach a little bit of mathematics at a local college, but I have never really pushed for and never been asked to do visiting lectures to undergraduate courses, and I think that is probably a shame that we are not asked to contribute to those degree courses.
>
> (40B: production manager, large steel manufacturer)

However, there is a sense in which employers could, if the will is there, forge closer links in various ways:

> Most organisations if they really wanted to could use people who are in education to do a lot more of their work rather than going to highly expensive management consultants, who

are only using the same processes anyway. The spin off for those things are: we get work done, we get it done cheap and often at quite a high level of competence. It is done well.

(77A: director of human resources, medium-sized health service contractor)

Current links

The nature of current links is diverse. In addition to the links established through placements (Chapter 8), there are a number of different, though not unrelated, ways that employers and higher education institutions engage in meaningful partnerships, although not all of these are formal or structured.

Many organisations have links with universities through teaching, research, student sponsorship or other initiatives. However, almost a quarter of respondents (23%) reported that their organisations had no formal links with higher education institutions that they were aware of. This reflects the findings of other research on employers' views of higher education (AGR, 1995).

The majority of the respondents discussed links between employers and higher education. Other than placements, the main links identified were careers guidance, teaching and external examining. About a fifth of those respondents who discussed employer–higher education interaction commented on such links. Research was identified by about one in ten and smaller numbers discussed a range of other links including sponsorship, involvement in training, resource development, student societies and participation in committees or governing bodies.

Careers guidance

Careers advisers have an important role not only in providing information and guidance to students, but also in advising employers, particularly smaller organisations, about the advantages of employing graduates. Careers services are key information holders about the current labour market and can provide essential links between stakeholders. The insights and information about the graduate labour market that careers advisers obtain can be helpful to their own institutions' future planning; close liaison between careers services, academic departments and key decision-makers is of growing importance in the increasingly competitive market of higher education.

However, there is a concern about the mismatch between jobs that students seem to want and existing vacancies (AgCAS/CSU/IER, 1996). The stakes are higher and selection tougher. Many able students are disillusioned and find it hard to keep trying when chances of success are slim. Careers counsellors are thus presented with numerous challenges, especially as there is considerable disparity in resources allocated to careers services in different institutions and variations in the extent to which activities in such institutions are supported or highly regarded. A recent study of student expectations revealed a 'concern that some university careers facilities are more limited than others, especially in the New University sector' (AgCAS/CSU/IER, 1996), a view echoed by a recent graduate in our study (40C).

Employers feel that higher education institutions could help students to focus more clearly on what they want to do in life and make them more aware of what they need to be effective in the workplace. It is generally perceived that careers services should be an integral part of the management structure of universities and should take a major role in helping to inform academic staff of careers options (Wallis and Harvey, 1994).

Recently there has been a shift towards encouraging students to be self-reliant in their career management (AGR, 1995) and a recommendation for higher education to review their careers-guidance strategies in the light of current employment trends and predictions for the future. However, careers guidance continues to be seen as playing a vital role in providing access to independent guidance and enabling students to find employment.

In addition, the information available refers predominantly to traditional graduate recruiters, large organisations who can afford to promote themselves (AGR, 1995). Some respondents in our study commented on what they perceive as the narrowness of career service information, a situation accentuated by the fact that the larger, regular recruiters produce far more material than some smaller, but very popular work areas:

> I did go to the careers service because I wanted to be a sports psychologist and no one could tell me anything so I just gave up. That's what I always wanted to do and basically I ended up having to do the whole slog myself. I came to the conclusion that I would have to go back and do a first degree in sports science, which I wasn't prepared to do. So I had to give up that idea. I think the careers service is very well geared up for people who want to work in the City and want to do management consultancy or accounting, or stockbroking. The actual links with industry, and industrial opportunities available, just weren't discussed. Which is probably a snobby Oxbridgy thing – they tend to get most of their people into City jobs.
>
> (32C: graduate recruiter, large tele-communications organisation)

Small firms are increasingly seen as potential graduate recruiters, providing more jobs for an increasing student population. Their needs are diverse and their access to information is limited by resources. This places a heavy responsibility on careers guidance providers to ensure that students have access to sometimes less 'glossy' information about smaller firms, and that the firms have information about potential recruits. Careers services have been establishing closer links with small and medium enterprises (SMEs), sometimes as part of TEC/LEC initiatives, sometimes through DfEE-funded projects. Other links are through well-established networks within institutions (AGR, 1995). The issue was raised by respondents in our study:

> I certainly don't remember seeing anything other than local jobs advertised [for school leavers] via local career services... So I think career services could do more as well in promoting the smaller companies. They are going to have to anyway because there aren't that many graduate training schemes in comparison to the number of students now with the explosion in higher education. Where are they all going to go?
>
> (28C; project manager, small design and communications company)

> I also think because the smaller companies don't have the resources to get in and tell the career services about the opportunities that are there, because of people who take career services to lunch, invite them to London, etc., then by-and-large they will talk about those companies before they talk about their local employers.
>
> (04B; project director, small corporate literature specialists)

Despite the best efforts of higher education careers services, who are increasingly targeting second (or earlier) years and who run a range of careers education programmes, some managers thought that perhaps students have misguided expectations about what kind of career their degree will lead to. Students need to consider, with guidance, what their options are before embarking on their course of study:

> I don't know how much effort, from day one, goes into helping a graduate focus attention on what he is going to do next in terms of career advice... I think a lot of graduates are fairly naïve as to what is available to them unless they do a pure degree like law or medicine. I think more time should be put into counselling people, certainly from the second year onwards into helping them work out what they are going to do when they finish.
>
> (26B: area sales manager, multinational business machines manufacturer)

> I would like to see better careers advice and better targeted courses really. It's very unlikely that I would recruit someone from a media degree. It's too broad. If they have done that then decided radio is their thing and gone onto a one-year post grad they are much more likely to get into radio.
>
> (13A: news manager, medium-sized private local radio station)

For one respondent, the onus is on the student, although more guidance at university would not go amiss:

> I don't know that higher education really can help, basically people need to focus more on what kind of occupation they want. A lot of people have come in and not really been suited to finance... I don't know at university, certainly in my time, that you get very much help at all as to what you ought to be looking for, what you're profiled for. A lot of people are just throwing themselves into the pot and hoping that they come to the surface... People need to know what they are good at, what they should be looking for, maybe what their profile suits them for... Perhaps more direction at university as to what is available and what particular people are good at.
> (22B sales manager, multinational reprographics equipment manufacturer)

There is some tension among employers on the issue of who can best provide careers guidance. Those attending the *Employer Satisfaction* seminar (Harvey, 1993) agreed that such guidance should remain the brief of careers experts. However, the CBI suggests that 'all those involved with students' education, not just careers specialists, need expertise in careers guidance. University tutors and departments can have as much influence on the careers choices of graduates as careers services' (CBI, 1994). This view was reflected in the response from one graduate employee:

> Certainly, but now it is monstrously hard. You do think, after all my years of education and my good marks why can't I just write to this organisation and they will give me an interesting job right now, but it's just not the case. I do think that universities are in some way so removed from that reality. They have a careers department but you will never catch a tutor showing an interest in your future career plans and giving you some constructive advice. It strikes me that is very negative of a tutor to see someone just swanning through a course knowing that they are going to be in trouble three years down the line because they haven't thought in advance of what they are going to do.
> (12C: trainee solicitor, large law firm)

Some thought that people who work in industry could help with careers guidance because they were able to give a more realistic picture of the world of work:

> The only thing I attended which was any good was the CRAC 'Insight to Management' course... young people coming in and saying, "Well, I work for Boots, and I work for this textile factory. You know, that was really useful because it was business... And that was the only thing that I had that made me think: "Right, this is going to give me some help when I decide what sort of job I am going to be doing."
> (28C: project manager, small design and communications company)

> The people who run [careers services] certainly need to have a practical awareness of what is happening in the world today. It is very important that they get that knowledge and understanding. Quite how they do it I am not certain... I think those who are working in industry are best placed to advise people who are asking what they need to do to get into the industry, what qualities do I need to develop.
> (39B: team manager, medium-sized software contractors)

Graduate employees in our study have had positive experiences of the careers services in terms of the information available, but recognised that it was up to them to make use of it:

> We had a good career service, if you used it you could find the information you wanted. There were lots of workshops running. They were nearly always fully booked and it was quite difficult to get on to them, but if you wanted to and were determined you could get the information you needed. By the time I done my tenth interview and my 20th application form I knew what it was about. I knew what they were all after. It was a long laborious process but there was the facility there and it was well worth using because it meant I had a job offer by the Easter holidays before my final term and that was very valuable for peace of mind. It probably lost me a grade on my degree the fact that I spent so much time filling in forms, going to first interviews, going to second interviews for two days. I did about six of those, which are really time-consuming.
> (47C: process engineer, multi national food manufacturer)

Some respondents expressed negative views about their experience of the careers guidance:

> I thought the careers guidance was appalling... I think the careers system needs an overhaul, it was very out of date... they don't seem to have the knowledge of what is really going on outside the university which is worrying when it is so hard to get jobs these days.
>
> (13C: news co-ordinator, medium-sized private local radio station)

> Well, I saw a bit of careers guidance at A-level and GCSE, and neither of those seemed particularly helpful. Being in electronics, when they suggested jobs early on, electronics wasn't in it. There wasn't the range of jobs in there, so it didn't seem worthwhile.
>
> (23C: electrical engineer, small medical lasers manufacturer)

Teaching and external examining

Experts in various fields of employment are clearly a valuable source of up-to-date knowledge and information relating to their particular disciplines or professions. Potentially, such individuals could provide a relevant and insightful input to many degree courses, enabling students to gain an understanding not only of the theory and practice of their particular disciplines, but also of what many employers term 'the real world of work'.

It was suggested by a few respondents that lecturers are lacking in awareness of what is happening in the world of work and that their knowledge is perhaps esoteric, out of date and badly communicated. This was by no means a typical perception of teaching staff. However, some employers thought that they might make a useful contribution to the delivery of courses, perhaps by 'doing guest lectures' (46A). A number of employers indicated that they already had members of staff who went out to colleges to provide some form of teaching or tutoring, who acted as external examiners for a variety of courses and exams, or who performed both these activities: 'A lot of partners and lawyers in the practice are lecturers in universities, locally and around the country' (06A). One strategic manager expressed the view that such arrangements helped to develop their staff:

> A lot of our managers... we actually try and get them to go into the university and help the university and colleges do sessions on things, because it gives them the exposure and practice at other skills as well. So we try and use that relationship both ways, so we can learn.
>
> (77A: director of human resources, medium-sized health service contractors)

It appears that such relationships are often undertaken on a 'personal arrangement' (03A) or *ad hoc* basis, rather than being formally structured and organised as company policy.

Research

Research plays a key role in many universities and colleges. For many employers, especially larger organisations, research is vital in the drive towards competitiveness and progression of the organisation. Research is varied and ranges from that undertaken to inform planning and policy, to technological development intended to maintain leading-edge products and that which aims to provide information designed to enhance the quality of service provision.

A few respondents expressed their research links with higher education in terms of funding or sponsorship of projects or research fellowships. One organisation, albeit an isolated example, had its own research company based within a university (29A).

Some employers develop or maintain research links with higher education on a 'practical' or 'productive' basis where their collaboration is geared more towards specific value-added outcomes:

> My remit is to [decide] what we need in terms of academic collaborations with university institutions and identify which institutions best meet those needs, and then basically target funding, usually this is Ph.D. and post-Docs. or contract research.
>
> (63B: research manager, large pharmaceutical manufacturers)

Research findings may be used to develop courses. One organisation has plans for one of its workers to use research findings as 'input on one of the nursing degrees at the local University' (19B). In a more directly collaborative research relationship, research and development is undertaken from inception to finished product. This kind of collaborative research effort benefits employers in terms of them being able to utilise research interests and also offer students (potential employees) practical work-related experience:

> In the past the firm has used the local university to design some marketing material as a competition... I must admit, at the moment... any links with higher education, we would probably view from quite a selfish perspective, i.e. we get cheap marketing.
>
> (17A: partner, small private specialist employment agency)

Whilst the majority of respondents who commented upon research links with higher education did so in a positive vein, others demonstrated less enthusiasm suggesting that they didn't 'particularly feel the need' to have research links (31A) or were concerned that the research project might get subverted:

> We are using them for testing, stress analysis, and basically we have been warned off by other people because sometimes, apparently, they tailor your job to their project so you don't get what you want. Then you get so far and the money has run out. We have heard complaints from various people in industry, they have put money in for research on [a specific project] and the money has been redistributed, the project has been tweaked.
>
> (18A: partner, small private design consultancy)

Sponsorship and funding

The majority of respondents who indicated that their organisation had some form of sponsorship or funding link with higher education acknowledged that it was mainly related to research. However, some respondents identified other forms of sponsorship or funding; in some cases this was aimed at targeting future potential employees: 'We might consider sponsorship with a view to catching future accountants early – getting our name implanted before they qualify as accountants' (17A).

Collaborative arrangements between employers, universities and other bodies emerged as a method of funding designed to engender industrial–higher education liaison. This highlighted the concern with costs and resources in that, without some external funding, such projects would be beyond the means of many employers.

> We also engage in collaborative arrangements with universities as part of attempts to stimulate liaison between higher education and industry... We probably wouldn't do these were it not for the fact that there's funding available, because we just couldn't justify the resources otherwise... it is good for the business because you can always tap into other resources.
>
> (23B: general manager, small medical lasers manufacturer)

Sponsorship to enable students to undertake courses as a matter of company policy demonstrates the value that some employers place on maintaining close links with higher education, although it is recognised that this would be unaffordable to many organisations.

> We sponsor people to do MBAs... so we have quite a lot of links with the MBA programme... We have a large number of people who are studying for a variety of qualifications at local institutions. We have a further education policy which basically says we will fund any relevant training for anybody. So that could be at any level.
>
> (47A: personnel manager, multi-national food manufacturer)

Feedback

Feedback is essential in maintaining a close and successful working relationship in any sphere of enterprise. The importance of clear and accurate communication in terms of what is happening in joint ventures between employers and higher education serves to inform both parties of the positive and negative aspects of the collaboration, which in turn will assist in the improvement of the relationship. Feedback clearly benefits the employer by ensuring that higher education knows what is required by a particular industry, business sector or profession, and that the course content reflects those requirements.

> We are very impressed by the graduates that are coming through, and I think, as far as the legal profession is concerned, that has been a result of quite close links that the legal profession developed and maintained over the years with higher education, and the feedback that has been generated to make sure that we are actually getting the types of graduate with the types of skills that we want, coming to see us. We meet on a regular basis with careers officers at education establishments and we talk to them and belong to recognised groups that provide a forum for discussion about needs requirements that the legal profession has of its graduates. This has had an impact on the compulsory content of undergraduate degrees and the Legal Practice Course.
> (06A: partner, large law firm)

Many employers pay substantial fees to have prospective or current employees undertake particular courses in higher education. As 'customers' of higher education, 'cost-flexible' employers want to know how a student is progressing, so feedback in this respect is important:

> We've had very little feedback to say how our employees were doing on the courses they were on, but over the last 18 months to 2 years we now get reports on the grades that staff have achieved, or a general report on their performance, which I think is helpful. Otherwise one relies on the employee to tell you, or you ask them, and are they telling the truth? If you are paying 75% of the fees you want to know that you are getting something back for your money.
> (37B: director of financial services, small housing association)

> We are sending people on this part-time degree and I virtually get no feedback... He has just passed his third-year exams but the college has not notified me – never discussed it. We are shelling out all this money and there is never any feedback from the tutors regarding our satisfaction or dissatisfaction with the quality of education they are providing to the student.
> (16A: office director, medium-sized quantity and building surveyors)

Developing future links

The majority of views on future links between employers and higher education were expressed in terms of 'market-driven relationships' (66A) in which employers are the clients or customers of higher education, looking for added value from the investment of time and resources:

> There definitely needs to be closer links between industry and universities especially within engineering, this is such an obvious area to have a close link because the closer link you have, the better the people coming out will be as they will be trained for what companies want. You often hear that universities think they know what people in companies want, and when people get out there they discover that somebody had got it wrong somewhere. There is a gap and they need to get together more and say these are the attributes we are looking for.
> (08C: graduate trainee, multi-national electrical products manufacturer)

Such views suggest that the nature of future relationships between higher education and employers will be driven by supply and demand. Yet, some employers who have been pro-active in building sturdy relationships with higher education institutions have taken the relationship further. Stakeholder-oriented approaches (Chapter 3) see benefits, not just in terms of higher education 'produce', but on a deeper level to actively promote the learning culture within their organisation and respond to the learning needs of students by providing opportunities and support for work experience. In short, to give real commitment to partnership.

Summary

- Links between higher education and employers provide opportunities for two different and independent cultures to establish meaningful relationships in which mutual understanding can flourish. Many respondents from a range of organisations indicated a strong desire for closer, more informed links with higher education, now and in the future.

- Employer links with higher education enable colleges to provide courses more relevant to a work culture, enabling students to develop the 'skills' they need to be effective in the workplace after they graduate.

- Such links allow members of organisations to engage with universities in activities that are potentially economically rewarding to both parties and improve communication between the two sectors.

- Students need a realistic picture of what the work culture is like. They should seek careers advice early and be proactive in their approach to job-hunting.

- Careers advisors have an important role in ensuring that students have access to information and guidance. Careers information tends to focus on the larger, traditional graduate recruiters who can afford to produce impressive brochures to promote themselves. Smaller companies need to self-promote as they are increasingly the recruiters of the future. Careers services could aid this process.

- Academic staff perhaps need more awareness of the employment market and be prepared to offer guidance to students.

- Most views expressed about higher education–employer links were positive. Some respondents clearly felt that it was very important for them to be involved with higher education and to develop and maintain links wherever possible.

- Respondents appreciated the value of having links with higher education to enhance understanding from both parties in terms of what is required to meet the needs of students and employers. There is clear indication that a good deal of collaborative activity already exists.

- British higher education may have to adopt 'new strategies' to help students to success at work, such as focusing on the transition from higher education to working life and thus will need to make more effort to engage with employer organisations.

- Although links with higher education can be costly in terms of time and staff availability, those who have established close links consider the investment to be worthwhile.

- When links are in place, employers want feedback. This is important to employers as 'customers', they want to know that they are getting value for money. However, taking a broader view, employers who invest substantial time and effort in relationships open up clear channels of communication and are engaged in continuous dialogue.

Training and lifelong learning

The majority of the organisations in the sample have some form of training for graduate and non-graduate employees. In some organisations graduates are recruited directly into training programmes for a fixed period of time. Other forms of training include informal workplace training, internal training sessions and the use of external agencies. Studying for further (often job-related) qualifications is seen as another form of staff development. Organisations have differing approaches to continual development and learning, ranging from assumed, but unmonitored, staff development to structured programmes for career development.

Graduate trainee schemes

Some of the organisations in the sample, especially larger ones, talked about training in terms of the initial training programmes designed for graduates who have joined the organisation through a graduate trainee programme. This initial training period can last from six months (39A) to up to three years (47A). The training schemes often involve placements within different areas, departments or teams within the organisation. Thus, even if graduates are taken on to work in a particular area, they are given a broader initial work experience to help them understand how the organisation, and the people within it, function.

> It is a bespoke programme lasting six months, the first four months is a core module, so every graduate joining the scheme will go through exactly the same training performance. It is approximately one-third classroom based – teaching management, technical and interpersonal skills, building those up, practising them – and then two-thirds out in the business, in the individual areas of the [organisation] to learn about the business and see what is happening. The last two months would be specific training, technical training, for the area in which they would first be placed.
> (56A: graduate recruitment manager, large financial institution)

These kind of schemes are often designed to train the managers of the future and are a way of accelerating promotion of those who successfully complete them. These schemes are very attractive to graduates, and large organisations are keen to select the 'best'. Employees who enter the organisation through this route often go on to make up a large percentage of the top positions within the organisation (Huddart, 1994).

> I think we will continue to hone and develop that [graduate trainee scheme], it is the key learning experience that gives the organisation the ability to put these people into positions of accountability at an early age.
> (36A: senior manager, large financial institution)

A number of managers and graduates highlight the need for the trainees to be doing 'real jobs from day one' as part of their training rather than just watching. One graduate felt that the six months training period had lacked this hands-on, real-job focus.

> I really want to get on and do my job but for six months out of the last eight and a half months I have just been sitting round with nothing to do. Part of the nature of the graduate training scheme I was on earlier was shadowing people, just watching them work and it was very frustrating.
> (39C: programmer, medium-sized software services contractor)

Training and retention

The intensive initial training periods that characterise these types of trainee programmes are an expensive investment and organisations are aware that they need to retain these employees to make their investment worthwhile.

> Taking on graduates is a significant overhead for us, quite a significant investment and, of course, they are free to move on when they have finished their training. So, we have to try and make sure we are cost-effective in the way we do it. I do think it's good to have graduates and when you find the right people, to invest in them, give them challenges and rewards that make them want to stay with the company. You grow them within the company until they become future management. (39B: team manager, medium-sized software services contractor)

A few respondents whose organisations have an initial training programme suggested that there were no appropriate structures in place for these employees to progress their careers (39A).

> We trip ourselves up because we provide very good training and then don't follow it through… I think we are missing a layer within the middle management and I think other companies are offering more attractive packages for people of our age and our calibre. (54D: assistant personnel manager, large international retailers)

> I am thinking of a couple of graduates now who looking at their last appraisal forms were saying things like, "I want to develop my job to where I can carry more responsibility, be responsible for more people". Reading those, you think to yourself, "Well, if we can't offer them greater responsibility soon then they are going to be looking elsewhere and we are going to lose them," which would be a shame when we have invested time and money in training them to do the job that they are probably doing very well but are now ready for a fresh challenge. (37A: deputy chief executive, small housing association)

For some organisations it is not viable to invest the time and money involved in graduate trainee programmes and, instead, they concentrate training resources on developing specific skills to meet current requirements.

Broad training vs. task-specific training

Training tends to be oriented to either specific jobs (or tasks) or to provide a more broad training to develop a range of skills and knowledge. In reality, most organisations have a mixture of these training approaches, though there is a difference in emphasis, depending on the extent to which there is a culture for more general training or whether the concentration is on specific skills needed for the job at hand.

Some managers talk about the importance of providing a broad-based approach to training and learning. This is particularly important if they are looking at the training needs of people for the future, making sure they are able to function effectively in senior positions in the company. This concentrates on employees who will push the organisation forward.

> The way you develop people is moving them, it is providing different opportunities, different experiences, different cultures, different parts of the business, working for different bosses, all of that is a crucial part of their development, and our development and training initiatives are very much focused around that premise. (32A: development and training manager, large telecommunications organisation)

> Well it might be something of a very deep interest to them and an area they want to move into, and we would support people in that as well… it just encourages people to look at the bigger picture rather than their word-processing skills or things on that level. (41A: general manager, small registered charity)

This approach is prevalent in 'fast-track' trainee programmes, although is also apparent in smaller companies who do not have a formalised initial training period. This kind of broader-based development of the individual is a financial investment from which some employers, with a cost-flexible approach, would expect some return in the future.

> As part of our management process, we do put a lot of effort into trying to assess potential as people move through and so we can look at the longer-term training and development needs rather than train for the immediate job… We need to make sure that, as a business, we are identifying those whom we regard as either business-resource or corporate-resource people. In other words, they are the managers of the future and we need to develop them, not just in the job that they are doing, but to provide them with opportunities and experiences, to test them out, to prepare them for future moves.
>
> (40A: manager of training and development, large steel manufacturer)

A cost-flexible approach clearly relates training to the needs of the organisation:

> You want well-trained people but it is expensive, especially if you lose 10% of your work force every year. I don't feel there is any incentive to train people once they are working for you, other than you want them to be good skilled workers.
>
> (49A: operations manager, computer-controlled systems manufacturer)

Others see it as important to encourage development, even if it means people move on to other jobs, and this reflects a response-flexible, inclusive approach that is interested in empowering employees who are seen as important stakeholders in the organisation.

> People coming here generally have a clear view of what they want to do, what they want to achieve in life, how they are going to get there. We can't always supply all of that, but as long as we are a stepping stone from which we benefit and they benefit I think it is beneficial. I think it helps keep and motivates people as well. They actually see that it is a two-way street in the job, and we have a very low turnover of staff.
>
> (23A: chief executive, small medical lasers manufacturer)

These two very different organisational approaches to training and development are summed up by Fisher (1994) in his comparison of the approaches of Ford and Unipart. Ford has an Employee and Development Programme which is not job-related and has the rhetoric of empowering individuals. This involves a wide range of personal development courses, foreign language courses and a variety of engineering-related courses. Unipart has a narrower approach, with the aim of building 'the world's best lean enterprise'. Development of staff is restricted to clearly business-related courses and to the inculcation of the company's operating ethos.

Approaches taken to training and employee development mirror the 'inclusivity' of the organisation (Chapter 3, Figure 3.2): whether an organisation is looking to enhance employees' competencies in a value-added approach, or whether an organisation focuses more on transformation through enhancing competencies and aiming to empower employees through a broader staff development.

Forms of training

Training is delivered in three ways: on-the-job; in-house; external. Typically, organisations use a combination of these forms of training, taking into account considerations such as the appropriate method for developing the required skills, available time and training budget.

> It can be quite formal off-the-job training, what we would call traditional courses, but also on-the-job opportunities as well. We try to encourage managers to develop their staff by coaching them and mentoring them. We offer secondments internally, which are across departments, inter-departmental, and that has been very successful.
>
> (42A: training and personnel manager, medium-sized private broadcasting company)

'On-the-job' training

On-the-job training involves the learning of skills and absorbing knowledge whilst actually doing the task. This is a form of training that all new employees (and established employees) are involved in as they learn and develop their job. This has its benefits in that it is learning from people who are already doing the job, that employees are learning things that are relevant to the job and that what is learnt can be put into practice straight away so the information is more easily retained.

> On-the-job training is just as good because you tend to find out all the pitfalls or where you are going wrong through experience… On-the-job experience is the best way to approach it. I think in a practical situation it tends to sink in more.
>
> (49C: project designer, computer-controlled systems manufacturer)

> I am trained all the time. Everything, pretty much, is new. There is no formal programme but I just learn on the job. They spend a lot of time, money and effort keeping up-to-date computer-wise which always means new equipment, new networks, building new computers or adding bits to them and I learn that as I go along.
>
> (18C: junior design engineer, small private design consultancy)

However, if it is the only form of training available to employees, this type of training can restrict access to new ways of thinking and impede the development of broader skills.

'In-house' training

On-the-job and in-house or internal training both happen in the workplace. Internal training refers to more structured sessions or seminars, often conducted by employees of the organisation, which may be cross-departmental. 'In-house' training is often developed in preference to expensive external courses (44B). It can also be more relevant as it is talking about the specific organisation and can spread ideas and good practice across different sections of the company. However, it too may be limited in that it may maintain the status quo and does not always mean that people are away from their place of work where they will be uninterrupted and be able to take a fresh look at their work.

> A lot of it is now provided locally and you then have the trade-off between freshness and sterility, because a lot of the time it is just people perpetuating the conventional ways of doing things.
>
> (43A: specialist journalist manager, large public broadcasting organisation)

External training

External training has the advantage of being conducted outside the workplace and can involve interaction with a wider variety of people. These types of courses are often developing generic skills applicable in a variety of workplaces and situations.

> There are externally-held courses, which would help people with complementary skills, whether that is interviewing or making presentations, or how to do disciplinary work.
>
> (54A: assistant to deputy chairman, large international retailers)

> Where I think the [corporation] has scored quite well in the past, is that the service providers have tended to be a long way away. I don't just mean distance, I mean removed from the people in their workplace. So if you go on a three-week basic journalism course, for example, it isn't in the place where you work, so you are getting new and refreshing ideas.
>
> (43A: specialist journalist manager, large public broadcasting organisation)

However, this is an expensive form of training, and can sometimes be too generalist and difficult for recipients to relate to their own organisation.

Continuous development and learning

Many organisations in the sample were of the view that they positively encouraged or facilitated continuous development through training and lifelong learning: 'I'm still learning, you always learn' (10B). Approaches to enabling lifelong learning reflected the differences in training provision. Some organisations saw lifelong learning in terms of continuous improvement and updating of job-relevant skills. Others adopted a more 'inclusive approach' that accommodated what Sir Charles Darby, Chairman of Bass Taverns, described as the 'moral responsibility' that employers have to offer employees the opportunities to continue to learn and develop. Employers can no longer guarantee lifetime employment but they can encourage continual development to help ensure that employees are equipped to continue to be employed (Darby, 1993).

> Our supervision and appraisal system is built around training and support, it is not a management tool to assess people's performance and kick their butts as such, it is about working with people to get them to take an interest in what they are doing and want to do it better, and part of that has got to be training…We also have a philosophy of personal and professional development and therefore I am quite happy to look at things from the point of view that, when somebody leaves our employment and goes on to another job, they should be in better position to get a better job. It might be something of a very deep interest to them and an area they want to move into, and we would support people in that as well.
>
> (41A: general manager, small registered charity)

Encouragement of personal and professional development may also be an important factor in building employee loyalty, when traditional incentives of a 'job-for-life', or a clear line of promotion, or high graduate wages are no longer a reality.

A number of organisations felt that continual professional development and lifelong learning was not part of their current culture, but that it was something that they wanted to develop more fully in the future.

> Training has got quite a way to go. We have got very small resources for training development and we would really like to build that in the future and kick off more of a learning culture.
>
> (68B: line manager, medium-sized insurance company)

> I think we have got a long way to go in developing life-long learning. We are committed to the Investors in People accreditation and that will help us to focus on where we can help to develop staff to the best of their ability – to tap in to people who thought they couldn't develop any further but have got potential that perhaps hasn't been realised yet. Sometimes it is questionable how relevant what they do is to their day-to-day work but it doesn't matter, because the very act of learning a new skill, getting more knowledge, must help in their day-to-day work as well, keeping their mind alert, ready to take on new challenges and so on. I have heard of some organisations who will support people going on evening classes for keep-fit and badminton, we have not gone that far, but I have heard it said by some employers that it is a worthwhile investment, because you are encouraging people to be outgoing and healthy minded.
>
> (37A: deputy chief executive, small housing association)

Both managers and graduates pointed to continual development as essential in order to do the job effectively and progress within the organisation. Some respondents emphasised a cost-responsive approach, arguing that if organisations or employees stand still and do not continue to learn then they will be left behind.

> If you are not prepared to take the best of what is available and apply it and change a process, then you inevitably fall behind, become less efficient, become less cost effective and are then unable to sell your product at a profit.
>
> (40B: production manager, large steel manufacturer)

Others adopt a learning-organisation approach (Arkin, 1993), much more geared to stakeholder responsiveness:

> Making our managers make the difference, and outlining some of the key skills and behaviours that are needed to be the agents of change to meet the challenges of the 1990s, innovation, empowerment, continuous improvement, results orientation.
>
> (47A: personnel manager, multi-national food manufacturer)

Appraisals

In some organisations continuous learning and development is based on an ongoing programme of appraisals and individual performance reviews, which identify training and enhancement needs.

> Each staff member has what we call a training profile which allows them to say what skills they think are needed to do their job, which skills on that list they have already got and feel comfortable with, and which skills they would like more training in. And then we prioritise those out and people just go looking for the suitable venues and courses. So training is very personalised in that respect.
>
> (41A: general manager, small registered charity)

The needs of individuals and the team, department or organisation are identified jointly by the employee and the line manager. However, the appraisal system is usually heavily weighted towards organisational requirements and is thus indicative of a cost-responsive approach. In some organisations the appraisal process is somewhat less 'top-down' in format:

> We have an annual appraisal and a personal learning plan that comes out of that. The plan is developed jointly between you and your manager with agreed target objectives for every three months. So they are very good on that front... At the appraisal sessions you get appraised by your manager and one of your peers, which I think is good because it is not just downward appraisals. They get other people to give a perspective because different people see you in different ways and you interact with them in different ways on different projects so you get much more of an all-round perspective – 360 degree appraisal.
>
> (28C: project manager, small design and communications company)

There are positive accounts of the appraisal process from line managers who see it as a way of developing 'delegated empowerment': giving people some choice in areas they want to evolve and giving them some responsibility for their own enhancement. Graduates are also positive about this involvement and having joint responsibility.

Cost-responsive, employer-requirement appraisal can easily become routinised and bureaucratic and some respondents indicated a need to review procedures:

> The appraisal form is broken down into a scoring system between 0 and 5, and it is used as an aid, but a lot of the criteria don't seem to be relevant to today's job. We are looking for ways of improving that system by looking at the key competencies within a job, a slightly different way of scoring it, and also looking at ways of your peer scoring you as well, so you are getting a contribution from other members of staff.
>
> (26B: area sales manager, multi-national business machines manufacturer)

> It will change because the company changes, and there will be changes in the forms and the layout. Now that is fairly trivial, except that it is quite important because if it isn't relevant to the work people are doing, then the process loses value. In fact the whole process was re-vamped and we have all had to learn to use new forms from January this year, and they are better.
>
> (46A: senior consultant, multi-national computer service company)

The importance of employees being active in the process of life-long learning is identified a number of times.

> The opportunities are there, it is down to the individual to take them. Nothing is given to you on a plate. It is down to you. It is there but you have to go and take it. But, just as in any career now, you have to stay ahead of the competition.
>
> (40C: graduate engineer, large steel manufacturer)

The stress is on the need for employees to be self-motivated. They should not just rely on developing in ways structured by the organisation, they should also have some input and impetus. This then needs to be supported by the organisation. Some organisations see this proactive approach to training as empowering employees.

> You take responsibility for yourself. The company will facilitate and help but you as an individual take responsibility for development and turn it into a life-long process. But it is quite difficult to get those philosophies through. Debates about empowerment are very often about managers refusing to give up power, there is another side in my experience and that is that some more junior employees are feeling very threatened by empowerment because they are suddenly responsible. They can't hide, they can't run to a boss and admit they have got a problem. We say to people, "You take the prime responsibility for your training, we will help you, we will guide you, come and talk about it. If you want to spend an hour in the learning centre during lunch time, after work or even during work sometimes, you decide."
>
> (11A: vice-president, multi-national food manufacturers)

Professional and regulatory bodies

Approaches to life-long learning within organisations can also reflect the requirements of particular professional and regulatory bodies, such as The Law Society, The Chartered Insurance Institute and so on (Harvey and Mason, 1995). In some organisations this involves encouraging employees to gain the relevant experience to become chartered:

> If we take on an engineer who has got an engineering degree, we would insist that they work towards chartership and, in doing so – following the training programme that we have worked out to meet our needs – they will also meet the institute requirement. And we can be fairly sure at the end of that they have got the technical knowledge and expertise to do a good engineering job within this industry.
>
> (40A: manager of training and development, large steel manufacturer)

> More recently we have tried to encourage our accountants to take on professional qualifications, some of them have already started the process others will need more encouragement. We do have a training policy whereby we pay 75% of relevant training expenses, we provide study leave and we provide day release to try and support the employees when getting a professional qualification.
>
> (37B: director of financial services, small housing association)

In other cases, support for life-long learning is directed towards continuous professional development (CPD), which is a requirement for continued membership of some professional bodies.

> Upon qualification we enter a Law Society regulated system, and the Law Society requires every qualified solicitor to obtain so many, what they call, CPD points every year. And to collect those points, you attend various lectures, it can be internal training, it can be these residential courses, and you get so many points for them.
>
> (09C: graduate trainee, large law firm)

> With the Institution of Civil Engineers you have to achieve so many training days a year, and you have to keep a record of that training, and at any time the institution can ask to see your training record and if you haven't kept it up to date you could find that you lose your status. So it is a continuous thing.
>
> (44A: business development manager, large international highway design engineers)

> To become a chartered surveyor you have to carry out CPD, Continuing Professional Development. We have had one or two in-house courses which qualify for that and we do provide training for specific aspects of the job, such as the CDM regulations which came in a couple of years ago. We have sent people on a residential course and trained people up to do that type of thing.
> (16A: office director, medium-sized quantity and building surveyors)

Support for continuous development and learning

Support can take various forms, including financial support, support through time and a more general supportive culture. Financial support could include paying for training courses, paying tuition fees for further qualifications, money for books or payment of conference fees and associated travel. This support is obviously restricted by the training budget. Support in terms of time could include time to attend courses, time to attend college, study time, and time to develop skills in the workplace.

> For the MBA, there is a summer school, which they have to go to. They take two days off a month. We will release them, they don't lose pay. Generally people here don't work 9–5 and I don't think it's right to actually say that they are not here for two days and deduct money for it when they are not really working the allotted time. It is not an equitable position to take.
> (23A: chief executive, small medical lasers manufacturer)

Financial support or support through time off is usually dependent on the perceived relevance of the activity to the job:

> If it was work-related I would want to do it in work time, but I would consider doing it in my own time, it wouldn't bother me, in fact I do read stuff at home and learn things at home in my own time.
> (39C: programmer, medium-sized software services contractor)

> You are allowed, if you wish, to identify the course and make the business case for doing this at the Bank's expense but at the very best you are fortunate enough to go away on a one year's Masters course. Some are allowed to do Masters part-time with half a day 'day release'. But you have got to make the case. You have, by and large, got to demonstrate to the Bank that it is a worthwhile investment and that you are one of the best of the bunch. It is not open to everyone.
> (27B: manager, large public financial institution)

There is also the restriction of how much time can be spared from the workplace, particularly in smaller organisations where there is no-one else to cover the work.

> Supporting people financially is not such a problem, but allowing people the time is problematic as we are so stretched.
> (39A: resources manager, medium-sized software services contractor)

> Because we are only a small organisation, obviously taking time out is very difficult, because in a large organisation there will be somebody covering me, whereas in what we are involved with, normally if you are out, you are out. There is nobody to cover you, so it might be a little bit difficult.
> (41C: project worker, small registered charity)

> What we are not committed to is giving people time off work to do it. We will financially fund them [on part-time courses], but generally we do not give people time off work.
> (09A: head of personnel, large law firm)

Even if the activity cannot be supported financially or through time, there can be positive support through encouragement of self-development. However, this general encouragement on its own may be unable to foster a culture of continuous learning: employees may need more concrete support in terms of time, money, promotion, and so on: 'I think they could encourage you more and make it more visible as to how your career might go' (22C).

Further qualifications

There was little enthusiasm for working towards post-graduate qualifications that are not directly linked to professional status or development of management attributes. A few organisations need postgraduate-qualified employees with specialist knowledge, especially in research and development departments. There was some reservation that postgraduate qualifications produced 'boffins' who were useful only in a limited sphere:

> If you want a boffin then fine, I don't mind having a boffin who sits there and does that specific job. It may be a particular niche that you are looking for. But generally speaking we are bringing graduates into this company to be the managers of the future.
> (60A: director commercial operations, large vehicle manufacturer)

Further qualifications, such as masters and doctoral degrees were, in the main, seen as a luxury with little intrinsic worth in themselves, and were closely tied to specialist discipline-related requirements:

> I don't know about postgraduate degrees because it comes back to whether it is a relevant qualification. It's probably going to be more about what vocational skills have you got that I can use. I don't care whether you can write 20,000 word thesis on something, I actually want to know can I send you out; can I put you on the 'phone; can I give you a job and know that it's going to be done.
> (28B: design manager, small design and communications company)

> There is no doubt, to do the sort of work we do on the economics front, you have got to have a second degree in economics, you've got to be a specialist and a good one at that. That's the area where it has gone the furthest. And that is irreversible. We are growing our own and therefore I would rather have as raw material people who I know are bright who I hope are adaptable.
> (27A: director, large public financial institution)

In some areas, albeit where specialised knowledge is at a premium, there are other advantages in having doctoral-level employees, although in the main they are likely to be recruited with Ph.Ds. rather than developed to doctoral level while at work.

> What training does a Ph.D. get that is different from a graduate? Certainly the level of science is significantly greater... as far as we are concerned usually organic chemistry, so from a science perspective you have to take it as read that they are bound to bring a different level of competence in. From a practical perspective, since we do a practical job, a Ph.D. comes in with normally 120 weeks of practical experience, so in terms of designing an experiment, interpreting the results of an experiment, they are going to be significantly more advanced. But the next thing I think that a Ph.D. differs in is that a Ph.D. thesis itself is an unsupervised construction, where they have to summarise what else has been done in the literature, they have to précis the reason for their doing the work in the first place, they then have to collate all of the data that they have gathered, draw conclusions from it and then present it in a logical, coherent fashion, and finally they have to stand up and be examined on it. And that tells you something different about an individual.
> (63B: research manager, large pharmaceutical manufacturers)

Although a few employees were pursuing postgraduate qualifications that were not linked to professional status, in the main, the small numbers studying, or intending to study, for postgraduate qualifications identified MBAs (part-time or through distance learning). However, some recent graduates wanted to undertake a masters course for interest, 'just to do it' (20C), rather than in relation to any specific career development:

> I think a Masters degree would actually be of use to me now, for the simple reason that it would give me an injection of new ideas and concepts that I could actually practice and bring into the industry. With a Masters degree you can consolidate the experience you

> already have in line with those concepts and take it forward... It is something I would like to do, so that I would have something to do other than work. There is a lot of pressure on people to work in their spare time, and I think if I had that it would give me something to fall back on, give me a bit more motivation to do some academic work, which is something I feel I have left behind in the last four years.
> (50C: performance analyst, large freight company)

In recent years, some organisations have had some internal training programmes accredited by particular institutions so that graduate employees would receive a qualification on completion. These organisations have identified that this is what graduates want; for example, a business qualification would give the graduates a 'competitive edge' (Hilton, 1993). One organisation in the sample also refers to their direct-entry graduate training scheme as now leading to a qualification (11C).

Some employees are negative about the thought of doing more qualifications, with some seeing further qualifications as irrelevant to the workplace.

> In this job I could go on to do an M.Sc. part-time – it is certainly not required. Perhaps if I asked to do it I would be allowed to but it wouldn't get me any further than a B.Sc. would here.
> (63D: research assistant, large pharmaceutical manufacturers)

> I'm just sick of doing degrees and courses I just want to earn some money. My views may change in a few years time. I may want to pursue that.
> (02C: art teacher, community school)

Several graduates have done further qualifications prior to employment and feel that this has allowed them access into their particular field of employment.

> The one year that gave me very specific skills for broadcast journalism, and because I had done that I got on to an organisation training scheme as well. This organisation has only got one journalism training scheme and because I had got all these skills, then they gave me a place. When I applied for the scheme the year before I did not even get an interview because I hadn't got the skills they were looking for.
> (43C: news producer, large public broadcasting organisation)

There is the feeling from some that as the number of graduates increases then graduates may have to consider undertaking postgraduate courses to make themselves more marketable.

> I think as time goes on the degree becomes more and more common and people will get a Masters. You are always going to need something else to make you stand out more from everybody else.
> (29C: buyer, medium-sized health product manufacturer)

Summary

- Graduate trainee schemes (GTS) are typically developed in larger organisations (though not exclusively) and often involve a number of placements within different sections of the organisation. They are often designed to train managers of the future.

- GTS are an expensive investment and, to be cost-effective, employers recognise the importance of employee retention. Thus, the need for career progression and opportunities in organisations for graduates who have completed a GTS is highlighted by graduates and employers.

- Broader training looks to develop a range of skills and often focuses on skills needed for future (management) roles in the organisation. Task-specific training concentrates on the immediate needs of the job, team or organisation and ensuring that staff have the necessary skills or knowledge.

- Training takes three broad forms: 'on-the-job', internal and external. Choice of training depends on appropriateness for particular training needs, cost and available time.

- It is important that employers strike a balance between training for immediate tasks, broader development of the individual and training for future needs.

- Continuous learning is something repeatedly cited by employers and recent graduates as an essential and integral part of working, highlighting the need to constantly develop in order to keep up with the demands of the job.

- Continuous development and learning is sometimes directed by the requirements of professional and regulatory bodies.

- Some organisations use appraisals and performance reviews as an on-going assessment of training needs and individual development.

- The negotiation of training needs and desired development between managers and employees seems to be, on the whole, a positive experience but one that usually prioritises organisational requirements.

- Both graduates and managers in the sample recognise that the organisation and the employee have a joint responsibility in developing continuous learning. The organisation needs to create the appropriate climate, for example, encouraging development through financing activities and allowing employees time to undertake these activities. The employee also needs to take an active role in their process of continuous development.

- Postgraduate training and qualifications tends to be linked to specific job-relevant skills and knowledge. There was little enthusiasm for post-graduate qualifications not directly linked to professional status or development of management attributes.

References

AGCAS-CSU-IER, 1996, *Great Expectations.* London, DfEE.

Allen, M.G., 1991, *Improving the Personal Skills of Graduates: Final Report 1988 – 91.* Sheffield, Personal Skills Unit, Sheffield University.

Allen, M.J and Scrams, D.J., 1991, 'Careers of undergraduate psychology alumni', paper to the 99th Annual Convention of the American Psychological Association, San Francisco, 16–20 August, 1991.

Appleyard, D., 1996, 'A schooling in real life', *Independent Education*, 7 November, 1996, p. 11.

Arkin, A., 1993, 'A formula for a learning organisation', *Personnel Management*, 25, no.7, July 1993.

Association of Graduate Recruiters (AGR), 1993, *Briefing: Assessment Centres.* October, Cambridge, AGR.

Association of Graduate Recruiters (AGR), 1995, *Skills for Graduates in the 21st Century.* Cambridge, AGR.

Association of Graduate Recruiters (AGR), 1996, *Graduate Salaries and Vacancies 1996 Summer Update Survey.* Brighton, AGR.

Atkins, M.J., Beattie, J. and Dockrell, W.B., 1993, *Assessment Issues in Higher Education.* Sheffield, Employment Department.

Ball, 1989, *Aim Higher: Widening access to higher education.* London, Royal Society for the Encouragement of Arts, Manufacturers and Commerce.

Ball, 1990, *More Means Different: Widening access to higher education.* London, Royal Society for the Encouragement of Arts, Manufacturers and Commerce.

Banta, T. *et al.*, 1991, 'Critique of a method for surveying employers', paper to the 31st Association for Institutional Research (AIR) Annual Forum, San Francisco, 26–29 May, 1991.

Barnett, R., 1994, *The Limits of Competence.* Buckingham, Society for Research into Higher Education (SRHE) and Open University Press.

Binks, M., Grant, A. and Exley, K., 1993, 'Assessing the output of institutions of higher education: a pilot study', in Harvey, (Ed.), 1994, *Proceedings of the Second QHE Quality Assessment Seminar*, 16–17 December, 1993, Birmingham, QHE, pp. 18–28.

BOC plc and London Business School (BOC/LBS), 1994, *Building Global Excellence.* Study of 21 UK companies. London, BOC/LBS.

Bolton, J. E., 1971, *Small Firms. Report of the Commission of Inquiry on Small Firms.* London, HMSO, Cmnd. 4811.

Boyer, R. (Ed.), 1989, *The Search for Labour Market Flexibility: The European economy in transition.* Oxford, Oxford University Press.

British Telecom (BT), 1993, *Matching Skills: A question of demand and supply.* London, BT.

Brown, S. and Knight, P., 1994, *Assessing Learners in Higher Education.* London, Kogan Page.

Burrows, A., Harvey, L. and Green, D., 1992, *Is Anybody Listening? Employers' views on quality in higher education.* Birmingham, QHE.

Business-Higher Education Round Table, 1991, *Aiming Higher. Commissioned Report no. 1 of 1991 Business-Higher Education Round Table Education Surveys.* Camberwell, Victoria, Business-Higher Education Round Table.

Business-Higher Education Round Table, 1992, *Educating for Excellence: Business-Higher Education Round Table 1992 Education Surveys.* Camberwell, Victoria, Business-Higher Education Round Table.

Cannon, T., 1986, 'View from industry' in Moodie, G.C. (Ed.), *Standards and Criteria in Higher Education*, Guildford, Society for Research into Higher Education (SRHE) & NFER/Nelson, pp. 145–56.

Caulkin, S. 1996, 'Flexible working is no friend to jobs', *Observer*, 20 October, 1996.

Causer, G. and Jones, C., nd, 'Responding to 'skills shortages': recruitment and retention in a high technology labour market', *Human Resource Management* Journal, 3. no.3.

Clark, K., 1996, Chancellor of the Exchequer's Budget Speech. London, House of Commons, 26th November, 1996.

Confederation of British Industry (CBI), 1994, *Thinking Ahead: Ensuring the expansion of higher education in the 21st Century.* London, CBI.

Confederation of British Industry (CBI), 1995, *A Skills Passport: A vision for our future.* London, CBI.

Council for Industry and Higher Education (CIHE), 1992, *Investing in Diversity: An assessment of higher education policy.* London, CIHE.

Council for Industry and Higher Education (CIHE), 1996, *Helping Students Towards Success at Work: Declaration of intent*. London, CIHE.

Council of University Classical Departments (CUCD), 1990, *Classics in the Market Place: An independent research study on attitudes to the employment of classics graduates*. Exeter, CUCD, Department of Classic, University of Exeter.

Darby, Sir Charles, 1993, 'Quality assessment and employer satisfaction', keynote presentation at the *QHE* 24-Hour Seminar, Scarman House, University of Warwick, 16–17 December 1993, in Harvey, L. (Ed.), 1994, *Proceedings of the Second QHE Quality Assessment Seminar*, 16–17 December, 1993, Birmingham, QHE, pp. 36–8.

Davies, G., 1993, 'HEFCE quality assessment methodology: how it addresses employer-education links', in Harvey, L. (Ed.), 1994, *Proceedings of the Second QHE Quality Assessment Seminar*, 16–17 December, 1993. Birmingham, QHE, pp. 32–6.

Department for Education and Employment (DfEE), 1996a, *Labour Market Skills and Trends*, London, DfEE.

Department for Education and Employment (DfEE), 1996b, *Skills and Enterprise Briefing*, Issue 2/96, February.

Department of Education and Science (DES), 1987, *Higher Education: Meeting the challenge*, White Paper, Cm.114. London, HMSO.

Department of Employment (DE), 1981, *Higher Education and the Employment of Graduates*. Unit for Manpower Studies, Research Paper No. 19. London, DE.

Department of Trade and Industry and Council for Industry and Higher Education (DTI/CIHE), 1990, *Getting Good Graduates*, London, HMSO.

Duckenfield, M. and Stirner, P., 1992, *Higher Education Developments: Learning through work*. Sheffield, Employment Department.

European Commission (EC), 1991, *Memorandum on Higher Education in the European Community*. 5 November 1991. Brussels, Commission of the European Communities, Task Force, Human Resources, Education, Training, Youth.

Fisher, P., 1994, 'Some degrees of coercion', *Guardian*, 3 March, 1994, pp. 14–15 of the Special Supplement to mark Human Resources Development Week.

Flanders, S., 1995, 'The coming of the blue-collar graduate', *Human Resources*, May, 1995.

Fulton, O., Gordon, A. and Williams G., 1982, *Higher Education and Manpower Planning*. Geneva, ILO.

Ganguly, P. and Bannock, G., 1987, *UK Small Business Statistics and International Comparisons*. London, Harper and Row.

Gordon, A., 1983, 'Attitudes of employers to the recruitment of graduates', *Educational Studies*, 9, no. 1, pp. 45–64.

Green, S., 1990, *Analysis of Transferable Personal Skills Requested by Employers in Graduate Recruitment Advertisements in June 1989*. Sheffield, University of Sheffield.

Greenwood, R.G., Edge, A.G. and Hodgetts, M., 1987, 'How managers rank the characteristics expected of business graduates', *Business Education*, 8, no. 3, pp. 30–4.

Guirdham, M., 1995, *Interpersonal Skills at Work, (second edition)*. Hemel Hempstead, Prentice Hall.

Harvey, L. (Ed.),1993, *Proceedings of the QHE Quality Assessment Seminar*, 21–22 January, 1993. Birmingham, QHE.

Harvey, L. (Ed.), 1994, *Proceedings of the Second QHE Quality Assessment Seminar*, 16–17 December, 1993. Birmingham, QHE.

Harvey, L. and Knight, P.T., 1996, *Transforming Higher Education*. Buckingham, Society for Research into Higher Education (SRHE) and Open University Press.

Harvey, L. and Mason, S., 1995, *The Role of Professional Bodies in Quality Monitoring*, Centre for Reseaerch into Quality, UCE, Birmingham.

Harvey, L. with Green, D., 1994, *Employer Satisfaction*. Birmingham, QHE.

Harvey, L., Burrows, A. and Green, D., 1992, *Someone Who Can Make an Impression. Report of the employers' survey of qualities of higher education graduates*. Birmingham, QHE.

Higher Education Quality Council (HEQC), 1996, *Graduate Standards Programme*. London, HEQC.

Hilton, P., 1993, 'An accelerated route to the top for graduates', *Personnel Management*, 25. no.7, July.

Hogg, C., 1994, 'Foretaste of work', *Human Resources*, Spring 1994.

Huddart, G., 1994, 'Degrees of choice', *Personnel Today*, 5 April, 1994.

Huddart, G., 1994, 'Yes Minister', *Personnel Today*, 12 July, 1994.

Hutchinson, S. and Brewster, C., 1994, *Flexibility at Work in Europe: Strategies and practice*. A report prepared for the European Association of Personnel Management. London, Institute of Personnel and Development.

Industrial Research and Development Advisory Committee (IRDAC), 1990, *Skills Shortages in Europe: IRDAC Opinion*, November, Brussels, EC.

Industrial Research and Development Advisory Committee (IRDAC), 1994, *Quality and Relevance: The challenge to European education: unlocking Europe's potential*, Brussels, EC.

Institute of Directors (IoD), 1991, *Performance and Potential: Education and training for a market economy*. London, IoD.

Institution of Directors, (IoD), 1996, *Business Opinion Survey*. London, IoD.

Institute of Management (IM), 1996a, *Are Managers Under Stress?* London, IM.

Institute of Management (IM), 1996b, *Management Development to the Millenium; New priorities.* London, IM.

Institute of Management and Ashridge Management College (IM/AMC), 1996, *The Qualified Manager.* London, IM.

Institute of Management and University of Cambridge (IM/UC), 1996, *Developing Managers for the Smaller Business*. London, IM.

Institute of Manpower Studies (IMS), 1981, *Graduate Employment and Careers*. IMS Report No. 30. Sussex, IMS.

James, M. L., 1992, 'Essential topics and subtopics of business communication: are we teaching what employers want?', *Business Education Forum*, 46, no. 4, pp. 8–10.

Jones, B., Scott, P., Bolton, B. and Bramley, A., 1994, 'Graduate engineers and British trans-national business: élite human resources or technical labourers', *Human Resource Management Journal*, 4, no. 1, pp. 34–48.

Johnson, D. and Pere-Vergé, L., 1993, 'Attitudes towards graduate employment in the SME sector', *International Small Business Journal*, 11, no. 4.

Kay, J., 1993, *The Foundations of Corporate Success*, Oxford, Oxford University Press.

Khawaja, S. *et al.*, 1991, *Technical Education: Its relevance to job market. A research report*. AEPAM Research Study, no. 90. Islamabad, Ministry of Education, Academy of Educational Planning and Management.

Knapper, C.K. and Cropley, A.J., 1985, *Lifelong Learning and Higher Education*. London, Croom Helm.

Kotter, J.P. and Heskett, J.L., 1992, *Corporate Culture and Performance*. New York, The Free Press, Macmillan.

Lindley, R., (Ed.), 1981, *Higher Education and the Labour Market*. Guildford, Society for Research into Higher Education (SRHE).

Middlehurst, R., 1995, 'Changing Leadership in Universities', in Schuller, T., (Ed.), *The Changing University*, Society for Research into Higher Education (SRHE) and Open University Press.

MORI, 1993, *Attitudes of University Finalists: Participants' report*. March. London, MORI.

National Board of Employment, Education and Training (NBEET), 1992, *Skills Required of Graduates: One test of quality in Australian higher education*. Canberra, Australian Government Publishing Service. (Also referred to as Skills Sought by Employers of Graduates on front cover of published report).

NEDO, 1986, *Changing Work Patterns*. A report by the IMS. London, HMSO.

Organisation for Economic Co-operation and Development (OECD), 1985, *Education in Modern Society*. OECD, Paris.

O'Leary, J., 1981, 'A crisis of our own manufacturing', *Times Higher Education Supplement*, no. 450, p. 8.

Pardesi, U., nd, *Marketing in Indigenous and Asian Small Firms in the West Midlands*. Birmingham, University of Central England in Birmingham, Ph.D. dissertation.

Pearson, R., 1976, *Qualified Manpower in Employment*. Sussex, Institute of Manpower Studies (IMS).

Personnel Today, 5 April, 1994.

Phillips-Kerr, B., 1991, *A Survey of Careers Destinations: 1985 Modern Language Graduates of the Universities of Bradford, Hull, Newcastle Upon Tyne, Sheffield and the Polytechnic of Newcastle Upon Tyne*. Newcastle, University of Newcastle Careers Advisory Service, May.

Policy Studies Institute (PSI), 1990, *Britain's Real Skills Shortage*. January, London, PSI.

Quality Support Centre (QSC), 1995, *Guidelines for Good Practice in Supporting Students in the Workplace*. London/Sheffield, DfEE.

Quibble, Z. K., 1991, 'Writing competences needed by business employees', *Delta Pi Epsilon Journal*, 33, no. 1, pp. 35–51.

Ratcliff, J. L. and associates, 1995, *Realizing the Potential: improving postsecondary teaching, learning and assessment*. Pennsylvania: National Center on Postsecondary Teaching, Learning and Assessment.

Rainnie, R., 1988, *Your flexible friend? Small firms in the 1980s*. Hatfield, Hatfield Polytechnic, Local Economy Research Unit.

Reich, R.B., 1991, *The Work of Nations: Preparing ourselves for 21st-Century capitalism*. London, Simon and Schuster.

Reichheld, F.F., 1993, 'Loyalty-based management', *Harvard Business Review*, no. 93210, March-April, pp. 64–73.

Reichheld, F.F., 1994, 'Loyalty and the renaissance of marketing' *Marketing Management*, 2, no. 4.

Research into Sandwich Education Committee (RISE), 1985, *An Assessment of the Costs and Benefits of Sandwich Education*. London, DES.

The Royal Society for the encouragement of Arts, Manufactures and Commerce (RSA), 1995, *Tomorrow's Company: The role of business in a changing world*. London, RSA.

Smith, C. and Elger, T., 1996, 'The new workplace', presentation at 'Shaping a new century – challenges for the centre-left', London, Commonwealth Institute, 29 November.

Teichler, U., 1989, 'Research on higher education and work in Europe', *European Journal of Education*, 24, no. 3, pp. 223–47.

Thomas, G.V., Robinson, E.J., Torrance, M., 1992, 'The writing experiences of social science research students', *Studies in Higher Education*, 17, no. 2, pp. 155–67.

Thompson, P., 1996, 'The new workplace', presentation at 'Shaping a new century – challenges for the centre-left', London, Commonwealth Institute, 29 November.

Trades Union Congress (TUC), 1989, *Skills 2000*. London, TUC.

Unit for the Development of Adult Continuing Education (UDACE), 1992, *Learning Outcomes in Higher Education*. Sheffield, Employment Department.

Wallis, M. and Harvey, L., 1994, 'Careers advisory services and recruitment: the role of the 'milk round'' briefing paper in Harvey, L. (Ed.), 1993, *Proceedings of the Second QHE Quality Assessment Seminar*, 16–17 December, 1993, Birmingham, QHE.

Waterman, R., 1994, *Frontiers of Excellence – Learning from companies that put people first*. London, Brealey.

Weiser, C.R., 1995, 'Customer retention – keeping customers for a lifetime', *RSA Journal*, 143, no. 5459, pp. 10–11.

Wright, P. 1996, 'Mass higher education and the search for standards: reflections on some issues emerging from the graduate standards programme', *Higher Education Quarterly*, 50, no 1.

Appendix 1   Outline details of respondents

01A	training and safety officer, medium-sized private leisure and entertainment complex
01B	head of leisure, medium-sized private leisure and entertainment complex
01C	duty manager, medium-sized private leisure and entertainment complex
01D	events manager, medium-sized private leisure and entertainment complex
02A	head teacher, community school
02B	head of science, community school
02C	art teacher, community school
02D	special needs assistant, community school
03A	head teacher, small private school for children with special needs
03C	teacher, small private school for children with special needs
03D	care assistant, small private school for children with special needs
04A	owner, small corporate literature specialists
04B	project director, small corporate literature specialists
04C	marketing assistant, small corporate literature specialists
05A	principal officer for policy, publicly funded youth service
05B	service manager, publicly funded youth service
05C	youth worker, publicly funded youth service
05D	senior community worker, publicly funded youth service
06A	partner, large law firm
06C:	trainee solicitor, large law firm
07A	deputy chief executive, regional arts board
07C	executive officer, regional arts board
08A	graduate recruitment and training manager, multi-national electrical products manufacturer
08C	graduate trainee, multi-national electrical products manufacturer
09A	head of personnel, large law firm
09B	graduate recruiter and training manager, large law firm
09C	graduate trainee, large law firm
10B	manager business banking, large financial institution
10C	supervisor, large financial institution
11A	vice-president, multi-national food manufacturers
11B	head of management recruitment and training, multi-national food manufacturers
11C	marketing officer, multi-national food manufacturers
11D	graduate trainer, multi-national food manufacturers
12A	personnel director, large law firm
12C	trainee solicitor, large law firm
13A	news manager, medium-sized private local radio station
13C	news co-ordinator, medium-sized private local radio station
13D	broadcast journalist, medium-sized private local radio station
14A	owner, small design and print agency
14B	studio manager, small design and print agency
14C	project manager, small design and print agency
15A	partner, small chartered accountants
15C	computing supervisor, small chartered accountants
16A	office director, medium-sized quantity and building surveyors
16C	building surveyor, medium-sized quantity and building surveyors

17A	partner, small private specialist employment agency
17B	office manager, small private specialist employment agency
17C	graduate recruitment consultant, small private specialist employment agency
18A	partner, small private design consultancy
18C	junior design engineer, small private design consultancy
19B	project manager, small publicly funded community health centre
19C	community worker, small publicly funded community health centre
20A	director, small publicly funded support and advice centre
20C	photographic adviser, small publicly funded support and advice centre
21A	director of human resources, multi-national communications company
21B	customer service manager, multi-national communications company
21C	network support engineer, multi-national communications company
21D	hostmaster, multi-national communications company
22A	human resource manager, multinational reprographic equipment manufacturer
22B	sales manager, multinational reprographic equipment manufacturer
22C	car fleet manager, multinational reprographic equipment manufacturer
22D	pricing manager, multinational reprographic equipment manufacturer
23A	chief executive, small medical lasers manufacturer
23B	general manager, small medical lasers manufacturer
23C	electrical engineer, small medical lasers manufacturer
24A	senior executive, multi-national information systems company
25A	managing director, medium-sized shop-fitting manufacturer
26B	area sales manager, multi-national business machines manufacturer
26C	salesman, multi-national business machines manufacturer
27A	director, large public financial institution
27B	manager, large public financial institution
27C	recent graduate, large public financial institution
27D	equity markets analyst, large public financial institution
28A	business manager, small design and communications company
28B	design manager, small design and communications company
28C	project manager, small design and communications company
28D	project manager, small design and communications company
29A	supply manager, medium-sized health product manufacturer
29C	buyer, medium-sized health product manufacturer
29D	promotions buyer, medium-sized health product manufacturer
30A	owner, small design consultancy
30C	junior designer, small design consultancy
30D	graphic designer, small design consultancy
31A	managing director, medium-sized house builders and regenerators
31C	senior quantity surveyor, medium-sized house builders and regenerators
31D	senior quantity surveyor, medium-sized house builders and regenerators
32A	development and training manager, large telecommunications organisation
32B	recruitment and development manager, large telecommunications organisation
32C	graduate recruiter, large telecommunications organisation
32D	programme manager, large telecommunications organisation
33A	production director, medium-sized refractory materials manufacturer
33B	commercial co-ordinator, medium-sized refractory materials manufacturer
33C	technical manager, medium-sized refractory materials manufacturer
34A	strategic manager, multi-national petro-chemical company
35A	acting divisional manager, local authority landlord
35B	research and policy officer, local authority landlord
35C	recent graduate, local authority landlord
36A	senior manager, large financial institution
36B	area manager, large financial institution
36C	branch manager, large financial institution

36D	branch manager, large financial institution
37A	deputy chief executive, small housing association
37B	director of financial services, small housing association
37C	management accountant, small housing association
37D	management accountant, small housing association
38A	head of branch, civil service
38B	director of personnel, civil service
39A	resources manager, medium-sized software services contractor
39B	team manager, medium-sized software services contractor
39C	programmer, medium-sized software services contractor
40A	manager of training and development, large steel manufacturer
40B	production manager, large steel manufacturer
40C	graduate engineer, large steel manufacturer
40D	chemical technician, large steel manufacturer
41A	general manager, small registered charity
41C	project worker, small registered charity
42A	training and personnel manager, medium-sized private broadcasting company
43A	specialist journalist manager, large public broadcasting organisation
43C	news producer, large public broadcasting organisation
44A	business development manager, large international highway design engineers
44B	line manager, large international highway design engineers
44C	recent graduate, large international highway design engineers
45A	senior advisor, small public watchdog organisation
46A	senior consultant, multi-national computer service company
46B	line manager, multi-national computer service company
46C	recent graduate, multi-national computer service company
47A	personnel manager, multi-national food manufacturer
47C	process engineer, multi-national food manufacturer
48A	editorial training officer, medium-sized newspaper publisher
48C	district news editor, medium-sized newspaper publisher
49A	operations manager, computer-controlled systems manufacturer
49C	project designer, computer-controlled systems manufacturer
50A	planning and analysis manager, large freight company
50C	performance analyst, large freight company
51B	research and information manager, medium-sized community health authority
51C	information analyst, medium-sized community health authority
51D	information analyst, medium-sized community health authority
52A	graduate recruiter, large international corporate accountants
52B	manager, large international corporate accountants
52C	graduate trainee, large international corporate accountants
53A	chief executive, small private research organisation
53B	research manager, small private research organisation
53C	research officer, small private research organisation
54A	assistant to deputy chairman, large international retailers
54B	deputy general manager, large international retailers
54C	foods manager, large international retailers
54D	assistant personnel manager, large international retailers
55A	managing partner, small quantity surveyors
55B	associate, small quantity surveyors
56A	graduate recruitment manager, large financial institution
56C	graduate trainee, large financial institution
57A	senior executive, large brewing company
57B	channel director, large brewing company
57C	category manager, large brewing company

57D	operations manager, large brewing company
58A	development co-ordinator, small publicly funded arts publishers
59A	head of career development, large financial institution
59B	line manager, large financial institution
59C	personal assistant, large financial institution
59D	business change manager, large financial institution
60A	director commercial operations, large vehicle manufacturer
60B	group taxation manager, large vehicle manufacturer
60C	finance controller, large vehicle manufacturer
61A	operations manager, international fast-food chain
61B	store manager, international fast-food chain
61C	assistant manager, international fast-food chain
61D	first assistant manager, international fast-food chain
62A	manager, large management consultants
62C	new graduate, large management consultants
63A	human resources manager, large pharmaceutical manufacturers
63B	research manager, large pharmaceutical manufacturers
63C	assistant research scientist, large pharmaceutical manufacturers
63D	research assistant, large pharmaceutical manufacturers
64B	graduate recruitment officer, large police force
64C	recent graduate, large police force
64D	police superintendent, large police force
65A	human resources manager, large gas suppliers
65B	contract manager, large gas suppliers
65C	account administrator, large gas suppliers
65D	risk monitor, large gas suppliers
66A	recruitment manager, multi-national petro-chemical company
66B	dealer analyst, multi-national petro-chemical company
67A	managing director, small journal publishers
67B	marketing manager, small journal publishers
67C	recent graduate, small journal publishers
67D	non-graduate, small journal publishers
68B	line manager, medium-sized insurance company
68C	recent graduate, medium-sized insurance company
68D	non-graduate, medium-sized insurance company
69A	strategic manager, small design agency
69B	line manager, small design agency
69C	recent graduate, small design agency
69D	non-graduate, small design agency
70A	strategic manager, multi-national petro-chemical company
70B	line manager, multi-national petro-chemical company
70C	recent graduate, multi-national petro-chemical company
71A	strategic manager, large international accountants
71B	line manager, large international accountants
71C	senior auditor, large international accountants
72A	strategic manager, automobile supply company
72C	zone manager, automobile supply company
72D	zone manager, automobile supply company
73A	operations manager, medium-sized motor part manufacturer
73C	recent graduate, medium-sized motor part manufacturer
73D	non-graduate, medium-sized motor part manufacturer
74A1	personnel director, multi-national engineering company
74B	human resource manager, multi-national engineering company
74C	employee development consultant, multi-national engineering company

74D	management development assistant, multi-national engineering company
74A2	graduate recruitment manager, multi-national engineering company
75A	human resources manager, medium-sized public hospital
75B	biochemist, medium-sized public hospital
75C1	laboratory technician, medium-sized public hospital
75C2	doctor, medium-sized public hospital
75D	laboratory technician, medium-sized public hospital
76A	senior executive, medium-sized, motor component manufacturer
76B	business manager, medium-sized, motor component manufacturer
76C	graduate trainee, medium-sized, motor component manufacturer
76D	industrial engineer, medium-sized, motor component manufacturer
77A	director of human resources, health service contractors
77B	line manager, health service contractors
77C	recent graduate, health service contractors
78A	trainee recruiter, large, international law firm
78B	line manager, large, international law firm
78C1	recent graduate, large, international law firm
78C2	recent graduate, large, international law firm
79A	strategic manager, large, chartered accountants
79B	line manager, large, chartered accountants
79C	auditor, large, chartered accountants
80B	bottling manager, medium-sized brewing company
80C	sales co-ordinator, medium-sized brewing company
80D	export manager, medium-sized brewing company
81A	software development manager, small, operator-systems design firm
81C	software engineer, small, operator-systems design firm
82A	head of technology strategy, large power company
82B	line manager, large power company
82C	recent graduate, large power company
82D	senior technician and safety officer, large power company
83A	strategic manager, large retail company
83B	deputy store manager, large retail company
83C	trainee store manager, large retail company
84A	head of administration, emergency service
84C	brigade statistician, emergency service
85A	director of resources, medium-sized charity
85C	human resources administrator, medium-sized charity
86A	management development manager, medium-sized leisure company
86B	line-manager, medium-size leisure company
86C	recent graduate, medium-size leisure company
87A	strategic manager, publicly funded small black arts and media organisation
87C	recent graduate, publicly funded small black arts and media organisation
88C	recent graduate, small, publicly funded black media organisation
89A	strategic manager, small civil engineering consultants
89B	line manager, small civil engineering consultants
89C	recent graduate, small civil engineering consultants
90A	regional and central divisional director, public information collection bureau
90C	assistant information officer, public information collection bureau
91A	head of department, large charity
91C	recent graduate, large charity

Appendix 2   Defining the size of organisations

Identifying the 'size' of an organisation is complicated by the lack of a generally accepted definition of a 'small firm', either internationally or within the United Kingdom. *Ad hoc* definitions frequently use the number of employees, but there is little consistency on the limits for small and medium organisations. In Britain and Sweden the upper limit for small businesses in some sectors is 200 employees, while in Germany a 'small' business has no more than 10 employees (Ganguly and Bannock 1985). Indeed, such limits are difficult given that a firm of 75 employees in the car industry would be regarded as tiny but 75 employees in a firm of architects would be regarded as substantial. Government departments use a variety of definitions including those based on employment, sales turnover, the size of premises and the value of exports or profits. For example, the 1981 Companies Act classified a firm as small if, for the financial year and the one immediately preceding it, two of the following three conditions apply:

- turnover did not exceed £1.4 million
- balance sheet total did not exceed £0.7 million
- average weekly number of employees did not exceed 50.

The VAT classification, based on sales turnover, is also used to define small businesses, however, it is unreliable as an indicator of small firms as it excludes those organisations with turnovers below the registration threshold (Pardesi, undated). The lack of clear definition is not new, indeed the Bolton Committee (Bolton, 1971) found it impossible to define a small firm adequately simply in terms of employment, assets, turnover, or any other *single* quantitative measure.

A qualitative approach, based on that adopted by the Bolton Committee, would suggest that a small firm is one:

- that has a relatively small share of a competitive market;
- that is unable to influence prices or, if it is a non-profit organisation makes little significant impact in its area;
- in which the management has close personal involvement in all aspects of the decision-making. In a commercial organisation they are likely to be the owners or part-owners;
- is independent, with the owners/managers having effective control of the business or activities of the organisation, although they might be limited in their freedom of action by obligations to financial institutions or funders.

An alternative way to classify a small employer organisation is to see it in terms of type (Rainnie, 1989), one suggestion would be as follows:

- *dependent*, a small organisation that exists to serve the interest of larger organisations through sub-contract arrangements;
- *dominated*, a small organisation that competes with larger organisations through intense exploitation of capital or labour or operates with small margins;
- *niche*, an organisation that operates in a safe 'niche market' unlikely to be invaded by a larger organisation because the profit or growth potential are low, within this niche market the organisation may well be a major player but remains vulnerable to competition and normally must constantly attract new business;
- *innovative*, a small organisation that develops new products, services or ideas but is vulnerable to takeover or to competition once the innovative product or service appears to have potential.

The classification used in this report is based on this qualitative approach. Organisations are assessed in terms of their market share, nature of their activity, impact, managerial and control structures, as much as on their turnover and size, in determining the appropriate classification.